The PEASENHALL MURDER

To the memory of
THOMAS
and for
JOHN, STEWART and WILFRID

The
PEASENHALL
MURDER

Martin Fido &
Keith Skinner

ALAN SUTTON

First published in the United Kingdom in 1990 by
Alan Sutton Publishing Limited · Phoenix Mill · Far Thrupp
Stroud · Gloucestershire

First published in the United States of America in 1991 by
Alan Sutton Publishing Inc · Wolfeboro Falls · NH 03896–0848

British Library Cataloguing in Publication Data

Fido, Martin
The peasenhall mystery.
1. Suffolk. Peasenhall. Harsent, Rose. Murder. Trial of
Gardiner
I. Title   II. Skinner, Keith
344.2052523

ISBN 0-86299-695-3

Library of Congress Cataloging in Publication Data applied for

Typeset in 10/12pt Times.
Typesetting and origination by
Alan Sutton Publishing Limited.
Printed in Great Britain by
Dotesios Printers Limited.

Contents

Foreword

by RICHARD WHITTINGTON-EGAN

Rose Harsent, full-blown, came, like Dylan Thomas's Nogood Boyo, to a bad end. 'Very enjoyable!' Six months pregnant, a cache of obscene letters beside her bed, she died in the full deflowering of her youth.

The goodly chapel-folk of the tiny Suffolk village of Peasenhall and its satellite townlets and hamlets were not surprised, but registered, with sage head-nodding and pious knee-bending, sanctimonious satisfaction at witnessing the fulfilment of their prophecies that the vengeance of the Lord would be visited upon sinful Rose. The sole question troubling these unfailingly charitable Christians was whether or no that stout pillar of local Primitive Methodism, choir-master and Sunday school superintendent, William Gardiner, had been the instrument of the Lord.

One thing at least was certain, it was not the hand of the Almighty that had lifted her nightie and cut Rose's plump young throat from ear to pink-shell ear. Yet someone, someone who had a lover's tryst with that concupiscent village belle, came out of the darkness, in from the pouring rain, and, to the accompaniment of flashing lightning and ominous, earth-moving thunder, slaughtered her, leaving a crumpled, plucked Rose at the foot of the kitchen stairs of aptly named Providence House.

Eighty-eight summers on, the old mystery still tantalizes and intrigues. The authors of this beautifully ordered book, putting back the clock, take the thatched lid off a seemingly idyllic country village to reveal rustic scandal seething like Eden's serpent in the hedgerows, bucolic gossip masquerading as pietistic righteousness, the Christians Militant ubiquitously condemnatory as usual, and nasty-minded local yokels hiding beneath the smock of innocence a prurient delight in eavesdropping upon love play behind the clay walls of the austere 'Doctor's Chapel'.

Knowing the case well, and having first visited Peasenhall some thirty years ago, at which time I was able to make the acquaintance of Rose's niece, Mrs Rose Annie Self, and several of the gnarled survivors of that

vii

unforgettable, unforgotten June, I was especially interested to see how the 'new generation of crime historians, using scholarly methods' would set about tackling the perplexment.

I have found the thoroughness and ingenuity of their research methodology most impressive. Attaching, quite rightly, supreme importance to the attempt to discover the authorship of the anonymous assignation note received by Rose on that fatal last day of May, the first thing that they did was to try to track down a specimen of Gardiner's handwriting. For seventy years no one had examined a sample for purposes of comparison independent of that made by the contemporary graphologist, Thomas Henry Gurrin, called, and relied upon, at the trials. Their persistence unearthed facsimiles of letters written by Gardiner and printed in the old *Sun* newspaper. Their next mammoth undertaking was to locate and compare with the calligraphy of the trysting note every surviving scrap of handwriting of those who dwelt in and about Peasenhall in Gardiner and Rose's day.

They made a point, too, of actually going to Peasenhall to ferret out every Ancient Mariner extant, and sat beneath many an octo- and nonagenarian's rheumy eye. The result of this new, practical get up and get out of the study approach has been revolutionarily ground-clearing.

It may be that the truth lies buried for ever somewhere in the graveyards of Peasenhall and Sibton, Yoxford, Halesworth and Saxmundham – alongside the young men and women who gossiped and flirted, laughed and cried, in that long-ago summer of 1902. But this book, far more successfully than any social history ever could, resurrects them all before our eyes. We see, not only them, but, in precise detail, village society, a world that is gone for all eternity – as through a glass blood-redly!

Rose Harsent of Providence House emerges as a most beguiling and seductive victim, taking her place in the remembrance of things past beside her East Suffolk sister-victim, 'no better than she should have been' Maria Marten of Polstead's Red Barn.

William Gardiner, dark, bearded, saturnine, macho man in his prime, more than ten years Rose's senior, and with a quiverful of six children of his own at home – and no taste for away goals – strides the stage well as Victorian melodramatic villain-figure-with-a-motive. But *was* that his real-life role?

The case finally boiled down – or up – to a problem in cubicular acrobatics: the issue was not simply whether Gardiner could, figuratively, get *into* Rose's bed without his wife's knowing it, but whether he could get *out of* his wife's bed without *her* knowing it. Doubt as to his prowess as a sexual athlete, questions as to his uprightness and as to whether there was Methodism in his badness, served him well.

The authors' assiduity has taken the story past the full-stop of previous accounts, beyond the fall of the *nolle prosequi* judicial curtain, out with the black limelight of two inconclusive appearances in the dock 'into the sunlight', as Marshall Hall would have put it, of, then, leafy Southall, in Middlesex, whither Gardiner, his great black bush of beard – symbol of his monarchic masculinity? – shaved off, flitted.

That John Rowland, whose much more superficial study of the case appeared in November 1962, had at least an inkling of the Gardiners' aftermath, is indicated by an article which he wrote in the short-lived magazine, *Criminology*, in May 1963. Therein he disclosed, among other things, that Mrs Gardiner's hair turned snow-white after her ordeal.

I am happy to be able to step into the witness-box and testify that this monograph is, without question, the most carefully researched and balanced consideration of the perplexing Peasenhall affair yet published. By virtue of their sterling work, the authors command respect for the conclusion at which they have arrived, but it is put to the reader with the pleasing politeness of those whose confidence is such as not to require the tactics of the bludgeon, and whose courtesy embraces the reader's right to render his own verdict after due consideration of the new and important material that they bring to the bar of posterity.

Acknowledgements

The authors met in 1987 when we had each published a book on Jack the Ripper. So had five other people. We were impressed with the unusually serious investigation and genuine new facts in each other's work.

At the time, Keith Skinner had already done a good deal of work on the Peasenhall Murder which involved his grandfather as a witness. He collaborated with the script-writer/actor, John Gleeson, who was and is interested in compiling a television drama around the subject. When John met Martin Fido, he was agreeable to our continuing the research with a view to producing this book in the first instance.

John had met Stewart Evans, a Suffolk policeman who had worked out the first reconstruction of the crime to explain convincingly how William Gardiner did it. Ever since he introduced us, Stewart has been invaluably associated with our work. He has been a welcoming host in Suffolk; has provided transport to Peasenhall, Ipswich, and Lowestoft. He has introduced us to some of the old Peasenhall people who had not been trawled in already by Keith and John's net. He has shared all his information with us. He has commented on our chapters as the work proceeded.

As we interviewed people in Suffolk, we found that others had preceded us. We were not much concerned about the gentleman from the Society for Psychical Research who thought that a photograph revealed Dr Lay's guilty ghost in the hedgerow behind Rose Harsent's grave. But the late Mr Dennis Jaques of Trimley had clearly covered the ground very seriously. Once he had been accompanied by a 'Mr Goodman' from London. We assumed this was crime historian Jonathan Goodman; it proved he was not, but he gave us generous encouragement to go on looking into this famous murder.

We discovered, at length, that Mr Jaques's partner had been Mr Wilfrid Goodman of Ickenham. He had carried out the London and Southall ends of the research while Mr Jaques covered Suffolk. Wilfrid told us that with no publisher's deadline, he didn't really know when to stop after Mr Jaques's death. He has generously made available to us an astonishing quantity of information about the case and the background to people in the case. Finally he checked our references exhaustively at the proof stage, and saved us from perpetrating a multitude of small errors.

Richard Whittington-Egan, doyen of crime historians, has been his usual enthusiastic and encouraging self, and gave us the fruits of his interview with Rose's niece in 1950, and the first really good photograph of her ever to be made public.

And the following have helped us with vital information and guidance: Mr Hubert Aldridge, Mrs Ruby Davis, Mr Herbert Denny, Mr Eric Godward, Mr Harold Mills, Mrs Joan Moore, Miss Brenda Pepper, the late Mrs Dora Pepper, Miss Gertie Rose, Mr Billy Rowe, Mr Fred Rowe, Mrs Elizabeth Skinner, Miss Elizabeth Watthews, the late Mr Wesley Whincup.

We are also grateful for the time, help and hospitality offered by: David Banthorpe, Evelyn M. Barnett, Paul Begg, Messrs Bentalls (Tunbridge Wells), John Bentley, Messrs Birkett, Westhorp & Long, Roger Carey, Dr Dorothy Chown, Ray and Joan Cole, Mr D.A. Escott, Paul Evans, Michael and Jana Ferguson, Rosalyn and Dave Fryer, Mrs Kitty Gardiner, Carol, Clare, Jonathan, Lucy and Basil Gleeson, Erika Gmeinhart, Messrs Gotelee & Goldsmith, Margaret Grantham, Peter Harsent, Mr M.D. Hocking, Audrey and Bartie Hotchkiss, Inspector Les Jacobs, Mr P. Jerrey, Mr J. Levett-Scrivener, Mr J.D. Mitson, Dr Colin Owen, Mrs Phyllis Packer, Alison Peacock, Mrs Pyemont, Mr J.W. Ripman, Richard Sharp, Ingrid Smith, Mr John Staunton, Gwen Stern, Mrs J. Stockeld, the Revd Jack Thickitt, Mike and Sue Trovell, Mr E. Warren, Molly Whittington-Egan, Gladys Wilton and the late Harry Wilton.

The Suffolk County Records Offices at Ipswich and Lowestoft have been unfailingly helpful, as have the staff at: the Norfolk County Records Office, Norwich; the British Library; the British Newspaper Library, Colindale; the Guildhall Library; the Library of the Museum of London; the Methodist Archives in the John Ryland University Library of Manchester; the General Registry of Births, Marriages and Deaths, St Catherine's House; the Principal Probate Registry, Somerset House; the Public Record Offices, Chancery Lane and Kew; the Census Office, Portugal Street; the Lord Chancellor's Office; the Commissioner's Reference Library, New Scotland Yard; BBC Written Archives, Caversham; Surrey Record Office, Kingston upon Thames; Southall History Society; and the Society of Genealogists. The Chief Constable of Suffolk kindly allowed us to spend a day working in the Constabulary Museum, Martlesham Heath.

We have also met and corresponded with members of the Gardiner family. None of the children alive at the time of the murder is still on earth. But we have come as close to William as is possible today. The misfortune of 1902 is not a happy family memory, and while Gardiner's descendants have been perfectly frank and helpful with us, they are not, by and large, delighted to have the matter raked over again. They definitely do not want any intrusion on their privacy. For this reason we take full responsibility for ascribing certain information to 'the Gardiner family' without specifying names and addresses of the descendants we have met.

Since we went to press, we greatly regret that our prime informant, Mr Herbert Denny, has died.

London/Heamoor/Bury St Edmunds
1990

NOTE

Describing a murder in which a specific defence was important and the events emerged in the court-room, we have found it essential to use two words with pedantic accuracy, disregarding colloquial usage.

Throughout this book, the word 'alibi' *always* means 'a defence of being elsewhere at the time of the crime'; *not* 'an excuse or exculpation'. 'Forensic' *always* means 'of or used in a courtroom'; *not* 'scientifically connected with criminal justice'.

We also find it preferable to use 'disinterested' with its correct meaning of 'not influenced by one's own advantage'.

New Road

brook

To Sibton Church and Yoxford

Wesleyan Chapel

To Poys Street, Sibton & Methodist Chapel

letter box

Huffen's Post Office

Mrs Dickinson's

Steammer's cottage

Burgess's cottage

The Causeway

Mrs Pepper's

Gardiner's cottage

washhouse & privy

SWAN INN

footbridge

The Street

The Ancient House

Emmett's Store

Centre Cottage (Davies's)

Doctor's Chapel

gate

Rendham Road

Church Street

Mill Lane

St Michael's Church

Smyth's Seed Drill Works

Providence House

Assembly Hall

Badingham Road

Wright and Sawyer's Lodgings

Bruisyard Road

To Badingham

Heveningham Long Lane

N

The village of Peasenhall

ONE

The Murder

here was thunder over East Anglia on the last night of May 1902. In many places, a picturesque lightning display was seen for an hour or more before the torrential rain fell. Alternating sheet and forked flashes lit up a sky full of dense clouds while the thunder rumbled and roared. In some areas people watched the electrical displays taking place in opposite directions at the same time. It was vivid and unforgettable, and found its way into the local press as the most remarkable thunderstorm seen for a considerable time.

The lightning did a certain amount of damage. A heifer was killed near Colchester. A cemetery-keeper was thrown from his doorstep into his house at Stowmarket as an oak tree opposite him was split in two. At Haughley Park, lightning came straight down the chimney, knocking a small grate out of place and melting the bell-wires in the wall.

The little village of Peasenhall, lying about seven miles west of Dunwich, between Halesworth and Saxmundham, awaited the downpour anxiously. There had already been another thunderstorm the previous evening, and the brook which ran alongside much of The Street, the half-mile-long thoroughfare that was almost the entirety of Peasenhall, was inadequately bridged at the crossroads to its western end, and it flooded the roadway if it ran too high.

At around ten o'clock that Saturday night many of the villagers were out on their doorsteps watching the lightning flashes in the distance and wondering whether they had a night of damage ahead of them. Mr Harry Burgess, a bricklayer who lived on The Causeway – an irregular line of houses and cottages facing the brook from its south side – went out to buy something before the rains came and the shops closed. He walked over one of the little footbridges spanning the brook, crossed the main road of stone chippings, and went into Mrs Amelia Pepper's shop on the north side of The Street.

As he came out of Mrs Pepper's at five to ten, he saw her next-door neighbour, a broad-built man of thirty-five, with black hair and a thick beard, standing on his doorstep. Mr William Gardiner, a family man with six children, was a foreman carpenter at the local seed-drill works. A fine workman and a power in his chapel, he had risen fast since coming from Yoxford to Peasenhall twelve years earlier, and was one of the most respected artisans in the parish. Now he stood in his doorway watching the storm anxiously, like many others up and down the road, whose flat shallow doorsteps and low sills offered little protection against flooded parlours.

Burgess went the opposite way from Gardiner's house to go home, and Gardiner left his door to walk out a few paces and speak to him. They knew each other through the Primitive Methodist Connexion whose local chapel was in Sibton, the next hamlet, lying east of Peasenhall, about a mile from Gardiner's house.

The two chatted for about a quarter of an hour – on business and the weather, Burgess said later. Then the bricklayer turned westward before crossing the road to make for the little footbridges leading back to The Causeway. As he did so, he glanced at the great gable end of Providence House, dominating the top of The Street, two hundred yards away. There was a light in the attic at the top, he noticed, where Rose Harsent, the servant slept. Nothing unusual struck him at the time: he usually saw Rose's room lit at that hour if he went down The Street.

But a few minutes later, Rose was no longer in her bedroom. She was saying goodnight to her employer, Mrs Georgiana Crisp, in the square main hall of Providence House. Mrs Crisp then went up the staircase from the hall to the principal bedroom, facing east down The Street, where she slept with her husband William, a retired tailor. Rose's attic was immediately above but it could not be reached from the landing. Rose had to go through the dining-room and into the little kitchen which was built out as a broad penthouse from the west wall of the building. From the kitchen, a boxed-in narrow wooden staircase ran steeply up into the roof, and from there a short passage from the west to the east of the house led to her bedroom.

Between eleven o'clock and half past the storm broke. On the other side of Gardiner's house from Mrs Pepper lived Mrs Dickinson, who ran her late husband's ironmonger's shop. Mrs Dickinson was frightened of thunder and recently widowed. Mrs Gardiner had told her that she would always come over and sit with her if anything ever alarmed her while she was on her own. Mrs Gardiner went across the narrow alley between their two houses to Mrs Dickinson's, while her husband checked that their six children were all right before following. He still had his carpet slippers on when he came into Mrs Dickinson's, anything up to half an hour after his wife, and the couple stayed with the nervous widow until the tempest eased at half past one, and they all knew that the first glimmering of daylight would come within the hour.

At Providence House, the fierce storm aroused the Crisps. Husband and wife prudently came downstairs to make sure water was not coming into the house. They did not go into the kitchen, but as Mrs Crisp closed the door between kitchen and dining-room, she vaguely noticed that the kitchen was remarkably dark. Everything seemed all right, so the two went back to bed and fell asleep again.

Some time later Mrs Crisp was awakened with a start by a thud and a scream from inside the house. The storm was still raging, but it seemed to her that she had been asleep for a considerable time, and, assuming that it was around midnight when she had been downstairs, she guessed it was now between one and two o'clock in the morning. She aroused her husband, who was very deaf, and asked him whether they should go and see whether Rose was all right. He thought there was no need, as the servant had permission to come into their bedroom if she were ever frightened. The two went back to sleep again.

In the morning, Rose's 62-year-old father William came to Providence House at eight o'clock with Rose's clean linen, as he did every Sunday. He went round the house to the back, where a small conservatory surrounded the kitchen window and door. He noticed that the conservatory door was open, which was unusual, and also that there was something dark pinned across the kitchen window. But nothing prepared him for the traumatic sight that met his eyes when he opened the kitchen door.

Rose Harsent lay on her back with her right arm outstretched toward the scullery wall, her head resting against the steps leading up to her attic bedroom, and her feet toward the outside door between kitchen and conservatory. A pool of blood spread from under her head and neck and to the left of her body, covering so much of the floor that Mr Harsent believed he must have trodden in it, although no footmarks were noticed later.

Rose's young body appeared almost naked apart from her stockings, as nearly all but the neck and shoulders of her nightgown and chemise had been burnt away from the sides. The burning had been particularly fierce on the right-hand side of the abdomen and the right arm, where the flesh was charred. The room stank of paraffin and charring.

Under Rose's head lay a copy of Friday's *East Anglian Daily Times*, folded in four and burned around the edges. But her hair and face were not singed.

Near to Rose's head, on her left, was the candlestick she used to light herself up to her room, together with its little cone-shaped earthenware extinguisher. The candle had burned out.

Between the candlestick and the girl's head was the stand and well of the oil lamp which normally lit the kitchen. Lined up beside it, parallel with and a few inches from her body, stood its chimney and mushroom shade, both heavily smeared with blood and paraffin. These lamp glasses were unbroken. The well was three-quarters full of paraffin.

The conflagration of Rose's nightgown had singed the cloth on the kitchen table about eighteen inches away from her left shoulder, and a blue dress which lay on the table. But nothing else had caught alight.

The tongue-and-groove plank door to the little staircase was open, pushed back against the wall to Rose's left. There were splashes or smears of blood on the bottom of the door, and blood on the first two stairs.

A heavy wooden bracket on the wall to Rose's left – one of a row which supported a small shelf above the staircase door – had been broken, apparently by the door being flung open against it with some weight.

There was paraffin-drenched broken glass close to the candlestick and lamp stand, some of it smashed to powder. The most prominent piece proved to be part of a medicine bottle, with alarmingly sharp jagged edges. The neck of the bottle had rolled away past the table to end up in front of the fireplace. It still held its cork, so tightly inserted that it could not be extracted. From the smell, it seemed that the bottle had contained paraffin. A label round its neck was soaked in blood and paraffin, and could not be read at first.

This gruesome scene was dimly lit, for a thick Scotch shawl was hung over the window looking into the conservatory. One end was supported by a fork stabbed into the woodwork.

Mr Harsent went over and took his daughter's arm. It was quite cold. A great gash across her throat suggested how she had died. He covered her body with a rug, and moved the iron lamp stand that was close to her head to see where the pool of blood had come from. Then he went two doors away, to Mr James Crisp's house, William Crisp's shoemaker brother. James Crisp came over to Providence House, and Mr Harsent stayed with his daughter's body while others fetched professional assistance.

Between half past eight and nine, Mr Harsent went up the main staircase to the bedroom to tell the William Crisps that his daughter was dead. Mrs Crisp did not venture into the kitchen until the evening, when the body had been removed. Mr Crisp came down quickly, but his deafness meant that he was never called as a witness at any of the hearings, and there is no account of his actions on this sad Sunday 1 June.

At 8.40 a.m. Dr Lay, who lived across the road from Providence House, came and confirmed the death. Rigor mortis had set in, and he estimated that the girl had been dead between four and six hours.

His first thought was that she had burned to death in an accident with the lamp, and he examined the burns on her arms and up her right side, only to discover that the flesh was charred but not blistered, which indicated that she had been dead before the fire. Moreover her body and nightgown were unburned where they touched the floor: only raised pieces of cloth, like that in the small of her back, had caught fire underneath the body. Adding the fact that her face and hair were unsinged, it was clear that she had fallen before her nightgown caught fire. Dr Lay now attended to the blood, and realized that her throat had been cut.

She was twenty-three years old, unmarried and six months pregnant. A week or so before, when her condition was becoming visible, she had denied it to her mother, saying it was only an unusually thick bodice. Mrs Crisp had also asked whether she was pregnant, but Rose had denied it again, and Mrs Crisp said no more about it. Two years earlier, Rose had remarked that she would throw herself into a pond if she ever got in the family way. So it seemed that she had now committed suicide.

Dr Lay noted that the deep cut across Rose's throat ran from the angle of the right jaw to the angle of the left. She had died, he reckoned, by loss of blood from the left jugular vein, though the wound had also opened her windpipe which would in itself have proved lethal. Dr Lay thought that the throat had been cut from left to right. There was another wound running from the angle of the right jaw up under the chin. This, too, penetrated the windpipe and would ultimately have killed the girl had she not bled to death. Finally there was a stab wound starting at the juncture of the left collar bone with the breast bone which ran up to the throat and joined the largest of the three injuries.

If, as the police later suggested, the first hypothesis was suicide, Dr Lay's rough conclusions must have been that Rose first tried to stab herself in the neck with an upward thrust; then, realizing this had not killed her, tried to cut her throat from right to left with a stroke that slipped and ran up toward her chin; and finally managed to cut her throat across from left to right. She might have dropped the lamp in collapsing, so that it set fire to her nightgown.

There was also a bruise on her right cheek with some abrasion leading up to it from the cut at the right jaw. And there were some cuts on her hands which puzzled Dr Lay. A cut ran across the right forefinger, and there were cuts in her left thumb and forefinger and the ball of the thumb.

Just as Dr Lay reached Providence House, PC Eli Nunn, the village bobby, was told that Rose Harsent lay dead. He hurried to the scene of the fatality, noted the position of everything in the kitchen, and then, helped by Dr Lay, proceeded to search Rose's part of the house.

The two went up to Rose's attic bedroom. Her bed had not been slept in, though a depression showed that she had sat on it for some time. On her box next to the bed lay an envelope, addressed to her, with Peasenhall and Yoxford postmarks. It contained an unsigned letter which read:

D R
I will try to see you tonight
at 12 oclock at your Place if you
Put a light in your window at
10 oclock for about 10 minutes then
you can take it out again.
dont have a light in your Room at
12 as I will come round to the
back

PC Nunn searched the girl's chest of drawers, and found another bundle of correspondence. This consisted mostly of completely irrelevant family letters, and a few innocuous letters from local men. But two groups of documents were of interest.

One was a bundle of intensely passionate (or sentimental) love letters, mixed with indecent suggestions and dirty poems. These were all unsigned. The other was a pair of signed letters from the married Methodist, William Gardiner, written a year previously when he and Rose had been involved in a village scandal. These letters referred to the action Gardiner was taking to establish their innocence. It was agreed by everyone that Gardiner's handwriting was completely unlike that of the dirty poems and declarations of love and lust. It would become a matter of considerable controversy later whether his hand was or was not similar to that of the assignation note to D R, however.

Nunn quickly concluded that Rose had not killed herself, but had been murdered, and he sent for senior assistance. Superintendent George Andrews from Halesworth joined the police contingent in Providence House fairly late in the day. He found Dr Lay still there, and he may or may not have heard that the doctor thought death was self-inflicted. But no one could find the weapon with which Rose had supposedly killed herself.

There was, of course, the broken bottle. Dr Lay had instantly recognized it as one from his stock with a prescription in his writing, but he could not immediately read the blood and paraffin stained label. The standard printing said 'A sixth part to be taken every four hours', but the patient's name was smudgily obscured.

Dr Lay thought it was for Mrs Gardiner's sister. He had prescribed for her a few months earlier when she was taken ill while staying with the Gardiners in Peasenhall.

He thought that the broken glass could have been used to inflict the flesh wounds in the throat, but it didn't seem a likely implement for the puncture wound.

The doctor pocketed the bottle to see if he could identify its recipient more precisely, and the police gathered together all the fragments of broken glass. They found that their careful sweepings did not constitute the complete bottle, and this led them to wonder where the other pieces had gone. When they subsequently passed the pieces to the Home Office analyst on 9 June, he found that the debris also contained half a spent wooden matchstick, and a piece of blue woollen fabric, about three-sixteenths of an inch across.

Dr Lay's concern was still with the label, of course, but a week after the finding of the body he still thought it had been addressed to Mrs Gardiner's sister. Only when the Home Office had treated it and the paraffin had evaporated still further could he read the inscription clearly on a photograph they showed him: he had written 'Two or three teaspoonfuls' above the print, and below it, 'Mrs Gardiner's chdn'.

Dr Lay was a plain country GP. He wisely asked a colleague to give a second opinion when he undertook the post-mortem. So Dr Ryder Richardson of Saxmundham came to assist him, and Dr Richardson reached his quick and clear conclusions far more decisively than Dr Lay. He could not, of course, offer any comment on the time of death. Nor was he absolutely sure whether the throat was cut from the left or the right. But the wounds were definitely not self-inflicted, and he thought that the assailant had stood on Rose's right. The death of Rose Harsent was murder. The burning of her nightgown was no accident, but a calculated attempt to destroy evidence at the scene of the crime.

So who could the criminal be? One name instantly put itself forward. Whether it was for his sister-in-law or his children, the broken medicine bottle of paraffin had come from William Gardiner's house. Rose had preserved two letters from him. She was pregnant, and his name had been involved with hers in scandal the year before. Gardiner was interviewed at work on Monday and arrested on Tuesday.

What had this scandal been? Well, to understand village scandal fully, one must start by understanding the character of the village and the villagers and of the two people who scandalized them.

TWO

The Village

S uffolk is fine unspoilt agricultural country. Excellent, if shallow, peaty top-soil rests on a clay base. This is arable farmland. Suffolk's contribution to animal husbandry was the breeding of Suffolk Punches: the great cart-horses which supplied the power for farming before the tractors and automotive machinery which itself constitutes Suffolk's contribution to industry. Garrets of Leiston were the great manufacturers of traction engines and road-rollers. All manner of agricultural implements were made in the county, yet industrialization never despoiled its rural tranquillity.

This is a district where fresh air from the North Sea encourages longevity; where the dry eastern atmosphere alleviates the arthritis which makes old age a misery in western England; where something in the way of life seems to keep Alzheimer's disease to a minimum. Like others who have investigated Rose Harsent's death, we were to meet and interview Peasenhall's nonagenarians. We never encountered fumbling minds, hazy memories or senile repetitiousness.

Stewart Evans, a Bury St Edmunds policeman who has studied Rose Harsent's murder more closely than almost anyone else known to us, drove us across the county to the village in early May. We passed occasional windmills, and in one large field, a row of ten traditional scarecrows.

Peasenhall was utterly beautiful. The late spring flowers massed along the lanes into the village: frothing cow parsley, some stitchwort and a few dead nettles giving a base of white; brilliant yellow patches of buttercups and the half-hidden, duller celandines; with the odd poppy blazing out. Only the familiar magenta of campion was strangely missing. There were cowslips in the cemetery where Rose Harsent lies buried.

The village lies along a shallow valley running from east to west. If you leave the village by turning right or left at the crossroads at the western end, you trudge uphill, whether you go north or south. The Street runs for about a quarter of a mile along the north side of the

Yoxford Brook which is now a trickle in a concrete culvert. Today it is hard
to imagine its being in danger of flooding and inundating the road. The
north side of The Street is lined with old cottages, often in pairs separated
by narrow alleys leading back to little gardens and outhouses. Alma
Cottage, William Gardiner's old home, now has an attractive facing of
pale green plaster. Roofs are a variety of slate, thatch, and heavy S-shaped
tiles. Here is where the Angel Inn stood in 1902. Here still stand the Swan
Inn, and Emmett's General Stores. You cannot see past the houses to the
countryside beyond on the northern side of Peasenhall Street.

South of the brook, a band of grass fronts the narrow roadway of The
Causeway, and straggling houses and cottages lie on the other side.
Behind them, fields sloping gently uphill have been converted to
allotments.

The only hint of topographical complexity lies at the eastern end of the
village, where The Street forks, and a few buildings, including the fine old
Tudor Wool Stapling Hall, lie between the branches. To the right, the
Yoxford Road runs south-east past the Wesleyan Methodist chapel. To
the left the road curves away north and passes through flat fields to the
Poys Street section of Sibton, about a mile away.

Yoxford, two miles east of Peasenhall, is crossed by both the railway line
and the main road leading to Halesworth, five miles to the north, and
Saxmundham, four miles to the south. Poys Street, where Sibton Primitive
Methodist chapel stands, is important to our story.

But we are most concerned with the western end of the village. The
Street stops being so named when it is crossed by a road running north to
south. To the north, Heveningham Long Lane winds away uphill to
Heveningham and Ubbeston. Church Street, to the south, slopes uphill
again, passing Smyths' derelict seed-drill works on its right, and becoming
the lane winding away to the Kelsale and Rendham Road.

As its name suggests, Church Street is close to the church of St Michael
which lies about twenty-five yards west of it, obscured by a row of cottages
running up Church Street to the Drill Works. The church is about fifty
yards back from Hackney Road, as the main Peasenhall Street is renamed
when it runs west from the crossroads. Again, a few cottages have sprung
up along the south of the road. They face the village assembly hall lying on
the north: a striking Swiss chalet erected by the Smyth family for
community functions. Just west of the church and the assembly hall, the
Bruisyard Road runs south out of the village. And that completes the
complexities of Peasenhall geography.

The Heveningham Road crossroads is the focal point of our interest.
The bridge at Church Street as it crosses the Yoxford Brook caused all the

flooding, but there has been no further inundation since the stream bed has been re-dug and its water led through an engineered culvert.

In 1902 Emmett's Store was at the crossroads, as it still is. The shop dominates the north-eastern corner, opposite The Ancient House to the south of The Street. The pink-plastered classical eighteenth century frontage of The Ancient House lies at an angle to the corner. A large and beautiful garden runs behind the house alongside Church Street for a hundred yards, terminating almost opposite the drill works. On this land, twenty yards back from Church Street, stands a little barn-like thatched and cob-walled seventeenth-century structure, with square-paned leaded windows. Now disused, this was, until 1912, a Congregationalist chapel, known locally as 'the Doctor's Chapel'. Today nobody knows for certain whether this name refers to the fact that it was on Dr Lay's land – for he was the owner of The Ancient House in 1902 – or whether it goes back to his father or grandfather, also doctors, who owned the house and used to worship there.

The west side of Dr Lay's house looked across Church Street to Providence House. This is another splendid historic building, sited directly on the south-west corner of Hackney Road and Church Street, with its great gable end looking down The Street.

The original seventeenth-century Providence House, home of a Civil War colonel, has been divided in three. The section owned by Mr and Mrs William Crisp was the northern wing. A balancing wing up Church Street was Church House where Mr James Crisp lived in 1902, and the two are linked by the old middle and original front entrance of the building, now called Centre Cottage. This was occupied by the family of a wheelwright called Davis when Rose Harsent was murdered.

We were privileged in that Stewart Evans had arranged for us to be shown around the murder house. The front door is in the north of the house, off the little lawn between the building and Hackney Road. It has the feeling of a large side door, and was, indeed, probably constructed after the original building had been divided. It leads into the hall where Rose and Mrs Crisp bade each other goodnight for the last time. The door to the dining-room opens off from it to the right and the door to the parlour on the left. The present owners have lightened the deep square hall ingeniously by removing the lath and plaster that filled the wooden frame enclosing the first floor landing. With that landing exposed, like a tiny minstrels' gallery, the whole character of the entrance becomes open and welcoming, without losing its quaintness and historical feeling.

The front parlour and the master bedroom overlooking Church Street (where Mr and Mrs Crisp slept) are lovely light airy rooms, and there is no sinister feeling about the house.

The kitchen has changed substantially since Rose Harsent's day. The outside conservatory has been altered, so that the window now looks directly on to the garden. The penthouse roof has been removed, and a bedroom built over the kitchen, its walls cleanly and almost undetectably continuing the line and proportions of the main building. The little scullery which filled the western end of the kitchen-penthouse has gone, and Rose's enclosed staircase has been removed. Access to her attic is now via a new staircase off the first-floor landing. The overwhelming impression one carries away is of the small size of the room in which Rose died compared with the large size of the house. Her body and the kitchen table would almost have filled the little room, leaving just a square yard or so by the door and window.

The only sinister trace left in Providence House is darkening on the brick floor where Rose's body lay, spreading back under the point where the staircase would have been. Can this be Rose's blackened blood? Or carbon deposited by the burning paraffin with which her murderer tried to destroy the scene of his crime? No one knows, but it has seeped down into the bricks so that it cannot now be removed. And some people say the bricks have been turned over as there is even more staining on the other side.

So much for the village. What of the people? This lovely farming county was long the setting for intense social disharmony. Farmers and landowners kept labourers' wages depressed, and used the tied cottage system to hold their workers down in a state akin to paid serfage. Fortunately for the villagers farming was not a monopoly employer in Peasenhall's economy. The Smyths were the largest employers in the village. Josiah Smyth was the inventor of 'the original Suffolk Seed Drill' which had been exhibited all over the world. The company kept a sales office in Paris, and engaged about four hundred hands in Peasenhall.

The drill works dominated Peasenhall's working life. Men came from all the villages around to work there, and the inhabitants of Peasenhall set their clocks and watches by the factory hooter which Tich Kemp blew at 8.00 a.m., 1.00 p.m. and 6.00 p.m. every working day.

Like many of the men they employed, but unlike the landowning gentry, the Smyths were Nonconformists, worshipping at a nearby Congregationalist chapel. For the other great feature of historic East Anglian society was the prevalence of anti-episcopalianism. Oliver Cromwell was a fensman from Huntingdon, and his sect, the Independents, were powerful throughout the region. Each parish congregation, they felt, should appoint its own minister and manage its own affairs: hence their later title of Congregationalists.

Throughout the Commonwealth period the Peasenhall district was blessed with a notable Congregationalist minister. Mr John Manning became vicar of Peasenhall and Sibton in 1654. In 1662, when the Tory churchmen of the Restoration got round to clearing out Puritans from the rural parishes, he was ejected and embarked on a career which would make him a memorable local martyr for the truth. He noted that oath-taking was directly contrary to scripture. He was to be imprisoned repeatedly for refusing to take Oaths of Allegiance to the Crown. None the less, in 1672 he was licensed to give Congregationalist 'lectures' at his home in Peasenhall, and continued to do so until his death in 1694. It is almost certainly at this period that the Doctor's Chapel was built, although by 1902 its importance was dwarfed by the greater Congregationalist chapel at Rendham, and its services were conducted, under licence, by a visiting preacher from Leiston. The Crisps worshipped at the Doctor's Chapel, where Mr Crisp was a deacon, and made it one of Rose's duties to clean the little building.

At the end of the eighteenth century, Methodism spread through Suffolk. John Wesley's 'Methodist Connexion' was originally intended to comprise a group of Anglican Bible study classes and prayer meetings to prepare ticket-holders for conformist Holy Communion at their parish churches. Class-members should, of course, lead lives of strict and 'methodical' Christian morality. They were visited by peripatetic evangelists, and these preachers, copying Wesley's extremely emotional style of exhortation, followed him in encouraging the familiar conversion experience.

Even before Wesley's death, it was becoming apparent that converted Methodists would not always find it easy to accept that they were in full Christian fellowship with more Laodicean Christians, or respect a hierarchical clergy which had not experienced conversion. And so a separate Wesleyan Methodist Church emerged.

The emphasis on personal conversion led to further doubts as to whether ordained ministers were invariably the right people to lead the saints. Wesley's organization of separate classes gave great standing to the 'class-leaders' who collected subscriptions, issued tickets for attendance to those who were paid-up, and were entitled to refuse class-membership to those whose lives were scandalous.

By the 1820s, labouring men saw no reason why their ministry should not be as acceptable as that of the more educated. Many Wesleyan ministers were unwilling to yield authority to less educated men. And so major schisms began. In the south and west the 'Bryanites' or Bible Christians became the working men's Methodist church. In the north and east, the almost identical Primitive Methodists predominated. Both groups accepted some of the structure inherited from the Wesleyans, but gave the laity far greater power. Chapels were built and maintained by lay trustees from the Primitive Methodist community. Society stewards were responsible for organizing regular worship. Lay class leaders still handled subscriptions, but also took pastoral responsibility for members. Groups of a dozen or so chapels were organized in circuits, with a superintendent minister who convened and chaired regular quarterly meetings of lay representatives of the chapels. Unlike an Anglican priest, the superintendent minister could be outvoted and overruled by the lay majority. The murder in Peasenhall affords one of the most fascinating examples of the tense workings of this hierarchical democracy.

The Primitive Methodist chapel at Poys Street, Sibton, was the oldest in the Wangford Circuit, built in 1836. Here William Gardiner and Rose Harsent worshipped.

Peasenhall's Anglicans worshipped at St Michael's church. This was so thoroughly restored in the 1870s that its interior has entirely lost the period charm of most Suffolk churches. Only its north porch door exhibits fine East Anglian medieval stonework. A pair of cuddly toy lions symbolize strength and virtue on the pillars. Savage nature, by contrast, is represented in the dragon and the wodwose (or wild man of the woods) who scramble up the angles above the door. Wodwoses (the 'Green Men' of so many pubs) are a surprisingly popular Suffolk ecclesiastical motif. Dressed in leaves, ferociously bearded and unkempt, and armed with crude, untrimmed tree-trunk cudgels, they may represent either the innocence of unsophisticated natural man, or the brutal carnality of the unregenerate. Those Peasenhall villagers who have long said, 'You can see a picture of William Gardiner on our church door', clearly believe the latter as well as believing in Gardiner's guilt.

The existence of dissent and schism caused a good deal of tension in Victorian village England. Anglicans seemed to Nonconformists to be snobbish. Nonconformists seemed to Anglicans to be sanctimonious.

Knowing that such divisions had survived until quite recently in many rural areas, we were interested to note what seemed to be a rough division among the witnesses at the court hearings following Rose Harsent's murder. It seemed to us that Anglicans tended to testify for the prosecution, and it was clear that many Primitive Methodists rallied round a brother in distress. So we put a direct question to Mr Herbert Denny.

At ninety-five, Mr Denny is the oldest surviving villager with clear memories of William Gardiner and Rose Harsent. Moreover, his father, Jonathan Denny, worked under Gardiner at Smyths' for several years. Mr Denny's memories are vital for any crime historian in Peasenhall.

'Tell us, Herbert,' we asked, 'was there any conflict between the Anglicans and the Methodists in those days?'

'Conflict?' returned Mr Denny in tones of manifest astonishment, as he contemplated something like modern football hooliganism. '*Conflict?* No. Never. Nothing like that. Why, they never spoke to each other!'

This was the strongest of several indications that religious divisions played a part in the events of 1902.

Mr Billy Rowe is a few months younger than Mr Denny. His cottage is in Hackney Road, at the other end of the village from Mr Denny's. The brook, he told us, used to flow along a gravel and weed-lined bed thirteen feet below the road surface in 1902.

We asked Mr Rowe about the social and leisure life of the village. He painted a rather bleak picture of unrelieved labour. 'It wasn't like today,' he said. 'There wasn't much to do. There was no television or anything to go to. People didn't do very much except work.'

He had no idea what women and girls might do with their leisure if they ever had any. Men and boys had little enough. But there were small areas of relief. While most writers have thought of the church and chapel choirs as the obvious musical outlets in the village, Mr Rowe remembered the three bands that gave concerts in the assembly hall: the brass band, the string band and the nigger minstrels. In a village of about 800 souls, a goodly proportion must have been engaged in music-making to keep all three running.

There was also football, Mr Rowe remembered. Peasenhall and Sibton had a combined football club, and the village took great pride in it. One important trial witness whose name was already known to us turned out to have been a great footballer. Appropriately, he was called Billy Wright.

Mr Rowe's Peasenhall seemed a rather more unified community than Mr Denny's. One could envisage, in his memories, the side of village life where sectarian disputes were set aside from time to time: where gentlefolk like the Smyths would make presentations to the village church, although they did not worship there; where the whole village would contribute to a Jubilee Clock Fund or a Bell Fund, regardless of the fact that the Anglicans obviously benefited.

Billy Rowe remembered William Gardiner as an adult to respect. He remembered Dr Lay with very great respect indeed. Dr Lay treated the Rowe family in the best pre-National Health tradition of living on the fees from the rich and serving the poor without charge. 'We must have owed him hundreds of pounds when he died,' said Mr Rowe. And one begins to sense mutual support and charity operating in the community as long as religious beliefs are put on one side.

So the Seed Drill Works was the main employer. The countryside all around dominated everybody's lifestyle. Travel was rare. The churches' sectarian quarrels played much the role that politics does today in the minds of men. Old Peasenhall might best be described as something we have totally lost and forgotten today: a completely rural industrial village.

THREE

William Gardiner and Rose Harsent

W illiam Gardiner's rise to respectability was heroic. Sibton chapel's class leader, Sunday School superintendent, society steward and organist was the second of his young mother's three illegitimate children. The foreman carpenter of Smyths' Drill Works came into the world in the grim red-brick Blything Parish Union Workhouse at Bulcamp.

His mother cannot have enjoyed the experience. A district nurse who first saw the workhouse in 1928 gave a most unfavourable account of it:

> We called it the infirmary, but they called it the 'wuk'us,' and
> how they hated it!. . . I can remember visiting the workhouse at
> Blythburgh when I first came this way to nurse and I was
> disgusted. . . . A woman I knew had to inspect these Suffolk
> workhouses and she told me that Bulcamp was the worst place
> she'd been into. How dreadful it was!

George Gardiner, William's grandfather, was an agricultural labourer. In 1839 he married Ann Friend in Wangford parish church. She was his second wife and George already had two children, John and Sarah. There followed another six: Emma, George, Ann, Caroline, Jane and James. In 1840, the family was living at Great Street, Yoxford. Ten years later they had moved to Brook Street in the same village.

The middle two girls were a bit of a handful. Ann was about nineteen years old and unmarried when, in 1863, she gave birth to a son, Harry William Gardiner. He was born at his grandparents' home in Yoxford, and he was still attending school from there eight years later.

Less than two years after Harry's birth, his nineteen-year-old Aunt Caroline became a mother for the first time. On 2 November 1864, Anna Maria Gardiner was born in Bulcamp Workhouse. On

22 December 1866, William George Last Gardiner followed her. And on 28 May 1869, Caroline was delivered of her last workhouse bastard, Ada Jane Gardiner. Two years later, all three children were with their mother in their grandparents' cottage in Yoxford, along with Ann's Harry. Ann herself was not there. The only one of Caroline's brothers and sisters still at home in Yoxford was her younger brother James who had become a wheelwright.

Caroline was a domestic servant. She would have lost her job with each pregnancy. The only way for her to receive reasonable midwifery or obstetrics would be to declare herself without means and place herself in the workhouse with access to the infirmary. With the child safely delivered, she could then discharge herself from the dreadful place and stay with her parents until she found a new post (or, in her case, another pregnancy).

Who were the fathers attracted by this pretty young woman with one blue and one brown eye? We simply don't know, but William's third forename, Last, looks like a clue to his. Stewart Evans has spotted two families of Lasts on the Yoxford census registers, one in Brook Street, close to the Gardiners.

In 1873, Caroline Gardiner married a 34-year-old bachelor shoe-maker named Edward Coleman who lodged near her parents' cottage. The wedding took place in Yoxford Wesleyan Chapel, and the marriage was not blessed with issue for another two years.

William started his life with the enormous handicap of being 'a workhouse brat', and one, moreover, whose feckless mother had repeated her shameful pattern a third time over.

William was educated, presumably, at the Yoxford parish school, and learned to write a clear firm hand, with reasonable spelling and punctuation. By the age of fourteen he had finished with formal book-learning, however, and went out into the working world. In 1881 he was described as 'working at Wheelwrights'. He was always rather a stickler for precise titles and artisan qualifications, and when he became a journeyman wheelwright he so described himself. When he rose to become a foreman he added that rank to official documents.

By 1888 he was no longer just the 'boy' around the wheelwright's shop. He was a wheelwright, and described himself as such on his marriage certificate. This made him a very highly skilled woodworker. To make and balance a wheel perfectly requires accurate carpentry of the highest order, and he would have had no difficulty in turning his hand to any other construction work in wood.

Suffolk woodworkers lived close to their raw material. Well into the

Imaginative illustrations of Rose's fate from contemporary newspaper reports, and her death certificate

2

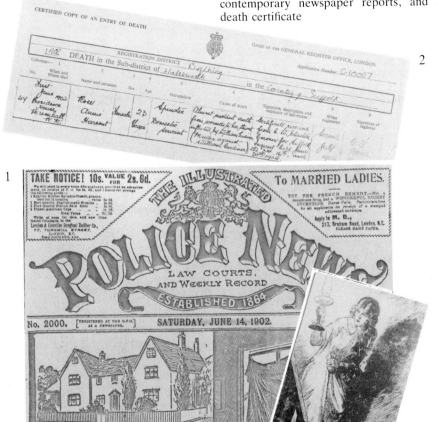

1

3

Tabloid press of 1902 envisages the discovery of the body, with discreet advertisements for contraceptives and abortifacients

1

Prominent features of Peasenhall, including an elevation of Providence House, and a diagram of its layout; a view of The Street from Rose's window; St Michael's church; and a view of the old drill works

Key

A = Rose's bedroom
B = Crisps' bedroom
C = Kitchen
D = Dining room
E = Front door of Providence House
F = Centre House, occupied by Davis family
G = The Church House, occupied by James Crisp
– – – Rose's route from her bedroom down rear stairs to kitchen

3

4

5

6

1

2

3

4

Gardiner in Peasenhall: his birth and marriage
certificates; a poster issued by his employers;
his cottage; a contemporary portrait of him;
and the wodwose on St Michael's church
which villagers mischievously designated his
likeness

6

twentieth century, the country carpenter did not look to a timber yard to sell him prepared lengths of seasoned timber. He went out into the woods; marked a tree suitable for his purposes; arranged for its purchase and felling; shaped his own planks and beams, and stored it himself for seasoning. This was a complete and satisfying working life.

On 16 October 1888, William Gardiner, wheelwright, married Georgianna, daughter of George Cady, dealer, at Westleton Primitive Methodist Chapel. The bride's father and Harriet Laura Davy were the witnesses. It seems to have been a shotgun wedding. The safe delivery of Ettie May Gardiner occurred two months later.

William's marriage certificate describes him as living at Elmswell, a village on the other side of the county near Bury St Edmunds. As far as we know, never before had he or any other unmarried member of his immediate family travelled so far away from the Yoxford district. The possibility that he ran away from the threat of paternity cannot be overlooked.

But parenthood seems to have been the making of him, giving him a new sense of responsibility and dignity. On Ettie May's birth certificate, for the first time, he dropped the name Last and added the qualification 'journeyman'.

Georgianna Cady was a Primitive Methodist. It is not known whether William Gardiner had had much to do with religion previously, but from now on he was decidedly active as a 'Prim'. And his marriage brought him into the family of one of the most colourful characters in the Connexion.

His father-in-law George Cady was originally a grocer and draper. But long before his daughter grew up he had entered the more exciting trade of horse-dealing, an unusual occupation for a Methodist local preacher. By profession, George was a worldlier man than most of his spiritual brethren.

By reputation, according to Allan Jobson the Suffolk historian, he was 'the biggest rogue in the community'. His most skilful horse-coping trick was dosing a broken-winded nag with shot to steady its breathing for the period of sale and delivery.

His combined reputation as a dubious horse-trader and hell-fire Methodist preacher raised a good many eyebrows. He even dressed for the two parts to extremes, wearing fustian cords with gaiters on weekdays; and a frock-coat and shovel-hat on Sundays.

But perhaps the most interesting thing about George Cady's Methodist horse-dealing was the hair-splitting scrupulosity which per-suaded him that he maintained his integrity. He would not deal on a

Sunday, but he would ask, 'Supposing this were not the Sabbath, how much would you be asking for that horse?' He would suppress the truth of a beast's weaknesses while selling it, but would tell you all the details honestly once your money was in his pocket if you chose to ask. And he would deceive with stickling half-truths.

George Cady was forty-eight in 1888 when his eldest daughter became pregnant. He lived in Great Street, Yoxford with his wife and seven children. Georgianna, named after George, was twenty, and had been apprenticed to a dressmaker.

George may have been a little slow in detecting his daughter's interesting condition. Perhaps some of his own troubles distracted him from the goings-on at home. He had offended the very weighty Primitive Methodist, Noah Etheridge. Noah actually took the matter to Quarterly Meeting, protesting that George owed him money and this must be sorted out. The elders of the church forced Mr Cady to explain himself and settle his debts.

And Saxmundham magistrates also wanted a word with Mr Cady in September 1888. He was fined 10/- (50p) and costs of 3/6d (17p) for letting two horses stray on the highway.

His granddaughter Ettie May Gardiner was born in Yoxford. But within a couple of years the Gardiners had moved to Peasenhall where William's steady rise to respectability would be achieved. It may have been at this time that Georgianna, at least, established the habit of reducing Ettie May's age by a year, so that she seemed to have been conceived in wedlock.

William went to work for a small carpenter and undertaker called Newberry. A number of artisans did this, putting themselves on the scene in case a secure vacancy should arise at Smyths' Drill Works. Gardiner was lucky. Within a short time he was employed by Smyths' as a wheelwright and carpenter.

He was an excellent workman. Every single recollection of him confirms this. His vice still stands fitted to the work bench of the wash-house behind Alma Cottage. He was clearly prepared to do serious work at home, for the vice is fitted with a well made wooden extension falling a couple of feet below bench level, to steady larger pieces of timber than most home handymen would use.

And in the early 1890s, two concurrent events in the Primitive Methodist Connexion must have boosted his self-confidence. William Gardiner started to rise in the church, while his father-in-law fell resoundingly. In 1892, Brothers Gardiner, Rouse, Barns and Jordan were appointed to form the Beccles Mission Board, under the direction of an accredited local preacher. Missions were part of the regular excitement of chapel life. Their particular attraction was the presence of missioners from outside the missionary territory. A poor man's church like the Primitive Methodists could not ship preachers all over the country, and the brethren running the Beccles Mission were only travelling a little distance north of their own circuit of Wangford. But it was the first definite responsibility the church had given Gardiner: his first taste of committee work, organization and administrative powers. And the extent to which it was probationary is clear, since a recognized local preacher was to oversee the work.

His fellow-missioner, agricultural labourer Henry Rouse, was to play a significant role in Gardiner's scandalous future. In the light of later events, it is extremely interesting to see that he also needed a local preacher to supervise him. Rouse was a very much older man than Gardiner, and not without ambitions in the church. Ten years later he would say that he had been a local preacher for twenty-five years. But this was evidently an exaggeration. In 1892 he was still at the bottom of the ladder of Connexion appointments, and if there should be spiritual competition among the brethren, he was competing directly with Brother William Gardiner, a man forty years younger than himself.

The following year on 6 March, Quarterly Meeting minutes recorded starkly,

'That we receive G. Cady's resignation as preacher & member,
he having become bankrupt; & he be reported to Dis[trict].
Com[mittee].'

How were the mighty fallen! The great George Cady was stripped of his church offices and thrown out of the Connexion less than five years after he had seen that the Yoxford scapegrace make an honest woman of his daughter. The shameless son-in-law was overtaking his wife's father, and starting on the route to esteem and respect in the church on his own account.

From the summer of 1893, Gardiner inevitably lost any sense of shamefacedness in his father-in-law's presence. His own family had been growing meanwhile with Ida Mildred born in 1891 and Ernest William in 1892. Then there was a four-year gap, during which Georgianna might have suffered one or more miscarriages. From 1896 children again came regularly to the Gardiners, though at a slightly lower rate of fertility. Bertie George was born in 1896; the twins Annie and Dora in 1898; Daisy May in 1901.

William's pride in his self-made respectability grated somewhat on his children. Ernest, in particular, resented the fact that they were always driven to chapel on Sundays in a trap borrowed from Smyths' Drill Works. It distanced him from his playmates unacceptably. And he hated, still more, being dressed up in neat clothes and forbidden to go scrambling in streams and bird's-nesting with other village boys. The girls were less resentful of being better dressed and turned-out than the generality of village children.

In 1900 William Gardiner was made society steward at Sibton chapel. Some time between 1897 and 1901 he also became class leader. The surviving minutes do not record his appointment, but they do record that of Brother J. Wright in 1894, with Harry Burgess as his Assistant. Burgess was also Sunday School secretary until 1897, when Gardiner relieved him of this office. Burgess seems to have held no further chapel positions until he became a trustee in 1908.

Was this rapid rise provoking envy among the brethren? Could this lie behind Gardiner's alleged 'Holy Willy' reputation, for which there doesn't seem to be a trace of evidence in any reliable contemporary report, or any old people's recollections? What does come resonating down the oral tradition of Peasenhall, however, is admiration for Gardiner the workman, and recognition of his strong personality.

Herbert Denny says his father, Jonathan, said he worked 'under Gardiner' for twelve years, which suggests that some form of seniority came very quickly to the young Methodist. Between 1898 and 1901 he was promoted to foreman carpenter and 'outside manager' with office space in the brick building above the works, next to the large office where, as Billy Rowe recalled, Mr Smyth 'did his scheming', or designed new agricultural machinery. Gardiner was now brought very close to Mr John Samuel Rickards the company secretary, who dominated the outer office. In 1900 the firm sent Gardiner to the Paris Exhibition to oversee their stand. It was a prestigious secondment, and it may have provoked some jealousy at the drill works.

The workmen to some degree feared his vehement character. Herbert Denny's father was hugely impressed by Gardiner's strength and 'nerve' or bold determination. He never forgot the occasion when Gardiner dropped a massive iron weight on his foot, crushing his toecap and breaking his toe. The black-bearded foreman roared with pain, and seized a mallet and chisel as if to amputate the offending toe on the spot. It took four men to restrain him.

There was also a dashing element to his very masculine personality. This shows in his surviving signatures, which are given ornamented underlining. And it showed in his almost personal claim to Smyths' black mare.

The drill works owned a number of horses. Old William Harsent was one of their carters for a time, nicknamed 'Old Strap' from his habit of taking off his leather belt to thrash any lads who climbed on to his wagon-tail.

But the black mare was part Arab, almost as large as a carthorse, and reputed to be the fastest carriage horse in the county. Gardiner took a pride in sprinting around the countryside with the mare pulling her trap at a fine clip. Even Mr Rickards turned to the firm's head carpenter when he wanted to be driven quickly to the market garden his wife ran for him at Kelsale. By 1901, 'Mr Gardiner' – ('Willie' to his family and intimates) – was a person to be reckoned with in working-class Peasenhall.

Where, with his background, did he learn to play the harmonium? Maybe he was a naturally gifted musician: one of those who simply find a keyboard, and quickly feel their way into vamping out basic harmonies. Certainly he became organist and choirmaster at Sibton Chapel. And chapel music brought Gardiner into close contact with a young woman who wanted to learn the organ; who is said by some to have played the chapel harmonium on occasion; and by others to have asked William Gardiner to give her organ lessons. This was a request to which he acceded with such alacrity, that the rumour still runs that the shared musical interest was a deep cover for something else. . . .

Rose Anne Harsent was a Sibton girl, the child of illiterate labourer William Harsent and his wife Elizabeth. She was the fourth, and then came four more brothers and one sister, and this large family had to go to work as soon as possible. Rose was educated at Sibton parish school, and the records show a good deal of absence with illness for her and her siblings, twice with ringworm.

Some time around 1898 when Rose was nineteen or twenty, she started attending the Primitive Methodist chapel. Her parents had been married in the parish church, but Sibton is a strange parish, strung out in hamlets around almost a square mile of fields. The church was half an hour's walk away from the Harsent home in Poys Street, while the chapel was just down the road.

But proximity is unlikely to have been the main attraction of Primitive Methodism for Rose. More probably, she was influenced by young Bob Kerridge, a ploughboy who may have been a distant cousin by marriage, for Rose's mother was the widow of a labourer named George Kerridge when she married William Harsent. Bob lived very near the Harsents in Poys Street, and within a couple of years he was so friendly with Rose that they were said to be engaged – or, at least, to have an understanding. And Bob was a keen Primitive Methodist.

There is also the possibility that Gardiner himself attracted her to the chapel. He may have known her or her family before coming to Peasenhall. For one Harriet Laura Davy, daughter of a wheelwright, who was a witness at the Gardiners' wedding, subsequently married a Harsent from Essex.

Whatever attracted Rose to Methodism, the choir and the church music became one of her continuing pleasures. As the *Illustrated Police News* astutely discovered, she told Bob Kerridge of her musical aspirations. From somewhere the young ploughboy found the money to buy her a small harmonium or 'American organ', even though the Kerridges were as poor as the Harsents. Cottage pianos and harmoniums were a major source of home entertainment for the poor, and they changed hands at low prices second-hand and at auctions. Rose's organ survived her understanding with Bob. It survived her. And the last pieces of it have survived Bob. In the 1920s Mr Herbert Denny bought it from Bob. When it passed beyond its playing days, he broke it up and used the case for timber. When we visited him, he showed us the two doorsills from his sitting-room into the passage and into his kitchen, which he made from Rose Harsent's organ.

In 1900 Rose went to work at Providence House. Away from home, she started to take an interest in less virtuous young men than Bob Kerridge. Gossip builds after an open scandal, and at this date it is hard to trust the views handed down to Billy Rowe that she was 'a bit warm' or 'a hot piece'. At the same time, it is unquestionable that she was pregnant when she died; that her name had been scandalously associated with Gardiner's in 1901; and that she enjoyed receiving salacious letters from Frederick Davis, the boy next door.

Frederick Davis was a most unfortunate young man. He attended the chapel at Sibton, and saw Rose every week, prominent at the front of the choir. Rose was no chocolate-box beauty, but the surviving photograph of her at about the age of eighteen shows a lively, vital and delightfully mischievous-looking girl with a trim figure.

Fred Davis was four years younger than Rose. He worked in Emmett's Store. As the grocer's boy, he had to deliver to the Crisps a couple of times a week. He came to the kitchen door at the back of Providence House, inside the conservatory. He did not always find Mrs Crisp there to chaperone his conversation, so he got to know Rose.

And through her, he made that exciting discovery for young men of sheltered upbringing: girls like to talk dirty, too.

Rose was interested in the lewd poems and verses that all the young men of Peasenhall knew, and Frederick agreed to write out copies of them for her. It is not known what they were, but certainly a number of today's rugby songs were already current in the 1890s. Davis probably wrote out a few verses of something like 'The Ball At Kirriemuir' or 'Kafoozelum, The Harlot of Jerusalem' for Rose. Harmless enough, but somewhat overexciting at a time when society decreed a quite impossibly sexless chastity for the unmarried.

This led Davis to think of Rose with a healthily sexy adolescent romanticism. He wrote her quite passionate love-letters, and stated shamelessly that his love included a carnal desire that he hoped she would satisfy.

And he used the literary allusions common to the pair of them to reinforce his mixture of passion and desire. He quoted from hymns and the Bible. His exact quotations were deemed too indecent or blasphemous to be made public. But he directed her to chapter and verse in the book of Proverbs. This might have been the optimistic chapter 13, verse 14: 'Hope deferred maketh the heart sick: but when the desire cometh it is a tree of life.' It might have been the beautifully complimentary chapter 5, verse 19: 'Let her be as the loving hind and the pleasant roe: let her breasts satisfy thee at all times; and be thou ravished always with her love.' But since it was regarded as rather ingeniously indecent, it was probably chapter 20, verse 27: 'The spirit of man is the candle of the Lord, searching all the inward parts of the belly.'

He also quoted from the hymn 'At even ere the sun was set'. It is not easy to find *double entendre* in its words, but the most likely lines which Davis might have sent Rose are:

> What if Thy Form we cannot see?
> We know and feel that Thou art here.

For these were overtly respectable young people, and while Davis evidently hoped that he and Rose might become physical lovers, what we know of his letters gives no indication that it happened. And when she first went to work for Mrs Crisp, Rose had been quite confident that she never would become pregnant until she was married. So it seems quite possible that for some time she contented herself with prolonged kissing and petting, and, if Davis was lucky, he may have felt what he never saw. Still, he was the young girl's confidant before she became pregnant, for he obtained for her a household marriage and medical manual which included advice on contraception and hints concerning abortion.

There's nothing dreadfully shocking about two young people discovering that they share an interest in sex. Davis was unlucky because Rose treasured his letters in her bedroom where they were found after her death, so that he was publicly excoriated when his authorship was proved.

Bob Kerridge was a simple sweetheart who wanted to marry Rose and gave her an expensive present. Frederick Davis offered the spice of sexy talk and letters – maybe even some cautious sexual experimentation. Were there other men, too, in Rose's life?

In 1901 it became known all over the village that there seemed to be at least one other.

FOUR

The Scandal

On Wednesday 1 May 1901, William Gardiner's work took him out driving one of Smyths' horses. It was not his favourite black mare this time, but a stallion.

He returned to the works at about half past seven in the evening, rubbed the horse down, watered it, and put food out for it. The horse made no attempt to eat, which worried Gardiner. As outside manager he was responsible for the horses. He went thoughtfully home for his tea.

In the Rendham Road he saw 20-year-old Bill Wright who worked under him as a wheelwright at Smyths'. They exchanged a few words, and Gardiner went on home. His tea, which he normally ate at six o'clock, was waiting for him. As soon as he had finished, he went out again to see if the horse was all right. If it was still off its feed, he proposed sending for the vet.

As he came back up Rendham Road to the drill works, he saw Wright again lounging around in the lane. This time the two did not speak. Gardiner went across the works yard to the stable, and found to his relief that the horse had eaten. By Gardiner's estimate it was somewhere between quarter to and quarter past eight.

As he stepped out into the lane, Rose Harsent called to him from the barred gate opposite, closing off the narrow path to the Doctor's Chapel. She had just cleaned it, but now the door was sticking, and she could not lock it. Gardiner went back to the door with her, and found the wood so rough and swollen that he had to slam it hard to make it close. He might have been three or four minutes at the chapel door as he forced it shut, locked it and tried it. The two spoke about the hymns for the forthcoming chapel anniversary service. Then they walked down the hill together, still talking, and parted at the crossroads. Rose went to Providence House and Gardiner went home.

The whole incident was utterly trivial, and he did not mention it to Mrs Gardiner. She was heavily pregnant, and her sister Annie was staying in Peasenhall for her wedding in three days' time.

That was Gardiner's story, and he stuck to it. He only made one significant change in the two retellings that have come down to us. In November 1902 he apparently placed the entire incident immediately after his arrival back at the works at half past seven. In January 1903 he described going back home for his tea and said he closed the chapel door at about quarter past eight, becoming a little irritable when pressed to be precise, and say whether it might not have been eight o'clock or quarter to eight.

But Bill Wright told a completely different story, and had the support of 26-year-old Alfonso Skinner, a fitter at Smyths'.

Between half past seven and quarter to eight, Wright came down Rendham Hill. He saw Rose come down the hill also (proceeding toward rather than from Providence House) and go into the alley leading to the Doctor's Chapel. He thought nothing of it. As he approached Church Lane he met Gardiner coming up the hill. They spoke briefly – presumably just to say, 'Good evening'. Gardiner then walked on past the chapel gate. Five minutes later, Wright saw him come down the hill again and walk back toward his home.

Between eight o'clock and quarter past, Wright was still mouching around the lane when Gardiner reappeared and started up Rendham Hill. This time Gardiner asked him how long he had kept a dog, and remarked that it looked like rain. Wright watched him go up in the direction of the drill works, and then turn abruptly into the alley on the other side of the road, leading to the Doctor's Chapel.

Wright sensed mischief. He hurried across the drill works yard, out into a path behind the church, and over to his stepfather Harry Redgrift's cottage, almost on the corner of Hackney Road and Bruisyard Road, where he shared a room with Alfonso Skinner. Gardiner was not Skinner's immediate boss, as he was Wright's, but he, too, would be entertained should anything scandalous emerge.

At about twenty past eight, according to Wright, the two young men made their way into the field to the south of the Doctor's Chapel, and crouched down behind a low hurdle fence opposite the south-west window. They were up on a high four-foot bank which hedged off the south side of the path leading from Rendham Hill to the chapel. They overlooked the window, but it was already becoming dark and they could not see clearly into the chapel. Skinner remained behind the hurdle for the best part of an hour, and Wright, with one break of five or ten minutes, was there for very little less.

First they heard talking and laughing. Then they heard rustling, and the window shook. Then a woman's voice cried, 'Oh! Oh!' and Wright said that he recognized the voice as Rose's.

There was then some further rustling which Wright evidently interpreted as the couple pulling their clothes on. He hurried back to the road, and went a little way up Rendham Hill.

Skinner stayed where he was, and heard a most interesting passage of conversation. The female voice, which he did not recognize, said, 'Did you notice me reading my Bible last Sunday?'

William Gardiner's voice returned, 'What were you reading?'

'I was reading about like what we have been doing here tonight. I'll tell you where it is. Thirty-eighth Chapter of Genesis.'

One or other of them then seems to have quoted the relevant verse, or part of it, since Skinner was later required to go over it in his courtroom testimony.

There can be no doubt whatever that the verse in question was verse 9. It was later to be characterized by learned counsel as 'that filthy stuff about Onan'. There is only one verse naming Onan which could be so described, and it also represents just about the only thing most people know about him:

And Onan knew that the seed should not be his; and it came to pass, when he went in unto his brother's wife, that he spilled it on the ground, lest that he should give seed to his brother.

Mealy-mouthedness and a misreading of this description of coitus interruptus led to masturbation being called Onanism by the Victorians. And Dorothy Parker delighted all her friends by calling her budgerigar Onan, 'because he spilled his seed on the ground'.

Skinner heard one more remark made in the woman's voice: 'It won't be noticed.'

After this exchange, Wright rejoined Skinner, and they both stayed behind the hurdle fence for about another quarter of an hour. Both men heard the woman say either 'I must go,' or 'You must let me go,' and Skinner heard her say, 'I shall be out tomorrow night at nine o'clock.' Wright and Skinner decided that they, too, had better make a move. Wright left first, and hurried away to the crossroads in the village and over into Heveningham Long Lane (often called Mill Lane as it led to a windmill).

Skinner followed slowly, and he saw Rose Harsent come out of the chapel and run down Rendham Road toward Providence House. Gardiner followed more cautiously, tiptoeing across the road according to Skinner, and then walking firmly down toward the crossroads.

Skinner followed him, and walked silently alongside him for the last twenty yards or so before the crossroads, where they separated. Skinner turned left in the direction of his lodgings, but he noticed that Gardiner did not turn right along The Street in the direction of his own home. Instead he crossed over the road toward Mill Lane.

There Gardiner encountered Wright once again, and continued the brief conversation they had earlier started about Wright's dog. This time Wright told him the dog had died.

The scandal about William Gardiner and Rose Harsent sprang directly from Skinner and Wright's account of the evening. They were frequently referred to as 'young boys', especially by those who wished to minimize the importance of their tale. So it is worth stressing that Skinner was twenty-six and Wright twenty. If mischief was in their minds it cannot be written off as a schoolboy prank.

Like Gardiner, the two clung tenaciously to their story, though they were confronted with vehement and bullying cross-examination on four separate occasions. The most determined forensic brow-beating did no more, however, than to leave some uncertainty in Wright's mind as to exactly how many times he had seen Gardiner in the lane before he went to the chapel.

Whose story was true? This was to be examined locally in a very short time. In less than a week, word reached Gardiner that the two were noising it abroad that he had been enjoying a spot of slap and tickle with Rose Harsent, and he decided immediately to protect his good name. He said nothing to his wife. She gave birth to a daughter just two days after the alleged Doctor's Chapel incident, so one can understand Gardiner's wish not to distress her.

He wrote to Rose from the works, put the letter in a blue envelope, and gave it to young Harry Harsent to take to his sister. The letter strongly suggests a manly confrontation of false accusations:

Dear Rose, –
I was very much surprised this morning to hear that there's some scandal going the round about you and me going into the Doctor's Chapel for immoral Purposes so that I shall put it into other hands at once as I have found out who it was that started it. Bill Wright and Skinner say they saw us there but I shall summons them for defamation of character unless they withdraw what they have said and give me a written apology. I shall see Bob tonight and we will come and see you together if possible. I shall at the same time see your father and tell him. –

Yours, &c.,
William Gardiner

Bob, of course, was Bob Kerridge. Clearly Gardiner could not leave Rose on her own to face any criticism from her family and fiancé. We do not know what was the outcome of that meeting between Rose, Bob, Mr Harsent and William Gardiner. We don't even know whether it took place.

He also spoke to Wright and Skinner at the works. It is possible that one or both of the young men spoke to him first, asking some teasing question. At any rate, there was a brief conversation on the shopfloor which ended with Wright protesting that he wasn't the only one to say that he had heard Gardiner and Rose in the chapel.

Gardiner was now under further domestic pressure. Daisy May Gardiner, born the day before Annie Cady's wedding, proved sickly. She was to die one month later on 2 June. Gossip and scandal around the works was a most unwelcome addition to his distress.

On 8 May, one week after the incident, Gardiner sent for both Wright and Skinner, and challenged them directly in his office. According to Gardiner he outlined the substance of the story he had heard they were repeating, and asked them if it was true that they were saying it. According to Wright he asked them what they meant by telling such lies about him. They insisted that what they had said was 'all right', and he responded that it was a lie. According to Skinner, Gardiner even maintained that he was not at the chapel at all that night. Certainly this was not something that he said on any other occasion.

Then Gardiner moved to using threats. If they did not give him an apology, he would bring an action against them for defamation of character. Both young men insisted that they would not apologize, for what they had said was true. Wright added that they didn't care, for all they owned was what they stood up in. According to Gardiner, one or other of them also said they could not retract, or they would be hooted all over the works. Both young men subsequently denied this, and on this unsatisfactory note the conversation ended.

Within a day or two Gardiner sent Rose another letter by hand of her brother.

> Dear Rose, –
> I have broke the news to Mrs. Gardiner this morning, she is
> awfully upset but she say she know it is wrong, for I was at
> home from half past eight till after nine and home again by 9.30
> so I could not possibly be with you an hour so she wont believe
> anything about it. I have asked Mr Burgess to ask those too
> Chaps to come to Chapel to-night and have it out there however

they stand by such a tale I dont know but I dont think God will forsake me now and if we put our trust in Him it will end right but its awfully hard work to have to face people when they are all suspicious of you but by Gods help whether they believe me or not I shall try and live it down and prove by my future conduct that its all false, I only wish I could take it to Court but I dont see a shadow of a chance to get the case as I dont think you would be strong enough to face a trial. Trusting that God will direct us and make the way clear – I remain, yours in trouble,

W. Gardiner

The inquiry at Sibton chapel took place on 11 May. It was not restricted to friends of Gardiner like Harry Burgess. Henry Rouse, the labourer who had been one of Gardiner's fellow-missioners to Beccles in 1892, took it upon himself to write to the Revd John Guy, superintendent minister of Wangford Circuit, asking him to attend.

The circuit superintendent minister was the most prominent figure a chapel could call in to help with a dispute. Mr Guy was a Berkshire man in his fifties. He had been a steady and successful superintendent minister at Wangford. He came to Peasenhall and spoke to Rose in her mother's presence before going on to chair the meeting. Nearly twenty members of the congregation were present, but Rose was not.

The meeting was lengthy. It started between seven o'clock and seven thirty. At ten o'clock, Wright and Skinner were allowed to leave. At half past ten the worthies decided to call the matter settled in Gardiner's favour.

Yet nothing had really been proven one way or the other. Wright and Skinner had told their story, and stuck to it through questioning by Gardiner and the brethren. Gardiner had told his story with equal firmness and had been equally unshaken. Some details which had been forgotten a year later probably came out then: Wright or Skinner, for example, probably mentioned having seen a match struck at one point in the chapel. But essentially, the hearing was confronted with a direct conflict of testimony, and they had simply to choose whom to believe.

It can't have been quite such an easy decision as Gardiner's defenders later suggested. It dragged on too long for that. But Mr Guy knew what the deciding factors were. There were two witnesses for the proposition, and two against (since the absent Rose was also reported to deny Wright's and Skinner's story). The two witnesses against were chapel members. Skinner, if he worshipped at all (and his daughter-in-law cannot recall his entering a church throughout the last twenty years of his life) was a churchman. Wright is not known to have avowed any denominational religion. The Methodists decided, under the circumstances, to believe their own.

Henry Rouse, the labouring local preacher, was present. He declared that the hearing convinced him that Gardiner and Rose were innocent of the scandal, as it did the rest of the meeting. The incident, it seemed, should be closed.

None the less, Gardiner tendered his resignation of all the offices he held in the chapel, and until Quarterly Meeting the following month the chapel lacked a class leader, society steward and Sunday school superintendent. This may have been the period during which Rose deputized for Gardiner as organist.

The following Sunday, Mr Guy and Mr Fidler of High House Farm met Rose and her mother together. On that occasion, Mr Fidler subsequently recalled, Mr Guy observed that he believed the whole scandal to be a 'trumped-up story'.

On 15 May, Gardiner's solicitor, Mr Harold Mullens of Halesworth, sent threatening letters to Wright and Skinner.

Sir, –
Mr. William George Gardiner of Peasenhall has consulted me in reference to certain slanderous statements which he alleges you have uttered and circulated concerning him and a young woman. I have to inform you that unless you tender my Client an ample written apology within seven days from this date legal process will be forthwith commenced against you without further notice to yourself. – Yours faithfully,
Harold A. Mullens

On 26 May, Mr Guy walked from Wangford to his home in Halesworth with Abraham Goddard, a farmer who was one of the most influential local preachers in the circuit, and a member of Quarterly Meeting. They were accompanied by another local preacher, the insurance agent Mr William Tripp. Both Mr Goddard and Mr Tripp gathered from their conversation that Mr Guy was wholly convinced of Gardiner's innocence.

At Quarterly Meeting on 26 June, Mr Guy gave an oral unminuted report on the inquiry. In the recollection of the Circuit's most powerful laymen, he affirmed that there was nothing to the scandal, and the meeting agreed that Gardiner should retain all his offices. Several would be lapsing at the end of the year in any case.

Abraham Goddard, Samuel Goddard, and the powerful old Blything farmer, Noah Etheridge, all clearly recollected Mr Guy's saying once again that the business was 'trumped up' and 'a fabrication of lies'. But they took less careful note than they might have done that Mr Guy also said there were two witnesses from inside the church and two from outside, and that he preferred to believe the two from inside.

All in all it seems that the local Connexion rallied together to defend themselves from scandal and stood loyally by their brother. There can be no doubt, however, that they would have stripped him of his offices and probably expelled him from membership had they felt that Gardiner was really guilty of adulterous impropriety with Rose. The Primitive Methodist archives from the period show that regular minuted disciplinary action, up to and including expulsion from the Connexion, was normal for any reported scandalous conduct. Mr Guy's assurances played a very large part in securing the elders' unanimous support for Gardiner and Rose.

Mr Guy's subsequent actions do not suggest that he was quite so convinced of Gardiner's innocence as he persuaded Quarterly Meeting that he was. Gardiner went to see him at his home in Halesworth to discuss dropping his proposed legal action against Skinner and Wright. Gardiner had probably gone to see Mr Mullens, and went straight from the solicitor's office to Mr Guy's manse in the same town. He was advised, he said, that it would be expensive and pointless to start proceedings. Skinner and Wright had no means, so that even if he won he would have to meet costs with no prospect of damages.

Mr Guy's conviction of Gardiner's innocence was shaken. It sounds rather as if Gardiner's firm declaration that he would take the matter to the courts had gone a long way to persuade the minister that he must be telling the truth. Dropping legal proceedings looked bad.

Gardiner was treated to a sympathetic but firm lecture. Mr Guy elicited his agreement that he had been 'indiscreet' – the nature of this indiscretion was not elaborated. But he had from time to time seen Rose home after chapel, and this might give rise to talk. Mr Guy warned him to be careful in his relations with young people, and hoped that the incident would be a 'life-lesson' for him. And Gardiner went on his way chastened, and assuring Mr Guy that he would be careful to keep out of Rose's company in the future. That should have been the end of the matter. But it wasn't. Gossip and sniggering continued and irked Gardiner.

On 17 December (Rose's birthday) there was a fire at Smyths' works which destroyed the blacksmith's shop. It began in the evening, when the men had gone home. Gardiner used to go to the works on his own of an evening, and on this occasion he went to the loft over the black-smith's shop for a piece of cotton waste. By Gardiner's account, the candle 'bent over' and set light to the cotton waste.

Smyths' were forgiving, however, and Gardiner was not sacked; possibly not even disciplined. Nor did they sack him when, shortly afterwards, he started yet another fire in the workshops. He was evidently a valued workman and an excellent foreman whose services could not be lightly discarded.

We might speculate that stress was making him careless. But Mr Herbert Denny's father Jonathan believed there was another reason. December 1901 was just about the time that Rose Harsent must have suspected she had conceived. Jonathan Denny was convinced that Gardiner started the fires deliberately in the hope of being sacked. It would justify a quick and quiet removal from Peasenhall to an anony-mous existence elsewhere, and would save him from the shame of exposure and the expense of a paternity order.

For the Dennys were among those villagers who had no doubt that Wright and Skinner had told the truth. Herbert, as a boy, saw Gardiner and Rose together from time to time. And he could not be mistaken about this: he knew them both well. The young Herbert was often sent to Gardiner's cottage to play with the twins, Annie and Dora. He couldn't tell them apart, and they loved to get adults to exchange the distinguishing red and blue ribbons they wore, so that he got their names wrong. And at Alma Cottage, he often saw Rose Harsent. On afternoons off she would sometimes pass the time there with Georgianna. Once she terrified little Herbert by picking him up playfully. The last person to do so had carried him among some beehives where he was stung, and the child feared it was about to happen again. So the only surviving man who was ever in Rose Harsent's arms ironically recalls it as a moment of terror during which he screamed and struggled!

None the less, Mr Denny's recollections of Rose are pleasant. Not so his memories of Gardiner. The big, black beard frightened him. And, young as he was, he had formed an impression of Gardiner as a domestic tyrant. For the instant she heard her husband coming home, Mrs Gardiner would press a piece of her home-made cake into Herbert's hands, and push him off out of the house.

Just before Christmas 1901, young Herbert saw another example of Gardiner's intimidating 'nerve'. Herbert was waiting beside the bridge at the crossroads for his father to come home from the works. On dark winter evenings he was not allowed to go up the lane to Smyths' on his own. Sitting on the rail over the brook was Tom Davis, Fred's father. As man and child waited there, Gardiner came out of the side door of the drill works, and made his way down past Church Lane toward The Street. He stopped at the bridge and chatted amiably with Tom Davis for a few minutes.

While they spoke, Rose Harsent came out of Providence House and walked past them up Rendham Hill. Tom Davis promptly grinned, and said meaningfully to Gardiner, 'There's a nice girl for you!'

Gardiner didn't speak. He walked firmly over to Davis and tried to throw him off the bridge and into the brook, thirteen feet below. Davis, a big man, slid quickly off the rail and defended himself. But the child was terrified at this spectacle of two men starting to fight over a trivial exchange.

The Doctor's Chapel scandal had an immediate effect on Rose's private life. Her engagement to Bob Kerridge came to a definite end. According to the Denny family, this was because Bob realized that she was dropping him at home on a Sunday night after chapel, and then waiting around for Gardiner with whom she would set off on long and presumably smoochy walks down the country lanes. According to the *Illustrated Police News*, however (the only contemporary newspaper which managed to learn anything about Bob), Rose took personal responsibility for dashing Bob's hopes.

> Both [Rose] and [Gardiner] denied that there was any cause for complaint, but the affair led to a rupture between the lovers.
> When reproached by a relative, who asked:
> "Rose, why are you treating Robert in this manner?" the girl replied, "Oh, he's too quiet for me. He has never anything to say. I like a man that's got some life in him."

That remark is obviously open to all manner of interpretations!

One night in February 1902, Herbert Rouse was walking home along the Yoxford Road when he encountered Gardiner and Rose going in the opposite direction. Rouse turned back to make sure he had seen them aright, and at the same moment they too turned back and made for the 'New Road' running from the Yoxford Road to the Poys Street Road beside the old Sibton schoolhouse, just east of Peasenhall village. The pair were at the entry to the New Road, standing just a foot or two apart, as Rouse walked boldly between them, saying, 'Good night, Gardiner. Good night, Rose.'

Neither man did anything immediately, but about nine days later, after a Wednesday night prayer meeting, Rouse drew Gardiner aside and took him out to the road for privacy. There he said, 'I am surprised that you should continue to walk about with that girl. There is so much talk, and it will do the chapel a great deal of harm.'

Gardiner replied, 'Have you said anything about it?'

'No,' said Rouse, 'I have not even told my wife.'

'If you do not say anything about it, it shall never occur again', Gardiner promised. Or so Rouse said. For Gardiner completely denied the whole incident when he was confronted with it.

Rouse claimed that he anticipated no further occasion to mention the subject. Then, at the end of the month, he was preaching in Sibton Chapel when he noticed with some shock that Gardiner and Rose were behaving curiously in their seats at the front of the choir. To quote Rouse, 'I saw Gardiner have his feet on Rose Harsent's lap. You gentlemen know what I mean by the lap of a person.'

Well, we can see what he meant by lap. Did he also mean 'knee' by 'feet'?

The strangest thing about this spectacle of indecent conduct was that it might have been seen by almost anyone in the chapel who chanced to look in that direction. Not surprisingly, Gardiner later denied it vehemently.

Rouse was tempted to reprimand them from the rostrum. But something told him not to: Rouse obviously thought it was the prompting of the Holy Spirit. Instead he decided to send Gardiner a discreet warning. He dictated a letter, for his wife to write out. It ran thus:

Mr Gardiner, –
I write to warn you of your conduct with that girl Rose, as I
find when she come into the chapel she must place herself next
to you, which keep the people's minds still in the belief that you
are a guilty man, and in that case you will drive many from the
chapel, and those that would join the cause are kept away
through it. We are told to shun the least appearance of evil. I
do not wish you to leave God's house, but there must be a
difference before God's cause can prosper, which I hope you
will see to be right as people cannot hear when the enemy of
souls bring this before them. I write to you as one that love
your soul, and hope you will have her sit in some other place,
and remove such feeling which for her sake she will do.

This remarkable unsigned letter in the unrecognizable hand of Mrs Rouse was posted to Gardiner. We don't know whether anybody else except Georgianna knew about it at the time, but it may have contributed to his decision to relinquish the class leadership when that came up for renewal in March, though he remained organist, choir-master and Sunday school superintendent.

The village was divided over Gardiner's guilt or innocence of an improper liaison with Rose, and to some extent crime historians have remained divided ever since.

William Henderson, in the *Notable British Trials* volume, sticks to the facts and reaches a sensible evaluation, but no conclusion.

> It must be recorded that he faced the situation like a man. . . .
> Whether he was innocent or guilty of this charge, these letters
> [to Rose] indicate that he was no weakling. . . . It is difficult to
> decide whether these are the resentful letters of an injured man,
> containing as they do his expression of trust in God and threats
> of legal proceedings against the slanderers, or mere camouflaged
> "instructions for the defence" written by a guilty man to his
> accomplice, notifying her that he is going to present a brazen
> front to the charge and warning her that she must do the same.
> If the truth of the matter lies in this latter interpretation of the
> letters, then they surely do credit to Gardiner's intelligence, for
> the closest scrutiny yields no indication that they are such.

What really happened at the Doctor's Chapel? We have given careful consideration to the evidence at all four hearings, and in our view Wright and Skinner were telling the truth. Their story was unshaken in its essentials, despite withering cross-examination, far exceeding that to which Gardiner was subjected. Unlike Gardiner, they had no possible reason to lie. From start to finish, from Gardiner's office to the majestic setting of the Assizes, they insisted that the reason they could not abandon their story was that it was true.

In Gardiner's favour stands his equal consistency whenever questioned about the events; also his firm directness in tackling the scandal head-on when it came to his attention; and the apparent clarity and sincerity of his two letters to Rose. Add to this his excellent reputation in the chapel as a man of probity, and the reasons for doubt are apparent. But Gardiner had very good reason to lie. The old question *cui bono?* finds against him immediately.

We are all sadly or cynically aware that men of outwardly devout lives may be secretly engaged in forbidden sexual activities. The Judaeo-Christian sexual ethic is not easily compatible with normal human desires and instincts.

Peasenhall village enjoyed a good sexual scandal. We know of a few which go back to Gardiner's time. The village's favourite womanizer was Mr Ludbrook, one of the Sibton chapel trustees. He lived on The Causeway and his wife provoked widespread mirth when she had been away for a holiday, and after her return asked all the village how one of her neighbour's garters came to be in her marital bed.

Gardiner's hands were already full, with a sickly baby and his sister-in-law's wedding to attend to. He could do without the addition of scandal. But how could a man of his probity bring himself to tell a blatant lie to resolve the situation? Well, there could be a loophole that his Nonconformist scrupulosity hoped to slip through: a loophole that led him directly into a trap when the young men stood up to him, and his own determination to stop the scandal left him with no alternative but to lie brazenly.

The story going around the village would have taken the form that Wright and Skinner saw Gardiner and Rose go into the chapel and then heard them commit adultery. It was too dark, of course, for them to have seen clearly through the windows.

Skinner was probably not sufficiently educated in the Bible to realize that Rose's quotation indicated that they had not heard quite what they thought. Those who did know exactly what 'filthy stuff about Onan' was always taken to mean, were too prudish to correct him openly. 'Onanism' is still defined in the dictionary as masturbation. It is probable that at most Gardiner and Rose practised coitus interruptus. It is possible that their erotic play did not go as far as penetration. Rose's remark, 'It will not be noticed', probably referred to the fact that some of Gardiner's 'seed' had indeed 'spilled on the ground'!

But the village was not being told the words Skinner actually heard Rose use: the words to which he swore at the trial. Mr Fred Rowe, the outgoing manager when Smyths' Drill Works closed, told us that local gossip repeated an alleged comment of Gardiner's: 'The House of God is above you and the staff of life is in you.'

A hair-splitting Nonconformist conscience may feel that there has been no real adultery as long as there has been no penetration or no intromission. Gardiner and Rose almost certainly had the same feeling. From Rose's point of view, it also had the advantage that she would avoid pregnancy. The precisian Gardiner could feel that in saying, 'I didn't do what you say I did', he was telling the truth, and could thereafter trust to the authority of his personality and the threat of the defamation laws to have everything put in the clear.

It didn't work. The young men weren't intimidated. And Gardiner would have been left with the sudden recognition that the half-truth that might satisfy his conscience could never be abandoned openly, as the whole truth would make him even more of a village laughing-stock. Having adopted the line of manly confrontation, he was finally reduced to a last ditch of barefaced lying.

This was not something he relished doing under oath in court. Four days before Mullens sent the solicitor's letter to Wright and Skinner, Gardiner had already assured Rose that the threat would never be acted upon and he would not force her to perjure herself. 'I only wish I could take it to Court but I dont see a shadow of a chance to get the case as I dont think you would be strong enough to face a trial,' he said. Why not, if their story were true?

Four days later he issued the threat, and immediately gave the signal to Mr Guy that it was only a threat. Naturally he didn't offer the wishy-washy excuse that he was not willing to put Rose through testifying to her innocence.

But what about his own protestations of innocence and his invocation of God? Did Gardiner think Rose would show the letter round the village as proof of her innocence?

Well, she would probably mention the letter to her parents or Bob Kerridge, and so his words would have to be guarded. We don't question that these letters show him to be, in Stewart Evans's words, 'very crafty'. We don't think their protestations of innocence can be taken at their face value. We think they rest upon the rather deceitful notion that incomplete intercourse is not adultery. We think Gardiner was, up to a point, revelling in the 'innocence' that only Rose could share with him. They were being wrongfully accused. They never went all the way. The word 'adulterers' could never *properly* apply to them. They were being despised and rejected, and God must pity their suffering at the hands of traducers.

Such smug self-deceiving piety is very unappealing. But it is also very common.

During the first half of 1902, somebody sent letters in cheap buff envelopes to Rose; letters that she did not preserve with her family mail and Gardiner's letters and Davis's outpourings. That somebody was probably her unborn child's father and probably Rose's murderer. Many people came to believe that person was William Gardiner.

FIVE

The Investigation

T wo days after the body was found, William Gardiner was arrested
for Rose Harsent's murder. It has always been believed that
Dr Lay's erroneous conclusion that Rose had committed suicide held up
the police investigation for twenty-four hours, and delayed his arrest.
Eli Nunn was quite forthright at Gardiner's second trial:

Q: Was not the first theory that this was a suicide?
Nunn: It was.

And Superintendent Staunton, who took charge of the case, was almost
as decisive at Gardiner's first trial:

Q: Originally, the theory was suicide?
Staunton: Yes, certainly; but after I had seen the body I could
            not think it was suicide.

This may be quite true as far as Superintendent Staunton was personally
concerned. But it is an inaccurate account of the previous day's police
conclusion.

Superintendent George Andrews's *Work Journal* has survived intact
and is displayed at the Suffolk County Constabulary Museum. Andrews
was stationed at Halesworth, and was the nearest senior officer to the
crime. His journal entry shows that he and Eli Nunn decided on the day
the body was found that they were dealing with a murder and Gardiner
was the probable murderer.

> SUNDAY 1 JUNE
> Office duty in the morning. At 1 PM called by PC Nunn to
> Peasenhall in consequence of the body of a singlewoman having
> been found dead in the kitchen of her master house Mr Wm
> Crisp at Peasenhall.
> Arrived at 2 30 pm found the body was that of Roseanne

Harsant aged 23 years The throat was cut from left to right
severing the Windpipe and left jugular Vein The Flanellette
nightdress worn by deceased was partially burned as was also
the Chemise. A quantity of broken glass was found near the
body which was that of a 10 oz Doctor Medicine Bottle. A
letter was found in deceaseds bedroom which was written by
some person but not signed asking for deceased to put her
candle in her bedroom window at 10 pm to leave it there for 10
minutes and that the writer would call on her at the back way
about 12 oclock. A man named William Gardiner is suspected.
Returned to Station at 6 PM. Reported to Head Quarters and
at 6.40 pm en route to LONDON.

This is fascinating. None of the three precise clues pointing to
Gardiner is explicitly indicated: his family name on the remains of the
medicine bottle; the similarity between his handwriting and that of the
assignation note (which should have been perceived by comparison with
his two letters preserved in Rose's drawer); and Rose's pregnancy which
supplied his motive.

Now, in support of Staunton's claim that suicide was reported, it may
be noted that Dr Lay was still unwilling to commit himself as to whether
or not Rose's wounds were self-inflicted when the inquest opened two
days later. But Staunton himself had no doubt once he had seen the
body. Nor, it seems, had Andrews and Nunn.

But why did they immediately believe Gardiner to be the murderer?
If Rose's pregnancy was the main clue, then the conclusion must have
been Nunn's, resting solely upon the well-known scandal. It would be
remarkably flimsy stuff on which to enter a suspicion in a *Work Journal*
that was regularly inspected by the Chief Constable. Andrews was an
old and experienced officer who had joined the force in 1869: he retired
in 1903. He was the son of one police inspector and the father of
another. It is surprising that he should have committed himself to
official suspicion on the basis of village gossip.

Yet it seems that Gardiner's handwriting was not instantly identified
with that on the assignation note. When Staunton went to question
Gardiner the following day, he took the second 'scandal' letter. But he
did not immediately suggest that it looked similar to the note. Instead he
compared the note with other samples of Gardiner's handwriting which
Gardiner produced, and only then drew attention to a mere two words
in the scandal letter – 'you' and 'again'. Neither of the scandal letters
was ever mentioned by the prosecution handwriting expert, although

Staunton told the second sitting of the Coroner's Court that all the letters found in Rose's drawer had been sent to him. We must conclude that the handwriting of these letters did *not* markedly resemble that of the assignation note.

Nevertheless, it was clear to the policemen that the assignation note was the most important clue. It must surely have been the work of the murderer, and it would be necessary to tie it to any suspect who was to be charged.

Prima facie, the likeliest clue to have fastened immediate suspicion on Gardiner was the medicine bottle. All the witnesses agreed that Dr Lay took the piece with the label attached, and recognized it as his own. But there is a good deal of evasiveness in the earlier hearings (at the magistrates' and coroner's courts) about the writing on the label. At one point Dr Lay was even stopped by the coroner (on Superintendent Staunton's request) from saying what the writing was until the adjourned hearing should be resumed. Why was this?

It seems fairly clear that once the words 'Mrs Gardiner's chdn' had been revealed under the smudges of blood and paraffin, the police and prosecutors wanted them well in the public eye. They were (and are) extremely damaging circumstantial evidence against William Gardiner. Yet it was universally acknowledged that Dr Lay could not decipher them until Home Office experts had cleaned the label. He identified the bottle as one prescribed for 'Mrs Gardiner's sister'.

Why should anyone be evasive about misreading the word 'chdn' as 'sister' beneath what was admittedly a difficult smudge? Especially as Dr Lay had, without question, prescribed medicine for both in the previous months?

The answer is that Dr Lay knew he had never labelled a bottle, 'Mrs Gardiner's sister'. He gave the lady her proper name, 'Mrs Culham' (as Nunn's evidence at the first trial and Staunton's at the second show). And once it was clear that Gardiner would be energetically defended, neither Staunton, Nunn, Andrews nor their legal leaders wanted that brought out too strongly. The misreading was so gross as to reveal that Dr Lay was being asked to confirm a prior suspicion: that the bottle did not lead the police to suspect Gardiner; rather their suspicion of Gardiner led them to anticipate (wrongly) the name on the bottle. They were lucky that the actual words suited their purposes far better than the ones Dr Lay had persuaded himself he could decipher.

Not that Andrews overstated the case in his journal. With his experience, he knew perfectly well that to say, 'a man is suspected' lies some distance from saying that he suspected him or would recommend charges.

It may be that the case would have been conducted more slowly and surely had Andrews remained in charge. But he could not. He was needed at the Old Bailey to give evidence against a fraudster named Rix, and did not return to Suffolk until Wednesday 4 June. By that time decisions had been made on the spot. Gardiner had been arrested, and Andrews's future contributions to the investigation were simply the routine ones of preparing detailed plans of Providence House and the Doctor's Chapel, and taking exterior photographs for submission to the court. The Constabulary Central Office at Ipswich handed the case over to Superintendent Staunton.

This was a move from one of the oldest and most experienced senior officers in the force to one of the youngest and newest in his rank. George Sydney Staunton had not even been born when George Andrews became a constable. He entered the force in 1893 at the age of nineteen, and walked the beat in Lowestoft for six years. In May 1899 he was transferred to Ipswich as chief clerk at headquarters and was promoted to sergeant in October. His rise was now meteoric.

In August 1900 he became an inspector. In January 1902 he became a superintendent. He was still under thirty.

We intend no disrespect to Staunton's memory in suggesting that this was a 'staff officer's' career of the kind mistrusted by men who work long hours in the field with the eye of authority so far distant that they can only expect promotion for remarkable achievements rather than admirable efforts. Staunton's subsequent career, though less fast and furious was sufficiently distinguished. He won the King's Police Medal before his promotion to assistant chief constable in 1916; the MBE before his promotion to deputy chief constable in 1919, and the OBE two years after his appointment as chief constable in 1933.

But the amazing spate of promotions between 1899 and 1902 distinctly suggests favouritism rather than noteworthy achievement. The two high points of Staunton's career were his determined investigation of the Peasenhall murder, and his magnificent work at the time of the General Strike, keeping public services in East Suffolk running while avoiding any friction between police and strikers. The vital early push to his career came from Chief Constable Jasper Mayne.

Mayne's written orders to the force are preserved at the Police Museum. He was typical of the gentlemen amateurs which most chief constables were at that time. His orders are serious, responsible, brief and to the point. Except for the annual occasion of the Police Sports, when Mayne issued pages of instructions: massive screeds directing exactly where the various bodies of police were to assemble, how the spectators were to be marshalled and everything done to ensure an excellent day's entertainment. In 1908 he even hired the Band of the Scots Guards for the occasion. The Annual Sports clearly engrossed Chief Constable Mayne more than any of his other duties. And the highlight was the tug-of-war, for which he presented a shield.

We have seen Staunton's photograph albums. They show a man with a wide range of interests including, year after year, team photographs of him as secretary with the Police Tug-of-War Team which he successfully coached and managed. A man after Jasper Mayne's own heart, making a positive contribution to the sporting activity which preoccupied the chief constable.

Now this is not to say that Staunton was promoted beyond the level of his competence. But it is true to say that he was a Head Office administrator who needed to demonstrate unusual skill in his profession to win the respect of his peers. He did so by his conduct of the Peasenhall investigation, throwing himself into it with an energy that impressed all observers. It was long remembered that, lacking other means of transport, he bicycled the twenty-four miles from Ipswich to Peasenhall to get himself on the spot immediately.

In spite of all this, however, he failed to achieve a conviction, and left us with a classic murder mystery.

On Monday 2 June, Staunton wired Eli Nunn from Ipswich that he expected to arrive in Peasenhall at around noon. Nunn did not hang around idly waiting for him. Between ten and eleven o'clock, he joined forces with Inspector Henry Berry of Halesworth and Sergeant Daniel Scarfe of Saxmundham. They went to interview Georgianna Gardiner: an action which was quite compatible with the investigation of a suicide (trying to see whether a quarrel with her former scandal-mate had unhinged Rose), except that they stationed PC Scott at the Drill Works to make sure Gardiner did not communicate with his wife.

Berry asked, 'What time did your husband leave home on Saturday?'

Mrs Gardiner said that he had driven Mr Rickards to Kelsale in the afternoon; had gone on to Leiston, and returned home at about half past nine.

'What kind of paper do you use in writing?' Berry went on. Mrs Gardiner fetched the family's ordinary penny packet of writing-paper, but it seemed to the policemen that she was a suspiciously long time in doing so.

Shortly before one o'clock Staunton arrived. He was shown the letters found in Rose's drawer, and went straight to the drill works to interview Gardiner.

Despite the presence of the constable posted by Berry and Scarfe, Gardiner's demeanour seemed completely innocent. He was apparently unperturbed by the police interrogation. Staunton was asked at the first trial:

Q: He gave you [his] account at once, freely?
Staunton: Yes, freely, very freely.
Q: He did not seem upset?
Staunton: No. That is what astonished me.

Why it should have astonished a superintendent who was merely investigating a report of a suicide is a question that was never put to him. Perhaps he felt that Gardiner, if innocent of murder, ought to have been more upset at being interviewed at all.

Staunton began by showing Gardiner the assignation note and asking if it was his handwriting. Gardiner said it was not. Staunton asked Gardiner to show him a sample of his writing, and Gardiner unhesitatingly pulled out a notebook in which he recorded workers' time shifts and wages for the firm. Staunton looked at it, and suggested to Gardiner that it was similar to the writing of the assignation note. Gardiner said something to the effect that there was a similarity but that he had not written the note.

There was to be some disagreement later as to how firmly Gardiner acknowledged that the handwriting was similar. So it would be of the greatest interest to find these notebooks. Alas, it can never be done. Many years later Mr Fred Rowe destroyed all the firm's outdated weekly records, including those kept by Gardiner, never imagining that a day would come when people wanted to examine these samples of his writing.

Staunton then showed Gardiner the second letter to Rose concerning the chapel scandal. Gardiner agreed at once that he had written it. Staunton pointed to the two words, 'you' and 'again', suggesting that they looked very similar to the same words in the assignation note. Gardiner made no comment. He may well have seen no need to. There were only ten words in the assignation note that did not also appear in the scandal letter. Another nineteen words were apparently so dissimilar as to invite no comment!

Staunton then asked about his movements on Saturday. Gardiner gave exactly the same account that his wife had given earlier. Staunton, Nunn and Berry then went back to Alma Cottage.

Sergeant Scarfe joined Constable Scott at the drill works to see that Gardiner did not communicate with his wife. This time Gardiner was left under no doubt that he was expected to stay with them. His legal advisers subsequently noted that he was effectively in custody, and should therefore have been cautioned. It was obviously to the advantage of the police to maintain that they were still investigating a suicide, so that they need not caution mere witnesses. But Staunton was noted for his scrupulosity, and some years later gained prestige when he prosecuted a magistrate for manslaughter in a serious driving case at some risk to his own career. So it is probable that at this point he felt some doubt about Eli Nunn's suspicion of Gardiner, and only began to share it after he had interviewed Georgianna. At any rate, he stated the following January that he only began to suspect Gardiner after he had interviewed his wife.

The return of the police alarmed Mrs Gardiner who asked where her husband was. She was reassured that he was in his office and would be home directly. It may have been at this point that Eli Nunn sympathetically told her she had nothing to worry about, which Gardiner's advisers later construed as a misleading indication that her husband was not under suspicion. Staunton asked her to describe her husband's movements on Saturday again. She said exactly what she had said before, and her story tallied exactly with Gardiner's. It was a story that gave him a perfect alibi for the murder, since at this time both Gardiners declared that they went together to Mrs Dickinson's at eleven o'clock and left together at half past one. The assignation note suggested that the murder had been committed around midnight, and Mrs Crisp's recollection of Rose's scream placed it at the height of the storm, so either way, by their account, both Gardiners were with Mrs Dickinson.

Staunton showed Mrs Gardiner the envelope which had contained the assignation note, and asked her if it was in her husband's hand. She agreed that the writing was like her husband's (and again, there would be subsequent dispute as to how much similarity she suggested), but she said categorically that it was not her husband's writing.

The policemen then returned to the drill works and relieved Scott and Scarfe. Gardiner may then have gone home.

At four o'clock, Staunton and two or three of the other police officers came to Alma Cottage yet again. There was dispute later as to whether Nunn accompanied them on this visit. He thought he didn't. Staunton thought he did. Mrs Gardiner was sure he did. The point was utterly unimportant to anybody, and nobody could conceivably have been lying. It acts as a timely reminder, however, that true crime investigation is quite unlike detective fiction. Most false statements are the result of faulty memory, not guilty deception.

This time Staunton homed in on the medicine bottle. Could Mrs Gardiner tell them anything about it?

'What medicine bottle, sir?' she asked.

Staunton proceeded to ask her whether her sister had stayed with her earlier that year, and been attended by Dr Lay. Georgianna agreed that she had. Had there been a medicine bottle labelled for Mrs Culham? She thought there had. Had she still got the bottle? She thought so, and went to look for it. But she could only find a couple of bottles without labels.

Under further questioning, she remembered giving Rose Harsent camphorated oil for a sore throat earlier in the year, and suggested uncertainly that she might have put it in the missing bottle which Rose must have taken away with her. This seemed very suspicious to the police. Why was the only witness to Rose's 'possibly' receiving this vital bottle before the murder the victim herself?

And it would look yet more fishy in weeks to come, when the bottle was shown to have been labelled for the Gardiner children and not Mrs Culham, yet it was *still* put forward as the one Rose 'must have' taken away with her. From start to finish, the evidence about the bottle looks very black for the Gardiners.

The next morning the coroner, Mr C.W. Chaston, opened the inquest on Rose in the Swan Inn. It was a brief and formal matter. William Harsent identified the body and described his discovery of it. His wife said that Rose had seemed happy and contented the previous Wednesday when she last saw her. Mrs Crisp described the night of the storm in Providence House. Eli Nunn gave an account of what he had found in the house. Dr Lay and Dr Ryder Richardson described the wounds on the body, and Superintendent Staunton stopped Dr Lay from saying anything about the label on the medicine bottle. The coroner noted that the initial theory of suicide was upset by the assignation note and the wounds, and adjourned the inquest for a fortnight to allow the doctors to conduct a full post-mortem and the police to continue their investigations.

It was probably during that morning that Gardiner behaved in a way that stayed in Jonathan Denny's memory. When he came to the drill works he did not go to his office or get on with his work. Instead he climbed up a high gantry above the works, and lurked there furtively all morning. Old Mr Denny was sure that he was hoping to be out of sight and avoid arrest if the police turned up. He always maintained that the incident took place on the previous day, but this was pretty certainly an error of memory, as Gardiner was in his office under police supervision for most of Monday morning.

At midday Gardiner declared that he felt ill and went home. From then on, his fellow-workers had little doubt that he murdered Rose Harsent.

That evening, young Billy Rowe went with his father to the butcher's. He saw a trap drawn up outside Alma Cottage. He saw Eli Nunn and three other policemen come out of the cottage, with Gardiner between them. All five men got into the trap and drove away.

'Where are they taking Mr Gardiner?' Billy asked.

'Just for a ride,' said his father. Up to then the Rowe family had liked and respected William Gardiner.

Staunton, Nunn, Berry and Scarfe had gone to Gardiner's house at half past eight. Since Nunn had been the first officer at the scene of the crime, his seniors left him to make the arrest. He read the magistrate's warrant issued by Captain Levett-Scrivener and cautioned Gardiner, who responded, 'I am innocent', and then fainted on the sofa. He had to be revived with brandy. Gardiner was undoubtedly a more nervous character than his reputation suggested.

When Gardiner had been revived from his faint, Staunton and Nunn asked Mrs Gardiner for his clothes. She gave them a shirt, undershirt, vest and coat. They asked her if any of them had been washed since Saturday, and she said, no, she only washed once a fortnight and her washing-day was a week ahead. They also took away her kitchen knives for examination. As her husband was led off under arrest, she too fainted.

Gardiner was searched at Halesworth Police Station, and a large clasp-knife in his trouser pocket was taken away. He was lodged overnight in Halesworth lock-up, and charged before magistrate Mr F.E. Babington at Halesworth Police Station the following morning. Gardiner had by now recovered his composure, and impressed onlookers with his detached indifference to the proceedings.

Mr Babington remanded Gardiner to Saxmundham Petty Sessions, and there Andrews and Staunton secured a further remand for a week to enable them to pursue inquiries and await instructions from the Public Prosecutor. The prisoner was lodged in Ipswich Jail.

While Gardiner was facing the law, Eli Nunn went back to Alma Cottage and asked Georgianna for all his boots and shoes. He was given a pair of boots and the carpet slippers he had worn at Mrs Dickinson's during the thunderstorm.

That afternoon Rose's body was brought from Sibton in a van to St Michael's church where the Revd Ernest Cooke, the vicar, read the funeral service. After this the coffin was carried the quarter-mile along the narrow lane to the cemetery, and she was laid to rest.

The next day Eli Nunn made another important discovery. Skinner and Wright lodged with Wright's stepfather, market gardener Harry Redgrift, whose brother George was Captain Levett-Scrivener's head gamekeeper. A man named James Morris worked turn and turn about for both brothers, as assistant gamekeeper in season, and gardener at other times. On Sunday, Morris had told George Redgrift an interesting story. At five o'clock in the morning after the great storm, he had walked along The Street from east to west, and turned up the Heveningham Road. As he passed Gardiner's cottage he noticed footprints in the soggy road surface. They seemed to start from Alma Cottage. They went down to Providence House and they returned back from Providence House toward Alma Cottage. Morris was sufficiently interested to cross over the road at Providence House and confirm that the footprints went up to the gate and came away from it. He noticed that the shoe sole was barred: a configuration which meant it must have been made of rubber. He mentioned it to gamekeeper George Redgrift later in the day. And word of this story reached Eli Nunn from Harry Redgrift on Friday 6 June.

He sent for Morris, who was unwilling to be involved, but confirmed the truth of his sighting. Nunn went to Alma Cottage again, and asked Mrs Gardiner whether her husband owned any 'indiarubber shoes' (the term that was persistently used, and led some people to imagine wrongly that galoshes were being described). Mrs Gardiner hunted about, and came out with an old pair of canvas shoes with rubber soles that her brother had given the family a week before. Nunn asked if there were any more clothes of Gardiner's in the house, and Mrs Gardiner produced a black coat and a vest that he had not worn for a long time. Nunn also asked about a new razor Gardiner was supposed to have bought in Leiston the previous Saturday. Mrs Gardiner pointed out that her husband did not shave, but produced an old razor that she used for trimming cloth.

On Saturday 7 June Nunn was back asking for Gardiner's mackintosh. Mrs Gardiner said it would be found at the drill works. On Sunday Nunn wanted a letter Gardiner had written to his wife from prison. Georgianna was understandably unwilling to let this go. But she agreed, on the undertaking that it would be returned to her within a week. And the next day she made the wise move of consulting a solicitor.

1

3

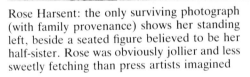

2

4

Rose Harsent: the only surviving photograph
(with family provenance) shows her standing
left, beside a seated figure believed to be her
half-sister. Rose was obviously jollier and less
sweetly fetching than press artists imagined

Rose's fiancé, Bob Kerridge, in
later life

Rose's father at her grave

The paired photographs of Gardiner and Rose were widely circulated at the time of the trials. Stewart Evans notes that Rose's picture appears to be a touched-up mortuary photograph, printed in reverse, with the bruise on the wrong cheek

1

2

The Primitive Methodist church at Sibton, where Rose Harsent was among Gardiner's pupils at Sunday school

3

Mr Herbert Denny, the last living witness to Rose and Gardiner walking out together

4

ENTRANCE TO DOCTOR'S CHAPEL.
showing the high hedge on the left, behind which Wright and Skinner were concealed. The entrance to Doctor's Chapel is on the right.

6

Interior and exterior views of the Doctor's Chapel and the path leading to it, with Wright and Skinner, the 'garpers', at the time of the trial

The witness Skinner, who corroborated Wright's story of a meeting between the murdered girl and Gardiner in the "Doctor's Chapel"

7

The Peasenhall mystery. The young man Wright, who was one of the principal witnesses for the prosecution.

8

1

I will try to see you tonight
at 12 oclock at your place if you
put a light in your window at
10 oclock for about 10 minutes then
you can take it out again.
dont have a light in your room at
12 as I will come round to the
back

The assignation note and the buff envelope in
which it arrived

Miss Harsent
Providence House
Peasenhall,
Saxmundham

2

Mr Arthur Sadler Leighton was to play a vital part in the Peasenhall case. He was an active and ambitious man in his middle thirties who had changed his surname from Bugg before taking articles with the firm of Birkett and Ridley (who, oddly enough, would be solicitors for the Crown in Gardiner's case). After completing his articles he set up his own partnership with Mr J.W. Aldous. At the turn of the century they took on Harry Scotchmer Gotelee, so that fifteen years later the one-time firm of Leighton and Aldous became Aldous and Gotelee. All three of these vigorous young solicitors threw themselves enthusiastically into Gardiner's case. It became a landmark success for the firm, and it made Mr Leighton's name well known with the general public as he made press statements and court appearances.

Leighton and Aldous's first decisive action was to call a halt to Eli Nunn's daily visits to Alma Cottage. The police now held every stitch of clothing Gardiner possessed, and poor Georgianna was understandably feeling persecuted.

But Leighton's most important decision followed his interview with Gardiner. He decided that Gardiner was innocent, and that positive conviction never wavered. It ensured that every fraction of energy Superintendent Staunton brought to assembling the prosecution case would be matched and bettered by another able young man, conscious that he was fighting for his client's life and convinced that an appalling injustice would result if he failed to win his case.

Mr Leighton did not waste time in opposing the weekly police requests for extensions of Gardiner's remand which continued until the beginning of July. He made his first appearance at the reconvened inquest on 16 June.

There were two small legal questions to be dealt with. Captain Levett-Scrivener was the foreman of the coroner's jury, and he thought he should be excused from further appearances since he was the magistrate who had issued the warrant for Gardiner's arrest. Coroner Chaston did not think this would prejudice him, and refused to excuse him. But Captain Levett-Scrivener's continuing presence brought out a very important point that Mr Leighton pounced upon, though Gardiner's defence never fully exploited it.

When Dr Lay told the inquest that the label on the medicine bottle was for Mrs Gardiner's children, the foreman of the jury raised the point that this was not what he had been told previously. Mr Leighton insisted over the coroner's mild demurrer that this should be explained, and Dr Lay now revealed that he had told the captain (in his capacity as magistrate) that the bottle was for Mrs Gardiner's sister. Over the past weekend the label had been returned to him, cleaned. And now he could read it accurately.

This meant, of course, that the original warrant for Gardiner's arrest was issued on the completely erroneous information that the bottle read 'Mrs Culham'. So it is clear that official suspicion against Gardiner, and even his arrest, pre-dated the discovery of circumstantial evidence against him.

The second legal matter was a request from Mr E.P. Ridley, the prosecution solicitor, that no fresh evidence be taken (and hence publicized) before the hearing at the magistrates' court. This came indirectly from Mr Sims the Treasury Counsel and from the Director of Public Prosecutions, who already felt that the case was 'a difficult one, and requires a considerable amount of care'. It was important that witnesses be examined in the presence of lawyers who had previously studied the depositions.

Under this pressure from on high, Mr Chaston decided to do no more than hear the full statements of the witnesses who had already been heard. Both Drs Lay and Ryder Richardson were now sure that the wounds were not self-inflicted. Dr Richardson corrected the original suggestion that parts of the medicine bottle were missing. He now knew that they had been ground into tiny fragments in the kitchen carpet. The bottle was fully accounted for.

Mr Leighton extracted two statements from Mrs Crisp that would prove useful later. She stated that Rose's scream had come in the middle of the storm. And that she believed the time was between one and two o'clock in the morning. Her vagueness would tend to confuse the prosecution.

Staunton and Andrews described two of the forms of inquiry proceeding. The letters found in Rose's room had been sent to Thomas Gurrin of Holborn Viaduct, the leading handwriting expert of the day. And on Thursday evening, Andrews had placed a candle in Rose's window, and Nunn had walked slowly into the street from Gardiner's doorstep until, at a distance of two yards from the cottage, it came into his view.

Mr Leighton read into the record that there was 'not a scrap of evidence against anybody' at that point, and it would be quite proper for the jury to reach an open verdict. The coroner noted that the Swan Inn was inconveniently small and stuffy, and suggested that the adjourned inquest should reconvene at Saxmundham in two weeks' time. The jurors hastily pointed out that Mr Smyth's Swiss chalet assembly hall could be used, and so spared themselves the unwanted journey on 30 June.

Eleven days before that hearing, Coroner Chaston joined Chief Constable Jasper Mayne among the privileged spectators at Saxmundham where Gardiner was brought before the magistrates for a formal hearing. Mr Ridley, as treasury solicitor, opened with a statement of the case against him. He described Rose's occupation, and had Superintendent Andrews exhibit his plans of Providence House. Then he went on to say, 'The case for the prosecution is that about twelve months ago, prisoner and this girl were having immoral relations.'

Mr Leighton was on his feet in an instant. 'I don't want to interrupt Mr Ridley,' he said, 'only I object to him saying what happened twelve months ago unless he proposes to call witnesses to prove that.'

'Of course I am going to call them,' Mr Ridley responded testily. He evidently disliked facing spirited opposition so soon. A magistrates' hearing should have been an easy run, with the defence reserved.

Mr Ridley went on to say that the Crown believed the illicit relationship had been kept up by letter, and started to introduce the assignation note. Mr Leighton was on his feet again.

'I understand that Mr Ridley has not his statements from experts in handwriting, and until he is prepared to prove that the letter was written by the prisoner, I object. He cannot make a statement unless he is ready to prove it.'

'I can tell you what the case for the prosecution is,' retorted Mr Ridley.

'Are you going to prove that?'

'Certainly, at the proper time.'

Mr Leighton still protested (correctly) that letters alleged to be by Gardiner should not be introduced with that allegation unless there was evidence to support his authorship. Mr Ridley simply steamrollered past this obstacle: 'I haven't said I have not got them. I am not going to tell you my evidence. I am putting the case for the prosecution before the Magistrates; it is for them to decide whether I prove it to their satisfaction or not.'

This was really naughty evasion. Mr Ridley had been caught trying to put in unsubstantiated opinion, and it was as well for Gardiner that the subsequent conduct of the prosecution was more scrupulous. Well, too, that his solicitor was an able court-room lawyer. Later in his career Mr Leighton was to leave the partnership and become a barrister.

Ridley suggested that the murderer had brought his medicine bottle of paraffin with him in order to destroy the body after the premeditated murder. But finding it was corked too tightly for him to open, he took the kitchen lamp apart to extract paraffin from its well. He described the assignation note and the two letters from Gardiner found in Rose's bedroom, without suggesting that they were obviously in the same hand. He did make the point that the envelope containing the assignation note was of an 'unusual' kind to which Gardiner had access because they were used in his office at Smyths' Drill Works. He declared that he would produce handwriting experts; tied the medicine bottle to Gardner by its label; and went on to the copy of the *East Anglian Daily Times* found under Rose's head.

Here he had an important point to make. The Crisps did not take the paper. Gardiner did. The copy must have been brought into the kitchen by the murderer.

He described the footprints seen by Morris; stated that Gardiner's clasp knife had mammalian blood on it and could have made the injuries to Rose; and gave the wider public its first intimation of the Doctor's Chapel story. He said that Mrs Crisp and the postman would confirm that letters like the assignation note had been delivered to Providence House between the Doctor's Chapel incident and the catastrophe, and that Rose's brother had twice carried letters either from Rose to Gardiner or vice versa. He stressed Rose's pregnancy as a motive, and suggested that Gardiner had committed the crime after he and his wife had returned from Mrs Dickinson's, creeping out of bed as soon as Georgianna was soundly asleep.

This was the prosecution case at that stage. It was obviously circumstantial, but the evidence of the bottle from Gardiner's house and the footprints seen by Morris was very strong indeed.

Mr Ridley's first witnesses were familiar names from the inquest. Superintendent Andrews described the building. William Harsent described finding the body. Eli Nunn described his findings in Providence House.

But now, for the first time, Nunn revealed that in addition to two letters from Gardiner and some family letters, Rose's drawer contained letters from men who were not her relatives. *Men*, we notice; not *a man*.

Staunton later confirmed that these included Davis's indecent missives, and other innocuous letters. He also added firmly that the indecent letters were not in Gardiner's handwriting, and the police had not yet managed to trace their author.

We should note here that there were about twenty letters in Rose's drawer. All were to be produced (though not all discussed) at Gardiner's trial, and with the addition of the assignation note and its envelope and two letters Gardiner had written to Smyths' from Paris when they sent him to represent the firm at the Exhibition of 1900, there were twenty-six documents in all. There were six of Davis's amatory and indecent items. We don't know how many family letters Rose retained, but it does seem that at least one man in addition to Gardiner and Davis was writing to her. It is most unlikely that he or they could have been her murderer without incurring some police suspicion. But the correspondence shows Rose to have been more free than coy in her approach to the other sex. These were still the days when an employer might warn a maid to have 'No Followers'. And some slight trace remained of the old feeling (illustrated by Jane Austen) that a private correspondence between unmarried, unrelated young men and women was somewhat compromising.

When Mrs Crisp came to repeat her evidence from the inquest, Mr Leighton cross-examined her severely. The poor lady was to spend the next few months as a forensic football. She had timed Rose's scream very helpfully for the defence at the inquest. Now she retracted, and said that she could not be sure what time she heard it. Moreover, she withdrew her original response to a juror's query, that she might have heard the clock strike twelve as she and Mr Crisp came downstairs to make sure the rain was not getting into the house. Now she said she could not have heard the clock for the noise of the storm.

Her revised evidence helped the prosecution. It gave them a free hand to place Rose's death when they liked. But Mr Leighton hinted that Staunton and Ridley had coached Mrs Crisp to change her tale. This she denied, but she was quite unable to explain why she had been definite about the times before, and now withdrew them.

To make matters worse, she had a nervous giggle. Cross-examining lawyers ask for nothing better.

'Has it occurred to you that a man's life is possibly at stake on your evidence?' asked Mr Leighton severely, bringing his examination to a conclusion.

'I don't know on my evidence alone', simpered Mrs Crisp.

'Or do you think it is a matter to laugh at?'

'No; I don't laugh, Mr Leighton.' But the *East Anglian Daily Times* had already reported her as testifying 'with a laugh' that Rose knew Gardiner.

In fact, Mrs Crisp was something of a village eccentric. As 'Old Tailor' Crisp's third wife she was the first who was younger than him, but like her predecessors, she brought money to the marriage. She lived on an annuity as a gentlewoman's spinster companion until she married at the age of fifty-two.

Her husband was on the Peasenhall School Board, and she paid the school formal visits, and occasionally marked the children's needlework.

Billy Rowe told us that the children all thought she was silly, and looked forward to her visits as occasions to laugh at her. But Fred Rowe told us more. After she had been wed a short time, she confidentially informed one of her friends about her sexual awakening:

'Do you know, Mr Crisp was rude the very first night!' she protested. The affront to her maidenhood rapidly passed along the grapevine of a delighted village.

Frederick Brewer the postman testified that Rose had asked him whether there was a letter for her on the Saturday morning before her death, when he delivered the assignation note. She had never asked such a thing before.

He was less positive as to whether he had previously delivered letters in similar envelopes to her. He couldn't, he said, swear to it. Mr Ridley would have challenged him hard with a statement he had made to the police, but Mr Leighton rescued him and preserved this useful uncertainty.

Brewer did not deserve to be humiliated over this: he was scrupulously refraining from releasing private information that reached him in the course of his official duties, as he was bound to do. When his superiors subsequently told him to tell the courts whatever they needed to know he was quite forthcoming.

Rose's young brother Harry was another new witness. He testified that he had taken more than one letter (he couldn't remember how many) from Gardiner to Rose the previous year, always in blue envelopes. He had carried an uncertain number of answers from Rose also. And in 1902 he had taken two letters from Rose to Gardiner, but brought back no replies.

He also regularly took the *East Anglian Daily Times* from Emmett's shop to the drill works for Gardiner.

Harry Burgess told about meeting Gardiner in The Street and seeing the light from Rose's window at the time proposed in the assignation note. Mrs Dickinson testified that the Gardiners had come to sit with her at eleven thirty and left at one thirty. James Morris described the footprints from Alma Cottage to Providence House and back again.

But the sensational new witness was Bill Wright. He told the story of the Doctor's Chapel very simply and with minimal suggestiveness. In fact, he said no more than that he had heard, 'laughing and talking in the chapel'. Mr Ridley did not extract anything apparently very damaging from him. But Mr Leighton set a precedent for bullying the young man and trying to discredit him by abuse.

'Have you played the part of an eavesdropper before?' he asked. 'An amateur detective, in fact?' And on getting no answer, he went on, 'Do you often make it your business to pry into other people's doings?'

On the strength of the evidence Wright had given, this was breaking a butterfly upon a wheel. But Leighton knew that Wright and Skinner would be very dangerous, and tried to spike this prosecution gun before it could be properly trained on his client.

The magistrates' court adjourned for another two weeks, and on 30 June the coroner's jury, in the comfort of the assembly hall, had their third bite at the cherry.

Mrs Dickinson's evidence had quietly changed to Gardiner's detriment now from that she had given before the magistrates. She now said that Mrs Gardiner came to her house at about half past eleven, and Gardiner followed at midnight, give or take a few minutes. She also said she had seen Rose come to Alma Cottage carrying a parcel at about nine o'clock that evening, although as far as she knew both Gardiners had been out. Mr Leighton did not brow-beat her as he had Mrs Crisp.

Morris gave his evidence. Captain Levett-Scrivener asked which way the bars on the soles went. Morris misunderstood the question – perhaps intentionally – and replied unhelpfully, 'backwards and forwards' (the direction of the footprints on the road). The police offered to show him the shoes given them by Mrs Gardiner, but Mr Leighton firmly stopped that. In the end, Captain Levett-Scrivener drew the outline of a shoe sole, and Morris sketched in bars running across it.

Mr Rickards gave evidence that Gardiner had easy access to office envelopes of the kind used for the assignation note. But the prosecution's suggestion that the envelopes were themselves unusual was undermined by Captain Levett-Scrivener who pointed out that he used similar ones on his farm, and Mr Rickards was then compelled to concede that they were in common use.

Harry Harsent's evidence about his messenger-boy service between Gardiner and Rose changed from what he had given the magistrates. He now said he had taken letters from Gardiner to Rose the previous year from June onwards. He could not remember how many, and he had taken a further two in 1902. All were in blue envelopes. He had also taken answers from Rose to Gardiner, but none more recently than a year ago.

The inquest was interested in checking the details of his delivery of the *East Anglian Daily Times*, and ignored this new confusion.

Harry Burgess told Mr Leighton that Rose's window was lit every night at ten o'clock. The coroner, with precisian severity, established that Burgess did not go out every night and pointed out that he could not know what he had stated for a fact. This exchange reveals some hostility to Gardiner on the coroner's part, or at least an unwillingness to let slipshod points in his favour pass.

Frederick Brewer, told by the coroner that the postal authorities had given permission for him to reveal information about the mails, now said that he had delivered letters to Rose in envelopes like the assignation note, addressed in the same handwriting. Mr Leighton was distressed at this change in Brewer's evidence, but the postman was right to claim that he had not denied it before the magistrates: he had simply said he could not swear to it.

When Superintendent Staunton gave evidence, Mr Leighton established that in addition to taking all Gardiner's clothes from his house, the police had also searched a disused well behind it. He also established that all the letters from Rose's drawer were now in Mr Thomas Gurrin the handwriting expert's hands. And the inquest learned that the police had at last traced the indecent letters and poems to Fred Davis.

Captain Levett-Scrivener was surprised when this was only casually revealed. Mr Cooke, the vicar, who was also on the jury, asked whether Davis had given a satisfactory account of his movements on the fatal Saturday night. Staunton replied that he had. But clearly the jury's spontaneous feeling was that some suspicion attached to him.

Bill Wright's evidence now became rather more sensational in response to Mr Ridley's questioning. He had heard Rose cry, 'Oh, oh!' followed by some rustling about.

Mr Leighton's cross-examination of him rested on the unreasonable proposition that he should have answered questions he had never been asked.

Leighton:	Why didn't you tell the whole truth before the Magistrates?
Wright:	I did.
Leighton:	What have you added now to that you gave before the Magistrates?
Wright:	I don't know that I have added anything.
Leighton:	Why didn't you tell the Magistrates you heard the girl say, 'Oh, oh'?
Wright:	Because they didn't 'ax' me.
Leighton:	You didn't tell them you heard rustling in the Chapel?
Wright:	They didn't 'ax' me. I only answered what they 'axed' me.

Alfonso Skinner supported Wright's story. He, of course, had heard the conversation between Rose and Gardiner which Wright had missed.

He reported hearing what the press coyly described as, 'some curious words' after Rose said she had been reading in the Bible 'about like what we have been doing here'. These were probably the words reported as 'The House of God is above you and the staff of life is in you,' when they reached Mr Fred Rowe, which do not occur in the Bible. But whatever words Skinner quoted, they were not the ones Mr Ridley wanted to hear, and over Mr Leighton's strenuous objection – 'What this man reads in the Bible has nothing to do with the case!' – he at last elicited the citation of the Onan verse, Genesis, chapter 38, verse 9.

Mr Leighton's cross-examination hinted at an area of ill-feeling between Skinner and Gardiner that was never followed up. Skinner did not recall Gardiner's ever saying anything to him on the subject of indecent photographs. This suppressed hint is the only contemporary trace of Gardiner's exerting a depressing 'holier than thou' influence on his juniors.

On Leighton's insistence, Mr Guy had been telegraphed to come and give evidence about the Sibton chapel hearing as a counter to Wright and Skinner. He proved far less satisfactory than the defence hoped as he had no recollection of telling prominent laymen that the charge against Gardiner was trumped up, and he concluded that the inquiry was deadlocked with two witnesses saying one thing and two another. At best, it seemed, Gardiner and Rose had been given the benefit of the doubt, and Mr Guy's last response was bleak: he had not expressed and never intended to express any opinion as to whether the charge against Gardiner was proved or not.

Fortunately for Gardiner's future defence, he did make one major error, recollecting wrongly that Rose was present at the chapel inquiry.

Nunn and Lay made perfunctory reappearances, largely to establish that Gardiner's clasp-knife could have caused Rose's injuries and Mrs Gardiner's table-knife could not. The coroner summed up with a fairly strong recommendation to the jury not to bring in an open verdict if they could fix responsibility upon anyone. After half an hour's deliberation they obliged by finding that William Gardiner had wilfully murdered Rose Harsent. The coroner directed that he should be sent for trial at the next Assizes.

So now the defence's only hope of undermining this was to overturn the inquest verdict with a dismissal of the case by Saxmundham Magistrates. The bench sat on 3 July to finish their hearing of the case. They met Skinner for the first time, and Mr Leighton treated him as he had Wright, accusing him of suppressing evidence before the inquest because he was now asked questions that had not been put to him then. His additions were not nearly as important as Wright's 'Oh, oh!' and the rustling, but Leighton's hammer-blow questions tell their own story:

Q: Why didn't you tell the coroner's jury about this interview with Gardiner?

Q: The usual thing – because I was not asked! Have you had your memory refreshed lately?

Q: Why didn't you say before the Coroner that you caught Gardiner up and walked with him?

This barrage of sarcasm is very unimpressive. It is an old legal dodge – with a weak case, forget the evidence and abuse the witness.

One other interesting little exchange was never followed up, and remains an intriguing sidelight on the Doctor's Chapel incident. Gardiner personally prompted Mr Leighton to ask,

Leighton: At the chapel enquiry that was held, did you say that while you were watching, a match was struck in the chapel?

Skinner: I don't remember.

Leighton: Was a match struck in the chapel or not?

Skinner: I can't say whether I said that or not; I don't remember saying so.

What on earth was this about, and why did Gardiner think it would help his case? We don't know, but it certainly goes to support our impression that dusk was too far advanced for Wright and Skinner to be able to see what was going on through the window.

Mr Guy came back and corrected his error of memory before the inquest. Mr Rickards identified two letters Gardiner had sent the firm from the Paris Exhibition. And Mr Thomas Gurrin, the handwriting expert, made his long-awaited appearance.

He was very cautious. He hedged nearly all his observations with the phrase, 'In my opinion.' He had to be forced to commit himself to the opinion that the Paris letters and the assignation note were in the same hand, even though that was the whole purpose of his presence.

More interesting than Mr Gurrin's tentative opinions, perhaps, is the fact that of all the Gardiner material available to him – including two letters to Rose, and the one from prison which Eli Nunn had taken from Georgianna – he only felt safe in using the two written from Paris in

1900 for his detailed comparison with characters in the assignation note.

One more important expert appeared. Dr John Stevenson, the Home Office analyst, had examined the physical evidence. He found that the bloodstained glass from the broken medicine bottle could not have been used to injure Rose as there were no miniscule traces of flesh on it. There was no blood on any of Mrs Gardiner's kitchen-knives. But there were traces of mammalian blood inside Gardiner's clasp-knife, which had evidently been scraped clean since the blood stained it. He found no blood or paraffin on any of Gardiner's clothes, footwear or pocket litter.

Among the fragments of the medicine bottle, Dr Stevenson had found half a spent wooden match-stick and a small piece of blue woollen fabric, about three-sixteenths of an inch long. The fabric had been exposed to heat and had subsequently got blood on it.

If it could be shown conclusively that this clue had not been accidentally included with the broken glass as it passed from Eli Nunn to Dr Lay or by whatever route it took to Dr Stevenson, this would be of the utmost importance. Prima facie it would seem to be a genuine clue. Its exposure to heat suggests that it was in the kitchen at the time of the paraffin conflagration, and the subsequent blood staining reached it from the bottle fragments with which it was wrapped.

The police were not fools. If the fabric seemed to have come from Rose Harsent's clothes or nightdress, they would have said so. If it seemed to have come from Eli Nunn's tunic they would have said so. They did say that it did not come from any of Gardiner's clothes in their possession. Today, with forensic scientific evidence playing a major part in murder inquiries, it would be the most important finding in the kitchen. In 1902, however, it was a tiny puzzle less than a quarter of an inch long, and nobody paid it much attention.

Mr Leighton called no witnesses and reserved Gardiner's defence. The magistrates felt that a case had been made out against Gardiner. They committed him for trial at the Assizes. Gardiner and his wife were allowed to sit together in the ante-room of the court for a little, where they both were seen to be crying. Then Gardiner recovered his composure, and bravely endured the public gaze as he waited for the train to take him back to Ipswich Prison.

SIX

The First Trial

G ardiner was to be tried at Suffolk Assizes in Ipswich Shire Hall on 6 November, before Mr Justice Grantham.

Mr Ridley, the prosecution solicitor, briefed Henry Fielding Dickens KC to lead the prosecution, with the Hon. John de Grey as his junior. Dickens was the only one of the great novelist Charles Dickens's many children to achieve success and distinction in his own right. He was a gentlemanly and sensible barrister, offering his clients hard work, serious thought, and no fireworks. He would proceed to the judicial position of Common Serjeant to the City of London and a knighthood.

He has been praised for his moderate and balanced prosecution of Gardiner, and this is just. On the other hand, he was briefed with an impossible case. On its merits, Gardiner should really have been found Not Guilty. We do not know, of course, whether the formal strategy presented to the jury was the outcome of Staunton's, Ridley's or Dickens's reflections on the evidence.

Leighton and Aldous briefed the young and unsilked Ernest Wild to lead Mr Claughton Scott for the defence. This turned out to be a brilliant choice.

Wild was thirty-three: just about the same age as the keen young solicitors instructing him. He was an East Anglian man, the son of a Norwich magistrate. He was a man of boyish charm with a most attractive voice. He was also a theatrical and emotional pleader, on the lines of his slightly older contemporary, Edward Marshall Hall. He conducted Gardiner's case in a temper of uncontrolled passion, treading the very edge of professional propriety. Still, this case made his reputation and was always regarded as his greatest achievement.

Why was this? Primarily because Wild, like Arthur Leighton, was absolutely convinced of Gardiner's innocence. He stayed with Leighton and his wife in Ipswich while the trials proceeded, which meant that he had no respite from partisan tension after each day in court. He flung himself unreservedly into the battle on his client's behalf, and at night, practised his speeches in front of a mirror like an actor. His energy might lead him over the top, but his fearless and determined advocacy made its mark on all onlookers.

Wild was spurred on to reckless forensic oratory by the fear that local prejudice would make it impossible for Gardiner to win a fair hearing in East Anglia. For example, Leighton and Aldous had already had to take out an injunction against a showman called Stewart who rented the Revolving Tower in Yarmouth, where he displayed a waxwork tableau of Gardiner in the very act of killing Rose. All the lawyers in the case were horrified by this prejudicial display.

After the coroner's and magistrates' hearings, both sides had a rough idea of the strengths and weaknesses of the case against Gardiner, and both set about to improve their positions.

The Doctor's Chapel incident was an obvious bone of contention. When the Sibton brethren considered it, Mr Guy inevitably concluded that 'somebody lies here'. There was a flat conflict of testimony.

Both sides carried out tests to see whether Wright's and Skinner's story could be demonstrably untrue. Eli Nunn took Wright, Skinner and Mr Burgess down to the chapel. He went and stood on the bank where they had hidden, while the others went into the chapel where the young men repeated the conversation they claimed to have heard. Wright and Skinner went through the Genesis passage, and Nunn heard it all clearly. Wright, Skinner and Burgess maintained that they spoke in very low tones.

Mr Leighton also visited the chapel, taking with him his assistant Mr Bullen, Methodist farmer George Fidler, and an architect and a quantity surveyor from Ipswich. They took turns in standing at the hedge and in the chapel and reciting unspecified verses of hymns and poems in what they believed to be normal conversational voices, but found that from behind the hedge they could hear nothing at all. From the lane they could distinguish two voices, but not make out any words.

These experiments could do little but persuade any jury that the legal teams engineered the evidence they wanted. The village believed that Leighton's team had carried out their test in the daytime, and the conversation was drowned by the noise of the drill works across the road.

For the record, we have also carried out our own test. We have experimented both from the hedge where Wright and Skinner stood, and also from a similar distance away on the opposite north side of the chapel, since the south wall by the lane has been rebuilt since 1902 and may be acoustically quite different.

Taking it in turns, we spoke from inside and listened from outside. The speaker quoted familiar, but unspecified poems, passages from

Shakespeare and the like. We started very quietly, and gradually increased the volume of the recitation until the listener signalled that he could now identify what was being said. We discovered that at Wright and Skinner's stated distance from the chapel it was completely impossible to make out words uttered in anything that could be called a reasonable conversational tone for the size of the building. It demanded strong and deliberate projection for words to be heard clearly. Even a listener stationed very close to the window could only hear what was said if the speaking voice was markedly firmer and clearer than we would assume to be normal in conversation between two people close together in a small room.

But we allow for the probability that ninety years ago rustic villagers normally spoke in louder voices than we do now. And our conclusion is that Wright and (more particularly) Skinner only heard excited high points of the hour-long conversation: moments when Rose raised her voice in ecstasy, or to show off her naughty knowledge of the Bible, and when Gardiner's tone increased in sympathy.

The prosecution was aware that one great weakness of their circumstantial case was the absence of any trace of blood or paraffin on Gardiner's clothing. Since Mr Leighton had objected to the repeated descent of Eli Nunn upon Alma Cottage, they strategically insisted that the house had never been properly searched, as for the first two days the death had been believed to be suicide. So Gardiner, they said, would have had time to destroy any bloodstained clothes.

Enquiries in the village unearthed Herbert Stammers who lived in a small building in the alley, between Mrs Dickinson's house and Gardiner's wash house. Shortly before the trial opened, the prosecution sent his deposition over to the defence advising them that he would be called to testify that Gardiner had lit an unusually large fire in the wash house the morning after the murder.

The prosecution was also resting on rather slender evidence when they claimed that Gardiner's liaison with Rose had continued between the Doctor's Chapel incident and the murder. Of course Rose was pregnant, and Gardiner was the only man whose name had been associated with hers in public scandal. But neither the magistrates nor the coroner had been shown any proof that Gardiner kept up an illicit correspondence with her beyond the fact that Mr Gurrin believed the assignation note to be in his hand, and it was reasonable to suppose that the author of that letter had written those others which postman Brewer had delivered and Mrs Crisp had seen.

Further enquiries in the village produced Herbert Rouse, now declined from farm-worker to road-mender. His deposition, too, was sent to the defence and resolved a minor mystery for the Gardiners. Georgianna had seen the anonymous letter William received after Rouse allegedly saw him put his feet on Rose's lap in Sibton Chapel. Since the letter did not mention that little exhibition, neither knew exactly what had provoked it. Nor did they know who had written it. They had never suspected Rouse.

They had kept the letter. Georgianna turned it over to the defence lawyers and it entered the case. But Wild, Leighton and Aldous were very indignant at receiving fresh prosecution depositions at such a late stage. They were convinced that the prosecution had sprung evidence on them at the last minute, confident that there would be no time for the energetic young defenders to uncover rebutting witnesses, and this introduced an element of bad blood among the lawyers in the case.

Sir William Grantham, the judge who was to try the case, was a handsome and elegant man whose face might have modelled for Solon the Lawgiver. But his cool, detached appearance was misleading since his was a notoriously unjudicial character. He was a model of the old-fashioned country gentleman, and retained the eccentric habit of wearing checks and riding a horse down the Strand to the Law Courts, long after that street was given over to wheeled traffic. But as an ex-Conservative MP he proved incapable of bringing dispassionate and unbiased attention to cases which aroused his prejudices. He was to be severely criticized for mishandling election petitions and publicly rebuked by the Liberal Prime Minister H.H. Asquith in 1911 for his indiscreet remarks from the bench. The *Dictionary of National Biography* says, 'he lacked the breadth of mind and the grasp of intellect necessary for trying great and complicated cases'. All in all Mr Justice Grantham was the wrong judge for the difficult Peasenhall case.

At half past ten in the morning of 6 November, he took his seat on the bench. Gardiner was brought into the dock, and allowed to sit in an old-fashioned armchair. He wore a dark suit, his beard was neatly trimmed, and it was noted that he took an intelligent interest in the formal opening of proceedings.

With the jury sworn in, Mr Dickens opened his case. He declared his intention to be judicial and temperate, and gave a very brief outline of the case against Gardiner. There was said to have been 'an immoral intercourse' between him and Rose which continued even after the Sibton Chapel inquiry; she became pregnant.

The time came when it was impossible to conceal her shame,
and if her shame was not concealed it was impossible to conceal

his. The case was that the prisoner wrote a letter making an appointment to meet her at her house at 12 o'clock on the Saturday night, and that he then murdered her in Providence House, and tried to destroy the body by fire. That was a short summary of the case.

Mr Dickens then drew out the case at greater length, naming the witnesses he would call and sketching in their anticipated testimony. Ernest Wild interrupted him once as he came to Henry Rouse and the letter he had sent reproving Gardiner after he had been seen supposedly playing footsy with Rose at chapel.

'The letter is undated and unsigned,' protested Wild. Mr Dickens gently pointed out that the envelope was dated 14 April.

'The defence did not hear this evidence until 1 November,' Wild objected.

'I think I had better not read the letter,' suggested Mr Dickens.

'I don't mind my friend reading it at all,' returned Wild.

Indeed he didn't! It had been given to him by Mrs Gardiner and brought into the case on his own decision. It would go a long way to discredit Henry Rouse in the courtroom, in his religious community, and in the eyes of posterity, by showing him up as a man who wrote anonymous letters. This whole interruption simply goes to show the strength of Wild's injudicious commitment to his client.

Mr Dickens had studied the transcripts of the earlier hearings. He spotted Mr Leighton's severity with Mrs Crisp, and now tried to spike the defence guns by telling the jury it was important that they should know exactly what she had said on the two occasions:

Substantially, before the Coroner she said she thought it was between one and two she heard the scream and thud . . .
Before the Magistrates, Mrs Crisp said she was asleep and had no means of judging what the actual time was. It was an undoubted fact from the evidence he should call that the prisoner and his wife from twelve till half past one were in the house of Mrs Dickinson.

Thus Mr Dickens hoped he had swept away the element of possible confusion introduced by Mrs Crisp's perfectly normal uncertainty about the timing of bumps in the night during a violent thunderstorm. But of course, he had not. His own case, as he stated it, exonerated Gardiner.

Fortunately for the prosecution, Mr Wild was so carried away by the theatrical and argumentative possibilities of cross-examining Mrs Crisp that he relegated this gaping hole in the prosecution's case to a minor position in his own. For Mr Dickens was calling Mrs Dickinson and giving Gardiner a complete alibi for the time at which the assignation note suggested Rose must have met her murderer. If Gardiner wrote that note, the inference would be that Rose sat up until at least half past one in the morning, hoping her lover would keep his word, even if the storm had delayed him. Since she would have to be up betimes herself before the Crisps arose, nobody who has reflected on this point has been persuaded by the prosecution's reconstruction of events. Rose, it is felt, would have said, 'He cometh not' and got into bed. But Dr Lay and Eli Nunn were quite clear on that point: her bed had probably been sat upon. It had definitely not been slept in.

Mr Dickens's opening statement made only one other important point which had not been brought out previously. He described the paraffin lamp standing in three pieces beside the body, and claimed that 'it seemed that some person had tried unsuccessfully to unscrew the top of the lamp to get out the oil'. According to one newspaper transcript of his speech he merely called this a prosecution theory. But another suggests that it rested on the definite appearance of the lamp.

What was this appearance? How could you tell that an unsuccessful attempt had been made to unscrew the wick-holder and open the well? No evidence was called on the point, yet it was and is manifestly important.

After opening his case Mr Dickens called his witnesses. Superintendent Andrews produced the maps of Peasenhall and plans of Providence House and the Doctor's Chapel on which he had lavished a lot of time and care. Bill Wright stepped up to repeat his testimony on the Doctor's Chapel incident.

The defence had been examining local gossip to see if he could be discredited, and Georgianna's mother produced an interesting titbit from the past. Mr Wild succeeded in reducing Wright to an embarrassed silence in the following exchange:

Wild: Have you never gone about what is called 'garping' in the country – seeing what is going on between young men and women?
Wright: I think not.
Wild: Don't you know?

Wright:	I know I have not.
Wild:	Let me just remind you. Don't you remember the time a few years ago when a young man named Ernest Cady [Georgianna's brother] was going to be married to a young woman?
Wright:	I know him well.
Wild:	Did you say then you saw them go into an orchard and behave improperly?
Wright:	No, sir.
Wild:	Did you see them go into your orchard?
Wright:	Yes, sir.
Wild:	What were you doing? Weren't you up in a tree?
Wright:	I was gathering apples. (*Laughter.*)
Wild:	Did you spread a scandal about these two people then?
Wright:	No; we mentioned it, but we did not mention any scandal about it.
Wild:	Did Cady come and ask you what it meant?
Wright:	Cady never came to me.
Wild:	Did Cady's mother ask you what you meant?
Wright:	Yes, Cady's mother did.
Wild:	Did you say there was another young fellow with you and he saw the same thing?
Wright:	I can't recollect. It is years ago.
Wild:	Was it true that you saw this indecency then?
Wright:	I never said anything about indecency.
Wild:	You thought that was bad?
Wright:	No.
Wild:	What did you talk about it for?
Wright:	(*Silence.*)

This was a well-prepared and beautifully executed cross-examination. Wright was set up for Mr Wild's scornful conclusion, 'I put it to you that is the way you and Skinner go about, trying to find out any filth you can.'

Yet it was not really pertinent to Mr Wild's case. A jury of countrymen would realize that 'garpers' usually saw what they reported. Wright had been trapped because he told the truth on matters which were hardly open to an innocent interpretation: Mrs Cady *had* reprimanded him; he *had* gossiped about an incident that he claimed entailed no indecency. Wright was an embarrassed young man. But he had not been shown to be a liar over the Doctor's Chapel incident.

The defence investigators then slipped up on one useful matter. Wild extracted from Wright that he and Skinner both lodged with a man named Redgrift. He went on to check that they had all talked about the Doctor's Chapel incident the following morning. But he had not been properly briefed as to Harry Redgrift's relationship to James Morris's gamekeeper employer. He laid a good foundation to suggest a nest of hostile village gossips building up mutually supporting stories against Gardiner, but could not use it when the proper time came.

Alfonso Skinner was luckier than Bill Wright. The defence had not been able to dig up any dirt in his past to embarrass him. He introduced a new sentence of Gardiner's that he remembered hearing just after the Genesis chapter 38 exchanges: 'Don't say anything about it. I shall be here tomorrow at 8 o'clock.' But he escaped without a mauling at Mr Wild's hands.

The judge put one question to him. Gardiner had claimed that the Doctor's Chapel story was 'nothing but old stuff'. The judge asked Skinner if he knew of any 'old stuff' which could be alleged against Gardiner. Skinner simply said, 'No.'

The following day Mr Justice Grantham made an apology and correction to the jury. Some East Anglians had pointed out to him that he misunderstood the dialect. 'Old stuff' did not mean stale gossip, as an outsider might assume, but a fabricated story. Gardiner's denial had been absolute from the outset.

Mr Guy was the next prosecution witness, describing the Sibton chapel inquiry and Gardiner's visit to him in Halesworth after he decided to drop legal proceedings against Wright and Skinner. It is doubtful whether his sententiousness can have created a good impression on most jurors when he claimed to have said at the inquiry, 'Somebody lies here, but the great God above alone will decide.'

Mr Wild treated him cautiously. He made the point that Mr Guy had inaccurately told the coroner that Rose had attended the Sibton inquiry, but did not press it. He suggested that Gardiner would not have been fit to hold the office of Sunday School superintendent if Wright's and Skinner's story were believed. Mr Guy suggested that it was 'only suspicion'. Mr Wild foreshadowed future witnesses by asking Mr Guy if he had not called the scandal 'a trumped up affair' at Quarterly Meeting. Mr Guy did not believe he had expressed any opinion at all.

It was, perhaps, fortunate for Gardiner that none of the lawyers involved in the case was familiar with Primitive Methodist priorities. He had offered to resign all his offices at the time of the scandal, and then, when exonerated, continued to hold them until they lapsed the following spring. After that, he continued as Sunday School superintendent, organist and assistant society steward. Outsiders naturally assumed that the position of Sunday School superintendent, with its responsibility for the moral well-being of young people, was Gardiner's most important post. Methodists were more impressed by the fact that he gave up the very senior chapel position of class leader. Nobody, they felt, ever gave up this office without a very strong reason. Gardiner's reason might have been a scrupulous feeling that the class leader must never be the subject of gossip, no matter how ill founded. It might equally, however, have been a guilty wish to escape from an exposed position. Mr Dickens should certainly have drawn attention to this possibility.

Henry Rouse now took the stand with his stories of seeing Gardiner and Rose walking out together, and Gardiner putting his feet in Rose's lap during chapel. Not only had his letter of reprimand to Gardiner been unsigned; he had dictated it to his wife so that his handwriting did not appear. The judge instantly pounced on this, ascertaining that Rouse did not know whether or not Gardiner would have recognized his writing. Nor had he received an answer. Since Rouse's deposition had arrived so recently, Mr Wild had to work with what he had. The anonymity was a perfect opening.

'You were ashamed of what you wrote?' he asked. And, 'What do you think of a man who writes a letter and does not sign his name?' Both questions tended to discredit Rouse by the fact that they could be put at all, regardless of what Rouse answered. The *East Anglian Daily Times* called Wild's cross-examination 'searching'. Apart from the last question – why didn't the anonymous letter make any mention at all of the feet-in-lap incident that had supposedly provoked it? – there was nothing that should have been difficult (as opposed to embarrassing) for Rouse to answer. The word 'searching' therefore presumably meant overtly hostile and very effective.

The last witness to the 'immoral intercourse' was Harry Harsent, Rose's young brother. His testimony at this trial was helpful to Gardiner. He said that he had carried 'two or three' letters in blue envelopes from Gardiner to Rose the previous year, the first of them in June. He had also carried several letters from Rose to Gardiner in the current year, 1902, but none from Gardiner to Rose. This supported Gardiner's admission that he had used Harry as messenger-boy for his two letters at the time of the scandal, and had received subsequent notes from Rose relating to choir business. Mr Wild contented himself with establishing that Harry took the *East Anglian Daily Times* to the works for Mr Smyth as well as Gardiner, and that Gardiner's copy sometimes had his name pencilled on it.

Brewer, the postman, was carefully questioned by both counsel and the judge so that his testimony became perfectly clear. On the morning of Saturday 31 May Rose had asked him whether there was a letter for her. This was unusual. In the afternoon, at about a quarter past three he had delivered the assignation note in the buff envelope. He had certainly delivered five or six letters to her in similar envelopes over the previous twelve months. One, two or three of them would have been in 1902. The Peasenhall and Yoxford postmarks indicated that the assignation note had been posted in Peasenhall between half past six on Friday 30 May and ten o'clock in the morning on Saturday 31 May. Nobody in the post office had noticed it was local, so it had been postmarked and sent on to Yoxford for sorting; postmarked again and returned to Peasenhall to reach the post office at about half past two.

There was only one question nobody thought to ask. Was it common for letters to be posted in the village for addressees in the village? The fact that no attempt was made to sort out village mail suggests prima facie that it was not. We have questioned both Mr Herbert Denny and another elderly villager, Miss Gertie Rose, about this, and received clear confirmation that it would be quite extraordinary to write to another villager through the mails in those days. Letters would be personally delivered by hand. Whoever wrote the assignation note had very strong reasons for not wanting to be seen approaching Providence House.

So much for the liaison between Rose and Gardiner. The prosecution at last came to the murder. Mrs Crisp was the first witness. Mr Dickens established two points of interest in his direct examination. Rose had been carrying the candle she used to light herself to bed when Mrs Crisp said good-night to her at a quarter past ten in the hall. The paraffin lamp was in the kitchen (at least, we take it, Mrs Crisp assumed it was. She was not asked whether she had actually seen it in place or noticed its light through the kitchen door.) We may infer that Rose had just brought the candle down from the bedroom, since Burgess saw a light there at around ten o'clock, and it is highly unlikely that Rose would have risked arousing Mrs Crisp's suspicion by removing the kitchen lamp for her signal. And this suggests that Rose had definitely followed the assignation note's instructions and set a deliberate signal in her room at the appointed time. It was mere coincidence that Burgess remembered always seeing a light in her room whenever he happened to be passing at ten o'clock.

Mrs Crisp also testified that the Scotch shawl hung over the kitchen window was normally kept in a tin box in the Crisps' part of the house, and she had last seen it there on the Saturday morning. Rose had, it seemed, taken very deliberate precautions indeed to keep her midnight tryst secret.

Mr Dickens had already outlined Mrs Crisp's conflicting testimony at the earlier hearings. He was content to let her say, now, that she did not know precisely what time she had come downstairs with her husband, or what time she had been aroused by the scream.

Mr Wild's cross-examination tried to get Mrs Crisp, as a deacon's wife, to confirm that the Doctor's Chapel door tended to stick at the time of the scandal, and had since been shaved down and repainted. Mrs Crisp knew nothing about it.

Then counsel turned to the timing of events during the storm. He rubbed Mrs Crisp's and the jury's noses in her conflicting testimony, eliciting the explanation that it was her husband who suggested to her that it was about midnight when they first came downstairs. Mr Wild persuaded her to admit that since she thought that Rose's scream meant she was frightened by the storm, it must have been still raging when she heard it. This was important, as it placed the murder at a time when Gardiner was undoubtedly in Mrs Dickinson's house.

And, for good measure, Mr Wild bullied the unfortunate Mrs Crisp quite unscrupulously. 'This is a matter of vital importance to me and my client. Could you have been paying attention when you were sworn before the Coroner?' he asked severely, and was no doubt gratified to receive embarrassed silence for an answer. He was happier still when Mrs Crisp gave a nervous laugh in one response. The *East Anglian Daily Times* was in no doubt that it was a wholly nervous reaction, but Mr Wild pounced.

'Mrs Crisp! Really, you've been laughing at me the whole time! This is a serious case. I believe you were corrected by the coroner for laughing.'

'I was not laughing; it is false,' replied the unfortunate witness indignantly.

Harry Burgess, the next witness, suffered even more from Mr Wild's forensic histrionics. He gave straightforward testimony to the light visible in Rose's room when he chatted to Gardiner in The Street at ten o'clock before the storm, and to the acoustic experiment conducted at the Doctor's Chapel by Nunn, Wright and Skinner. But under cross-examination he laid himself open to be made the bumpkin butt of Mr Wild's superior wit. When Wild asked him how loudly Skinner and Wright spoke (Burgess had already told Mr Dickens it was 'very soft') the witness replied, 'I ain't no scholar.'

'That is why the constable took you,' riposted Mr Wild, and was rewarded with general laughter. He raised another laugh when Burgess testified that he had slept through the storm, and could not say how long it lasted.

'I think it would take a pretty good storm to wake you,' gibed Wild, and again the court-room rocked at his sally.

It was a tactical error. Wild's next question to Burgess was really important. Had he not seen a light in Rose's room at ten o'clock on previous occasions? But the exposed position in the witness-box, probably coupled with the horrible stuffiness typical of Victorian court-rooms, quite overcame Harry Burgess. With a feeble affirmation, he fainted. Mr Wild's smelling salts failed to revive him, and he had to be helped out. Wild deserves no praise for that successful reduction of a potentially helpful prosecution witness to a limp rag.

The last prosecution witness that day, Mrs Dickinson, testified that Mrs Gardiner came to her house between eleven o'clock and half past, and Gardiner joined them at about midnight. She was not sure of the exact times. Gardiner had been wearing carpet slippers, she was sure of that, because one fell off during the evening. His manner was perfectly calm and untroubled throughout the storm. She was certain they left at half past one because she glanced at her clock as they went. For good measure, she said that she had sold paraffin to Mrs Gardiner but never to her husband. Mr Wild had no need to bully her. She was far more useful to him than to the prosecution.

After her evidence, the judge's attention was drawn to the fact that a juror was almost fainting in the vile fug, and the court was adjourned for the night.

Next morning, under-gamekeeper James Morris was the first witness. He described the footprints he had seen as made by 'Indiarubber bottoms with bars'. And then he shocked Mr Dickens by being unco-operative when the sketch he had completed at the inquest was produced. Had he drawn the bars on the outline sole? 'No,' he said.

The judge tried to correct him, pointing out that depositions affirmed that Morris drew the bars after Captain Levett-Scrivener had sketched the outline.

'I do not remember seeing this sketch before,' said Morris. 'I think it was a larger one.'

The lawyers were mildly disgruntled. They all knew that this was Morris's sketch, and he didn't seem likely to deny that it represented the way the bars had run on the footprints he saw. But Morris's intransigence had its desired effect. Both Dickens and Wild treated him gingerly, and were careful not to lay themselves open to an unexpected reply, or to draw attention to any that he gave.

For example, Morris confirmed having met George Redgrift, the head gamekeeper, three quarters of an hour after he had seen the footprints. The judge asked whether this was before he had heard of Rose Harsent's death (as indeed it was), thus opening the way for the point that it would be significant if he had noticed and commented on an apparent coming and going between Rose and Gardiner before he knew anything untoward had happened. Yet neither Mr Dickens nor Mr Wild dared ask Morris whether he had in fact mentioned the footprints immediately! It was merely left as a vague possibility.

Wild had several cautious strategies with which to undermine this damning witness. The first was to suggest that he had actually seen the pattern on the soles of the canvas shoes Mrs Gardiner had produced when they were exhibited at the Magistrates' Court, and had then drawn them appropriately at the inquest. Morris roundly denied having seen the soles in court, even if they had been a mere two yards away from him.

Wild's next attempt was to suggest that the road was so wet, with the gravel in places washed away, that the tracks could hardly have been seen even if they survived the storm. Morris stonewalled implacably while Mr Wild questioned persuasively on this point, so that, after reading the exchange, we ourselves had no idea what conclusion should be reached. So, over eighty years after the event, we questioned Mr Herbert Denny and Mr Billy Rowe about the old road surface, and learned from them that, as they remembered it, Morris was unquestionably right. The surface was untarred, dusty, white chippings. Even they, as little boys, left clear trails if they were carrying anything heavy. Footprints made in the road after a storm would be clearly visible; even footprints made during it might well remain.

Mr Wild had one signal success in his cross-examination, however. It was, once again, the outcome of Leighton and Aldous's patient detective work among the villagers.

Wild:	Did you say before the magistrates the road was very wet?
Morris:	Yes.
Wild:	Did you say, 'I never saw any other footprints'?
Morris:	I did.
Wild:	Did you say it had been raining fast during the night, and after the footmarks had been made?

Morris:	Yes.
Wild:	Is it true that you saw no other footprints?
Morris:	(*Silence*)
Wild:	Come now, sir! Do you say no to the question?
Morris:	I can't remember seeing any other footprints.
Wild:	Not any on your round?
Morris:	Well, I did, about half a mile off, on the Heveningham Road.
Wild:	Have you not heard that a witness was coming to say that he was walking along that road?
Morris:	No. But I've seen him here.
Wild:	Have you not heard that he was walking past Crisp's house on the road to Heveningham that morning?
Morris:	No.

Wild had successfully knocked two chinks in Morris's armour. That last negative might be strictly true, in view of the fact that Heveningham Long Lane led away from Providence House from the opposite side of the Hackney Road crossroads. But there could be little doubt, in the light of what was to come, that Morris knew he had not encountered an expectant defence witness who was going to say no more than that he had been walking half a mile away from the village that morning. Morris's laconic steadfastness had been made to look less like sturdy veracity, and more like deliberate unhelpfulness.

And, of course, the jury could guess that the forthcoming witness was going to challenge Morris's powers of perfect observation.

Satisfied with this effect, and with extracting from him the fact that he had not seen any footprints on Gardiner's doorstep and had not been interested to look, Mr Wild made no comment when Morris gave a quite absurd answer:

Wild:	It's a large square step coming into the road?
Morris:	No.

Why on earth did Morris tell this blatant untruth? Possibly because he took 'large' to mean remarkably or unusually large. But certainly his answer shows that defiance put truth at risk in his evidence.

Mr Wild's last line of attack was the suggestion that Morris had waited a long time before coming forward with his evidence, and only chose to do so on the Friday after the murder when he knew that Gardiner was under arrest. Mr Dickens set out to correct that on redirect by ascertaining that Morris had been out with gamekeeper (George) Redgrift looking after pheasants on the Thursday when Eli Nunn asked him to come back to the police house at Peasenhall. He confirmed that 'Mr Redgrift' had been there, and Mr Wild fumbled the opportunity this gave him.

'Is Redgrift the master of Wright and Skinner?' he asked. Morris gave his favourite response: 'No.' And Mr Wild pursued the matter no further.

Yet he seems to have been scenting the real possibility that Wright's stepfather, Harry Redgrift, had put the police on to Morris. That would mean that gamekeeper George Redgrift told his gardener brother about the footprints, so that Harry Redgrift might have talked it over with Wright and Skinner, as he had earlier talked over the Doctor's Chapel with them. If that line of transmission of information to Eli Nunn had been established, the possibility would exist that Wright, Skinner and the Redgrifts put it into Morris's head that the footprints started from Alma Cottage. But Wild lost the opportunity by asking if Redgrift was Wright and Skinner's 'master'. Gardener Harry Redgrift was actually their landlord. Mr Smyth was their master. Morris batted the question away like a fly.

The judge followed up to reinforce the importance of Morris's conversation at 6.00 a.m. on Sunday 1 June. Like Mr Wild, he may well have thought the gamekeeper was the only Redgrift in question. Sir William Grantham put the question Mr Dickens had funked: had Morris actually spoken about the footprints when he met George Redgrift in the early morning? Morris confirmed that he had described the trail between Alma Cottage and Providence House a good five hours before he learned of Rose Harsent's death. Mr Wild was left with rather unsatisfactory results from his cross-examination, and Morris emerged as a sly old countryman who had resisted all the smart folks' attempts to get him to embroil himself and his neighbours any further in this business.

Herbert Stammers struck the press as even more unforthcoming than Morris, and also as more prosperous than his neighbours. His testimony amounted to very little at first. He had seen Gardiner going towards the washhouse at 7.30 a.m. on Sunday 1 June and noticed there was a fire in there. Cross-examined, he confirmed that the Gardiners sometimes lit a fire in the washhouse and made breakfast there in the summer. And the washhouse was overlooked by Mrs Pepper's and Mrs Dickinson's houses as well as his. He had told the police about the fire when they asked him – he couldn't remember when that was. He knew nothing about his deposition's having reached the defence as late as Tuesday 4 November (two days before the trial opened). When really pressed, however, he admitted that it was only the previous day, Monday, that the police had approached him.

Mr Wild somewhat spoiled his effect when he protested that the deposition reached him improperly late, and Stammers's testimony had not come up to proof. The judge agreed that the defence had not been properly notified of this witness, and had Stammers recalled to question him personally. Sir William then brought out the vital point Mr Dickens had missed: that Stammers's attention had been drawn to the fire because he thought it 'an excellent blaze', or 'a large blaze'. Unusually large, the jury might infer. Mr Wild would have done better not to have protested, and to have left it as an ordinary fire in the washhouse.

Mr Rickards identified the letters Gardiner had written to the firm from Paris, and testified that both yellow and blue envelopes were kept in Smyths' office to which Gardiner had access: envelopes of the kind used for both the assignation note and Gardiner's personal notes to Rose. He gave Gardiner a good character, but may have been prejudiced against him by the strong feelings which were springing up at the drill works. For he said, 'I have not heard that anyone but Captain Levett-Scrivener had envelopes of the same sort, and should not have known this if he had not spoken of it.' This was putting a very prejudicial gloss of peculiarity on cheap business envelopes which Captain Levett-Scrivener had remarked were in general use, and Rickards himself confirmed were sold by the five and ten thousand in Ipswich.

William Harsent told his story of finding his daughter's body again, and Mr Wild wisely did not press an old man who evoked strong sympathy in the onlookers. But he showed his determination to fight hard when Eli Nunn took the witness-box. He asked that Superintendent Staunton should leave the court while Nunn's evidence was taken, and the judge, correctly, concurred. This was a signal that Wild would be looking for weaknesses and contradictions in the police account of their detective work.

In the event he was unable to shake Nunn greatly. He was a competent and experienced witness. The *East Anglian Daily Times* described the six-foot former bricklayer as 'a smart and highly-intelligent specimen of the Suffolk constable, with a dash of grey in his hair, and the aspect of an old soldier'. It added that he 'conducted himself under cross-examination as if to the manner born'. It noted only one moment at which Nunn seemed to have been foxed, when he accepted the word 'persecution' as a description of his repeated visits to Alma Cottage.

Scrutiny of the newspaper's full transcript of the cross-examination, however, shows a more significant exposure of some excess of zeal or lapse of memory. Nunn claimed that he had no notebook at Alma Cottage, and had not taken any record of the interviews with Mrs Gardiner. Wild persisted until the judge asked to see Nunn's notebook. Sir William then revealed that Nunn had indeed made a note of one of Mrs Gardiner's responses relating to the camphorated oil in the medicine bottle; had then struck it out, and written in its place, 'Mrs Gardiner states she offered to give Rose Harsent some camphorated oil, "but I am not sure whether I gave it to her or not".'

Still, Nunn acquitted himself well in the teeth of a quite ferocious cross-examination. Wild managed to bring in the suggestion (which Nunn denied) that he had indirectly tried to intimidate a witness by saying to Mr Pepper, 'Leighton has been after your wife – you had better be careful.' And he used Nunn's testimony to foreshadow Fred Davis's dirty letters to Rose.

It was agreed that most of them were too obscene to be read in open court. But the florid love letter was given in full (though the newspapers suppressed two suggestive phrases):

> My innermost yearnings have made me write down on paper a
> few lines about her that has enraptured my whole heart; a Rose
> among the many thorns that reside in our midst. Her shapely
> form and wavy hair makes her the idol that I worship. She
> means to me my very existence. You may smile, fair reader, at
> my nonsense, but since she crossed my path the very moments
> spent in her presence are like a breath from Paradise. The time
> may come when she may leave me to woo some other man, but
> Heaven only knows the pain that will [g]naw at my heart. Life
> will not be worth living, but should I win her heart for my own
> it would seem like heaven upon earth. A glimpse of her at any
> time will cheer me through the day. I hope the time is not far
> distant when [words omitted]. No other girl can [words
> omitted]. Like the old song:–
>> 'She's the lily of the valley,
>> The bright and morning star.'
> With her lovely charms she has won my very soul, and when at
> night I sleepless lie I think I see her face smiling at me as only
> those in love can know. I dare not think of her being out of my

reach. She has engraved her image upon my heart, and I pray that she will soon return my love. If not Heaven only knows the consequences. Burn this.

During the lunch adjournment the jury was given Davis's naughtier compositions to read. On their return they expressed their relief that this appallingly obscene matter had not been read in open court.

Superintendent Andrews was recalled to introduce his detailed plans of the Doctor's Chapel. The rotund and elderly officer attracted a jocular remark from Mr Dickens about being 'the RA of the police force'. He was quite uncomprehending when Mr Wild got a titter from the court by asking whether he had ever sent any pictures to the Academy.

Superintendent Staunton, who followed his colleagues, was the new model modern policeman. The *East Anglian Daily Times* stated that it would never have thought of him as a policeman at all. Essentially this seems to mean that a smart young journalist would not have felt the assurance to patronize him.

Staunton emerged from Wild's cross-examination unscathed. He was always prepared to yield the edges of points without giving up the centres, so that Wild could not make him look intransigent or biased.

Dr Richardson presented the post-mortem findings. Either of the two lacerations in the throat might have caused death. The cuts on the hands were probably made as Rose tried to ward off blows. The burning of the body had taken place after death. Suicide was ruled out. And, emphatically, Gardiner's white-handled clasp-knife could have inflicted all the wounds. Mr Wild had no questions for Dr Richardson.

Dr Lay described what he had seen on being called to Providence House and confirmed what Dr Richardson had said about the post-mortem. Mr Wild questioned him. He was anxious to ascertain that Rose's hair was unsinged, although the copy of the *East Anglian Daily Times* had lain beneath her head and was partially burnt. This would indicate that the body had been moved after the fire had started, and it would be most unlikely that the murderer could have avoided getting blood on his clothes.

Dr Lay spotted where Wild's questions were leading and became a little evasive. Wild pushed him strongly on the fact that he had said at the inquest that the newspaper was under the head. And he extracted two laughs when the doctor hesitated as to what he meant by saying Rose's hair was not so neat as it would be during the day; that it was not hanging down her back, but was up.

'Was it what is known as a bun?' asked Mr Wild, to laughter. And when Dr Lay said he didn't know, Wild asked him ironically whether he had really seen the body at all!

He changed from mirth to severity, however, on learning that a newspaperman had been allowed to watch the post-mortem. This was improper, even if the coroner had approved. The judge agreed, saying he had 'never heard of a more monstrous thing'.

Dr Stevenson, the Home Office analyst, had watched the proceedings from a seat of honour by the sheriff and his chaplain beside the judge's bench. Now he testified that there was no trace of paraffin or blood on any of Gardiner's clothing or property, except his knife. This had been sharpened on a whetstone, but also cleaned carefully by scraping inside the clasp. Traces of mammalian blood remained between the white casing and the brass, and between the blade and the spring. It was impossible for Dr Stevenson to say whether the traces were human or a rabbit's, but he was positive they were not more than a month old.

There followed the traumatic humiliation of Fred Davis. Mr Dickens had little to ask him. He lived next door to Providence House and was apprenticed at Emmett's Store at the time of the murder, though he had since gone to London. He identified the notorious dirty letters from Rose's drawer as his. He had not had immoral relations with Rose and had never walked out with her. On the night of the murder he had left work at about ten o'clock, stayed out till about half past, and then gone to bed. His brother slept with him, and he would have had to pass through the room where his father slept to get out again that night. His father was in court to confirm that he had not left the house, if necessary.

Mr Wild gave Davis an appalling battering. He repeatedly asserted that he was filthy. He accused him of unchivalrous cowardice in stating (no doubt perfectly truthfully) that Rose had encouraged his salacious correspondence. He openly accused him of fathering her unborn child. And he stopped so abruptly short of accusing him of the murder that he probably hoped the jury would conclude that Fred had done it.

He established, first, that Fred could easily visit Rose in the kitchen from the back gate of his home, and had done so in the past.

Wild:	When you were there on business you took the opportunity of giving her a beastly poem?
Davis:	Not without her request.
Wild:	Her request! you say that of a dead woman? That she requested you to give her this filth?

Davis:	Yes . . . She said she had heard of these poems being about, and she asked me to procure her some, and I did so.

Wild took Davis up on the suggestive words the newspapers tactfully omitted from the letter read out in court:

Wild:	In that letter you say, 'I hope the time is not far distant when . . . .' You meant what you said?
Davis:	I done it for fun.
Wild:	You are on your oath. Did you mean it?
Davis:	It was only a sportive flirtation.

Rose was not unique. This was a point that Mr Wild prudently dropped, as it seemed Fred might show that village parents knew about this rather normal adolescent activity, and took their own measures to control it:

Wild:	Were there any other girls in Peasenhall to whom you wrote in this tone?
Davis:	I think not.
Wild:	Don't you know?
Davis:	I was stopped.

Wild's most serious accusation elicited a determined denial:

Wild:	Do you mean to say on your oath that you were not the father of her unborn child?
Davis:	I can swear to that. (*And witness struck the box with his finger to reinforce the oath.*)

Mr Wild then suggested that Davis had owned rubber-soled shoes at the time of the murder, as had many young Peasenhall men including Fred's brother. Fred didn't question other young men owning them, but claimed he had not possessed any until he went to London.

Then Wild turned to a 'dirty book' Fred was supposed to have lent Rose. In fact, Eli Nunn had refused to characterize the publication in that way when cross-examined, merely calling it 'a pamphlet'. The judge described it as a leaflet, entitled 'Proper Discipline to be Observed by Married People with Regard to the Consequences of . . .' (presumably 'Marital Intercourse', or words to that effect). In essence it would be contraceptive instruction.

Wild:	Did you give her a dirty book?
Davis:	I lent her one.
Wild:	What was it?
Davis:	I forget the name of it. I borrowed it of a man named Grice.
Wild:	Was it not the book about the way to procure abortion?
Davis:	It was things like that.
Wild:	Knowing this girl was *enceinte* you lent her a book?
Davis:	I lent it to her over twelve months ago.
Wild:	What reason had you to lend her a book of that sort?
Davis:	Because she wanted one.
Wild:	What was the reason?
Davis:	I hoped she would like me more than she did, but she would not have anything to do with me afterwards.
Wild:	You wanted to take precautions?
Davis:	That was partly in my mind.
Wild:	You thought it might be useful to you afterwards?
Davis:	I thought it might.
Wild:	In what way?
Davis:	If I went out with her and married her.
Wild:	Is it not much more likely that you lent her the book in order to undo your handiwork?
Davis:	No, sir.

That was a revealing little exchange. Fred evidently believed his chances of having sex with Rose were very good indeed. And she must have been on terms of considerable intimacy with him if, in the moral climate of 1901, she asked him to obtain a contraceptive manual for her. This went beyond the request for copies of salacious verses, amounting to a confession that she was (or was contemplating) enjoying illicit sexual activity.

Since she dropped Fred as soon as she had the leaflet, we may assume that he was being manipulated: that his puppy-love amused her, but did not hold her interest for long. He was probably telling the truth when he said he had not had 'immoral relations' with her. He wanted to. He nearly made it, but in the end, he was too keen, and Rose got everything she wanted from him without going the distance.

Davis said that he had got the dirty poems from 'lads', one of whom

1

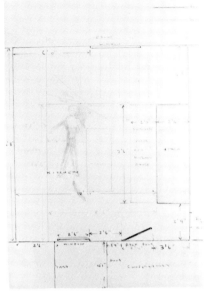

Reconstructed scene-of-crime sketch by Stewart Evans with only one error: the lamp pieces should be parallel and . not at right-angles to the body

2

Gardiner's washhouse

3

4

Cover page of Superintendent Andrews's *Work Journal*, with his account of Sunday 1 June 1902 in Peasenhall

1

Officials and witnesses involved in the case:

Revd Ernest Cooke

2

Dr Lay, centre second row in panama hat; on his left, Revd Ernest Cooke

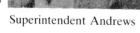

3

Superintendent Andrews

4

Superintendent Staunton with police
tug-of-war team rope at his feet

5

Chief Constable Jasper Mayne

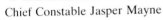

6

Dr Ryder Richardson

1

Handwriting evidence. Gurrin's prepared sheet offsets the words of the assignation note (left column) against specimens from Gardiner's Paris letters. Note, *inter alia*, the totally different capital Rs and Ps

2

Fred Davis's flowing hand (seen here on his marriage certificate) is totally different

3

The Burton confession letter is actually more similar than Gardiner's hand was named Smith and had since joined the army. And his cross-examination ended with Mr Wild's ringing accusation hurled at him for the jury to contemplate.

Wild:	How did she come to ask you for these verses?
Davis:	She repeated the first lines of one.
Wild:	Do you mean to say that Rose Harsent was the seducer in this case and she led you astray?
Davis:	That's about the truth of it.
Wild:	What a gallant, chivalrous young man!

Mr Dickens's brief redirect drove home that the contraceptive leaflet had been obtained in September 1901, three months before Rose became pregnant, and he offered to call Davis's father to prove his alibi. Mr Wild, however, disclaimed intending to suggest that Davis was the murderer. Fred's relief at this rather unmerciful deliverance was visible to reporters in court.

Wild:	My suggestion is that this young man is the father of the child. My suggestion goes no further, because it would be wrong.

Lawyers do not like overtly accusing a witness of the crime in a capital case. But Mr Wild believed passionately in his client's innocence and would evidently have loved to prosecute Fred Davis for the murder of Rose Harsent. He had to stop short of saying so, however, or the court might have reprimanded him for making a reckless accusation without having any evidence to shake Davis's alibi.

Fred's place was taken by Mr Thomas Gurrin the handwriting expert. He had prepared an elaborate chart of photographic comparisons. In the left-hand margin, each word from the assignation note was written down separately to form a long column extending for two pages. On the right, extracted letters, words, and fragments of words from the two letters Gardiner had written from Paris were laid out to exhibit similarities of character formation. Led by Mr Dickens, Mr Gurrin confirmed that letter after letter showed some unusual similarity of formation, until Mr Wild protested that Mr Dickens seemed to be the expert in the case. Thereafter Gurrin made his own selection of comments.

As the first and most prominent professional examiner of questioned documents in England, Mr Gurrin took an interest in the legal standing of expert witnesses. He was aware that Lord Russell had pronounced that they should point out factual details (like comparisons of letter formation) but not express opinions any more than other witnesses. Through Mr Dickens he asked his lordship whether he should state an opinion as to the authorship of the assignation note or not. Sir William said he should, and Mr Gurrin declared that in his conscientious opinion, the writer of the letters from Paris also wrote the assignation note. He later added that uncertainty about the validity of Lord Russell's pronouncement was the reason he had been so cautious before the magistrates.

Mr Wild's usual domination of the court-room failed him with this particular witness. He antagonized all his listeners with a cheap sally when Mr Gurrin referred to testimony he had given before 'the learned Magistrate'.

'Probably he was not so very learned; but still, go on,' jeered Mr Wild. The judge's eyebrows shot up indignantly, and some one in court gasped, 'Oh!' It was ill-mannered, in that the junior prosecuting counsel, Hon. John De Grey, chaired a bench of Suffolk magistrates. It is all the more puzzling in that Wild's own father was an East Anglian magistrate.

He recovered a little when Gurrin hesitated to offer an opinion on the syntax of the assignation note and Paris letters.

'Cease to be an expert and become a man!' pleaded Mr Wild. But Gurrin himself good-humouredly led the laughter at this shot, so it did him little harm.

His laborious testimony was inherently rather boring, yet the court, and particularly the judge and Chief Constable Jasper Mayne, paid close attention as Mr Dickens examined him. Their interest was apparently exhausted by the time Mr Wild cross-examined, even though he made occasional good points. He remarked, for example, that Mr Dickens had indicated that the S in Saxmundham was formed exactly like a capital T in the Paris letters, and Gurrin had let that stand as a point of similarity, whereas the unbiased observer would read it as the reverse. He showed that Gurrin was rather shakily suggesting that the assignation envelope was possibly in a disguised hand, while the note itself was undisguised. But the court was bored by the time Mr Dickens closed the prosecution case.

So, wisely, Mr Wild asked for the court to adjourn for that day before he opened the defence, claiming that he had so much matter to bring forward that he could not reasonably make a start in the time available. The foreman of the jury was outspoken in his approval of the adjournment.

'We've had enough of it for today,' he said when the judge hesitated.

On Saturday morning, everyone was refreshed and ready to hear what Mr Wild would say to undermine the prosecution. Their great court-room entertainer, who had evoked laughter and righteous indignation in equal measure, did not disappoint them. He started by reducing his client to tears as he painted a pathetic picture of his shamed widow and orphans should he be found guilty. He then moved to the case.

The motive rested heavily on the Doctor's Chapel incident. Mr Wild called Wright and Skinner 'lewd louts with lewd minds', who would leap at the chance to discredit a man of religion. He offered four reasons for doubting their story.

First, Wright claimed to have left the scene just at the point when events inside the chapel were becoming interesting. This was inherently improbable. Second, Skinner had related the Genesis chapter 38 conversation, word for word, parrot-fashion, which suggested that he had memorized a prepared statement. Third, he had changed his original story, 'We left together', to make it fit Wright's claim that he left first. And finally, it was utterly improbable that Gardiner and Rose would have talked loudly enough to be heard from behind the hedge.

The Sibton chapel inquiry completely exonerated Gardiner. Had there been any doubt in the Methodist elders' minds, they would not have let him retain all his posts 'with the exception of one or two subordinate offices which he was asked to accept again, but refused'. (As we have seen, this was a very misleading description of the class leadership.)

Turning to Rouse, Mr Wild called him 'the assassin who stabs in the dark, the anonymous writer who does not sign his name, nor date his letter'. He drew attention to the improbability of Gardiner putting his legs on Rose's lap in front of the whole congregation, and asked the jury to dismiss Rouse's evidence.

As to the murder itself, Mr Wild knew that Mrs Dickinson was his best witness. The evidence of the assignation note suggested that the murder must have happened soon after midnight. Mrs Dickinson's testimony proved that Gardiner could not have done it then. If he was waiting to keep his appointment with Rose all the time he sat with her, he must have been a consummate actor. If, as the prosecution suggested, he carried out the murder after one thirty, Rose must have sat up for an hour and a half in her nightdress and stockings, which seemed absurd. Anyway, Mrs Gardiner would testify that her husband had gone to bed beside her after they returned home from Mrs Dickinson's. And her account would be supported by Mrs Pepper's relating what she had heard from next door.

The handwriting expertise of Mr Gurrin would be challenged by two 'gentlemen, not professional witnesses', who were accustomed to looking for bank forgeries and believed that Gardiner had not written the assignation note.

Then Mr Wild indulged in an extraordinary passage of speculation whose propriety seems very dubious:

> Assuming that a man, whom we will call X, committed that murder, what would his business be? He would think, 'I must not appear in this matter. I must endeavour to point the guilt to somebody else.' Because a man who would commit a murder like that would hesitate at nothing. He therefore imitates the writing of Gardiner. He therefore carefully imprints those footprints which are said to have been seen by Morris. Assuming the man X to have done that, every tittle of evidence disappears against him.
>
> It is not for me to say whether it is likely or probable, but it is possible, that these suspicious circumstances are the work of the real murderer, in order to throw the blame upon the innocent man against whom a scandal has arisen.
>
> Gentlemen, you had for the first time yesterday a man in the witness-box whom we have not seen before – the man Frederick Davis; and I do suggest to you that, if it is a question of who was the father of the child, one can have very little doubt he was in the witness-box yesterday. You have read those awful letters. You have seen how, first of all, they described the lustful desires of a man, how next there were various experiences and acts minutely described. Here is a man who last September bought a book for this girl to tell her how to remove her trouble. He says it was last September. We have only his word for it. They always antedate these things in bastardy cases. I suggest to you that these improper letters point to one thing only to men of commonsense and men of the world, viz.: that the man who has had everything he wants, and who has held habitual possession, and who has gone too far – in order to prevent the evidence of his own misdeeds from coming to light, gave her a book for a certain purpose. It is not for me to point to the murderer of this unhappy girl. It would be too much to expect that, in order that the prisoner may be acquitted, he must show you who committed the crime. The law does not put that upon the defence, or else many an innocent man would be hanged by the neck until he is dead. But I am entitled to say, when they bring forward their Wright, and their Skinner, and their Rouse, as pointing to the

paternity to this child, I bring forward, or cross-examine, the man who is the undoubted father of this child.

Rarely has counsel looked more 'Willing to wound, and yet afraid to strike,' though no one could accuse Wild of a tendency to 'Just hint a fault and hesitate dislike.' He concluded by calling Davis 'a vile, lewd blackguard', and moved on to the footprints.

He noted that no cast had been taken of the footprints, and there was only Morris's word for their existence. He declared that he would bring rebutting evidence from James Hart, who had walked down Hackney Road and up Heveningham Road at four o'clock in the morning in hob-nailed boots. He had seen no footprints beside Providence House, and Morris had not observed Hart's until he was half a mile up Heveningham Road. From this, Mr Wild deduced that Morris's observation was imperfect and that the footprints, unseen by Hart, were made between four and five o'clock: too late for a murder that took place in the darkness as timed by Mrs Crisp's hearing the scream.

Mr Wild then came to a couple of his strongest points. There was not a trace of blood or paraffin on Gardiner's clothes or his canvas shoes. Nobody had been found to suggest he owned any clothes the police had not seen, and he would certainly have burned his canvas shoes if, as the police claimed, he had worn them at the murder, and then lit the fire in the washhouse to dispose of incriminating clothing.

The medicine bottle was harder to dispose of. Mr Wild mocked the suggestion that any murderer would take a labelled bottle to leave as a calling-card beside his handiwork, or imagine that a mere half pint of paraffin would serve to dispose of a body. He argued that Rose had retained the bottle Mrs Gardiner gave her and used it to keep paraffin in the kitchen. He did not explain how it came to be broken beside the body.

But he finished on another strong point, at least to our ears, attuned as they are to the success of forensic science in identifying minute traces of murderers' clothing or body fluids at scenes of crime. He drew attention to the tiny scrap of blue cloth Stevenson had found with the bottle fragments. Since it came from neither Gardiner's nor Rose's clothes, it must have been the murderer's, and he could not have been Gardiner.

With that, Mr Wild called Mrs Gardiner as his first witness. She had been seen around the court the previous day, looking distressed at her surroundings. Now she appeared self-possessed as she stepped up in a crimson bodice and lace shawl to give her evidence. Her large hat was trimmed with feathers and big blue silk bows.

Her account of the murder night was straightforward. Gardiner had come over to Mrs Dickinson's 'A very few minutes' after her. They left at half past one, and the clock struck two as they went to bed.

Very shortly after that, little Bertie woke up and cried, and she went and comforted him. She was out about five or ten minutes.

A little later – (the papers reported her as saying a little after one o'clock, but this must have been an error) – she came downstairs for some medicinal brandy as the storm gave her 'pains in her body', which, in fact, kept her awake until five in the morning. Her night was so bad that she heard the clock strike every hour.

She got up once again before five, however, as the twins awoke. She put one in bed with her elder sister, and brought the other in with her and Gardiner. Gardiner slept through this.

She and her husband rose between eight o'clock and half past on Sunday, and lit the fire in the washhouse. Gardiner's manner had been perfectly normal at all times, including his reaction to the dreadful news of Rose's supposed suicide. His wife knew all about the Doctor's Chapel scandal, but she had never believed in it, and it had in no way affected their excellent marital relations.

She believed Rouse was hostile to her husband because he was jealous of his position in the chapel. She knew that Gardiner had last used his clasp-knife to 'hulk' a rabbit. The judge first needed to be told that 'hulking' meant gutting (which he himself called 'paunching'), and then had to have it explained to him that villagers did not usually buy their rabbits ready cleaned from poulterers!

Mr Wild took Georgianna carefully through the police interview at which Eli Nunn had noted down her remarks about the medicine bottle, even though he forgot he had been present. Georgianna reported the following dialogue from the police interview:

Georgianna:	Well, I remember giving the deceased some camphorated oil in a medicine bottle.
Staunton:	Are you quite sure she took it?
Georgianna:	Yes, she took it, because I gave to to her.
Staunton:	Are you quite sure?
Georgianna:	(*No response*)
Staunton:	(*To Nunn*) You had better put it down, 'I gave Rose Harsent some camphorated oil in a medicine bottle, but I'm not sure she took it.
Georgianna:	I'm quite sure she took it!
Staunton:	(*No response*)
Nunn:	(*Wrote something*).

It is utterly improbable that anybody was deliberately lying over this matter. It is remarkably difficult to recollect exactly what has been said in conversations at times of stress, and there is no doubt that participants quite honestly and inaccurately tend to remember hearing what they expected to hear. Staunton, we believe, honestly thought Georgianna had indicated some doubt. She was convinced she had felt and shown none. Nunn genuinely forgot this particular occasion among his repeated visits to Alma Cottage.

The memory of Gardiner's arrest made Georgianna falter in her testimony, but Mr Wild produced his bottle of smelling salts and she recovered.

She set a curious mathematical problem for future generations that was not seized upon by Mr Dickens. Gardiner had been wearing one shirt when he was arrested, and she later handed over another that she said he had been wearing on the night of the murder, and that was awaiting washing. She washed every other Monday, and her next wash after the murder was due on 9 June. Gardiner slept in his shirt, and these two, she said, were the only two he possessed. Yet somehow he contrived to have one shirt on, one in the wash, and 'a clean shirt' on Sunday. Could there have been a third shirt that had been destroyed in the washhouse fire?

Mr Dickens cross-examined gently. His only trace of asperity came as she resisted his bringing out that she had never previously told the police about having a sleepless night after the storm. Her excuse was the one the defence had forced from so many other witnesses: she had not been asked.

There was then an interesting exchange about her and Rose. Rose came to Alma Cottage whenever she chose; there was no rule restricting her. Georgianna had always looked on her as a most respectable girl.

Wild:	And you never saw her with any man about the village?
Georgianna:	I could not say that.
Wild:	I mean in an improper manner?
Georgianna:	No.
Wild:	With the exception of the scandal about your husband and her, did you hear anything about her?
Georgianna:	I heard her and young Davis were on very friendly terms.
Wild:	But she still came to your house after that?

Georgianna:	Yes.
Wild:	Therefore, I don't suppose you thought there was anything wrong?
Georgianna:	No.
Wild:	With the exception of what you have mentioned, do you suggest she went with any young man?
Georgianna:	She was engaged.
Wild:	(*Interposing*) That was the young man, Bob [Kerridge] whom the prisoner wrote about in his letter with regard to the scandal.
Judge:	That was broken off?
Georgianna:	Yes.

Did the Gardiners direct Mr Wild toward his onslaught on Fred Davis? His was the only name Georgianna volunteered in connection with Rose. And why did everyone keep Bob Kerridge so discreetly out of sight? He had moved to Uggeshall where he was working as a ploughman at the time of the trials. Yet the prosecution might usefully have called him if he had broken off his engagement because he doubted Rose's denial of all connection with Gardiner, and he would have been equally helpful to the defence if he would swear that he had never believed the scandal. What did he believe, and why was he never asked? Why was his surname concealed from the press? It has never before been published.

Mrs Pepper was the first witness after lunch. Mr Dickens, quietly but effectively, reduced her claim to corroborate Georgianna's account of the night. She had sat up till four o'clock in the morning, she said, and had heard Georgianna come downstairs once, to attend to Bertie whose cries she heard. Georgianna, of course, claimed to have come downstairs three times: once for Bertie; once for brandy; and once for the twins.

Worse still, Mrs Pepper now swore that she knew it was Georgianna because she recognized both her light step on the stair and her voice when she spoke to the child. She further swore that she had told the police this. Mr Dickens was able to confront her with her signed statement to Staunton, made at the time. It read, 'I heard some one go downstairs at Mrs Gardiner's house, and, from enquiry I made of Mrs Gardiner, I believe it was her who came downstairs.' This effectively discredited her testimony.

Mrs Martha Walker of Sibton testified that she had known Gardiner for twelve years and found him a most respectable man under all circumstances. She also confirmed that Rose had suffered a bad cold at Easter, and recovered after using camphorated oil that Mrs Gardiner had given her, so that she was able to attend a tea meeting she had expected to miss.

At last Mr Wild called the prisoner at the bar.

Gardiner impressed onlookers by taking the stand with quiet confidence. His evidence directly confirmed Georgianna's and Mrs Pepper's about the murder night. He had gone to Mrs Dickinson's at around half past eleven, and stayed there till half past one. He did not notice the time when he was undressing. He heard Georgianna leave the bed twice: once to attend to Bertie and once for brandy. After that he slept till eight o'clock.

This corroboration was unsurprising since he had heard the testimony. As Mr Dickens realized, too late, it was normal for defendants who chose to give evidence to be called first by the defence. After that, the witnesses called to support their stories would be testifying quite independently, since only expert witnesses were allowed to hear earlier evidence. The prosecution might normally hope to find some contradictions between defendants' stories and those of their witnesses. Mr Wild had subtly and quite consciously avoided this danger. The witnesses who followed Gardiner into the box were all those whose testimony could not be used to contradict Gardiner's evidence.

Gardiner only differed from his wife in his speculations about hostile witnesses. He refused to be drawn into suggesting that Rouse was jealous of him.

'Is Mr Rouse somewhat inferior to you in the chapel?' asked Wild.

'I do not like to say', replied Gardiner. 'The man is as good as me.' But he agreed that his position was above Rouse's.

'I should have thought a preacher was above a superintendent,' interposed the judge, who was notorious for his inability to resist comments from the bench. 'I may be wrong.' Indeed he was. He mistook the term 'class leader' for a synonym for Sunday School superintendent, and so, like all the other lawyers, missed Gardiner's significant position of superiority and the curious fact that he relinquished it.

As for Wright and Skinner's hostile testimony, Gardiner could suggest no reason why Skinner should have spoken against him. He tentatively suggested that Wright might have been hostile because he and Mr Smyth had previously reprimanded the young man for a piece of bad workmanship. None the less, he agreed with the characterization of their story as 'a wicked lie'.

In Morris's case he did not suggest that any hostility motivated the witness, and he could offer no explanation at all for the footprints.

Mr Dickens seemed to lay the foundation for an interesting suggestion that Gardiner first saw Rose, helped her with the sticking door, and walked down to Providence House with her before he went home for his tea, thereupon arranging to meet more clandestinely later. This was not suggested in Wright's story, but it would have fitted with Gardiner's original timing of his movements at the Doctor's Chapel. It was never followed up, however, presumably because Wright could not conscientiously endorse it. Fourteen months after the event it is not surprising that memories were starting to get a bit shaky about who was in what lane and when on that noteworthy evening.

Altogether Gardiner's appearance in the witness-box redounded to his credit. He was not shaken in cross-examination. He answered firmly and promptly to all questions, only pausing once in disgust when Mr Wild asked whether he had in fact put his feet on Rose's lap in chapel.

'Do I really want to answer that question?' asked Gardiner. 'Is it consistent?'

When Gardiner stepped down, the Methodist farmer Abraham Goddard took his place and testified that Quarterly Meeting heard from Mr Guy that the Doctor's Chapel scandal was, as far as he could ascertain, a trumped up affair and a fabrication of lies. He had not said there was any dilemma over the evidence, rather that it was so contradictory that he could not believe it. Mr Dickens pointed out that Mr Guy had told the court that 'the boys' were not broken down under cross-examination and their story was not discredited, and that was what he had reported to Quarterly Meeting. Mr Goddard responded that he and Mr Tripp had definitely been told by Mr Guy that the scandal was a fabrication.

George Fidler had not been at Quarterly Meeting. He could, however, testify that he came away from the Sibton chapel inquiry satisfied that Gardiner was completely innocent. He did disclose a tendency to bias when he admitted that he would rather believe one Methodist brother than two outside witnesses. And he described the experiment at the Doctor's Chapel carried out by Mr Leighton and the two gentlemen from Ipswich.

Mr Leighton did something extraordinary. He went into the witness-box to give evidence on behalf of the client who was instructing him. He described the experiment at the Doctor's Chapel which had produced such different results from Eli Nunn's. And he was followed by

Mr Corder the architect and Mr Parmenter the surveyor who had accompanied him and Mr Bullen and Mr Fidler.

Ubbeston poultryman James Hart was the witness Wild called to scupper Morris's story of the footprints. He had stayed at his brother's in Hackney Road during the storm. Going back home at four o'clock, he had walked along the Hackney Road and up Heveningham Long Lane in his hob-nailed boots. He had not got far in his testimony when the judge protested that it was irrelevant and inadmissible. Mr Wild argued that it was necessary rebutting evidence, and, though not convinced, Sir William allowed it to be heard.

Mr Dickens brought out, from Superintendent Andrews's maps, that Hart's route would not have brought him anywhere that made it likely for him to notice the footprints at Providence House.

Mr Charles Larkin, a Norwich accountant who often had to detect forgeries and irregularities, was called in to rebut Mr Gurrin's hand-writing evidence. Mr Larkin was loftily superior to Gurrin's photo-graphic chart: 'Accountants never accept photographs.' He thought that the writer of the assignation note was better educated and more accustomed to writing than Gardiner. But he also thought the similari-ties between the note and the letters were so striking that the writer of the note must have been deliberately imitating Gardiner's hand! Like Mr Gurrin, he thought the envelope showed more evidence of deliber-ate imitation than the note itself. It was awkward for Gardiner that a defence witness perceived a similarity.

Mr Edgar Bird, a bank cashier who followed Larkin, also thought the assignation note was written by someone better educated than Gar-diner. His cross-examination degenerated into a dull wrangle about the likelihood of an educated man misusing capital letters. While Mr Larkin had preened himself on not being 'a professional witness', it must be admitted that these two amateurs ended the defence case lamely.

The court adjourned until Monday, with the jurors promised an outing to Felixstowe or somewhere similar on Sunday.

On Monday morning the jurors asked whether they could see the letter Gardiner had written to Georgianna after his arrest, and any others he had written in prison. It was suggested that they confine themselves to those written near the time of the murder. The particular one they requested had been returned to Georgianna and was in Peasenhall. Mr Wild immediately offered to send for it by motor-car. The driver was given tacit assurance that he would not be prosecuted for breaking the snail-like speed limits of the day, and he returned with the document by the luncheon adjournment, having travelled at a breath-taking average of 20 mph.

Everyone looked forward to Mr Wild's summation. And although it reads much less impressively than his opening speech for the defence, they were not disappointed. It contained great lachrymose passages at the beginning and end, portraying the inevitable damage done to the prisoner's unblemished reputation by this publicity, and the harrowing future for his widow and orphans should he be convicted. Gardiner was reduced to tears again.

There were flashes of Wild's familiar indignation and sarcasm. Skinner was 'of his own account . . . a filthy young man who goes about searching for what vice and sin he can discover'. With the knife, the prosecution, 'instead of starting a hare had started a rabbit'. The theory that it was the murder weapon 'was a pretty one – the sort of thing one reads in a comic paper'. If experts like Dr Stevenson were believed as to the age of blood particles, 'a good many men would go to the gallows'.

But the speech was less convincing than the opening as too much of it was taken up with repairing patches of defence evidence. Too many conflicting arguments were put forward to meet the possibility that this or that piece of the prosecution case might be accepted. Too much windy hypothesis replaced serious detail.

Much of the speech was taken up with boosting defence witnesses over the prosecution. Hart disproved Morris. Goddard disproved Guy. Larkin and Bird disproved Gurrin. Gardiner and Georgianna were so convincing that they disproved the prosecution case.

The best argument put forward in the speech was a very short summary of three genuine points in Gardiner's favour:

The first was – struggle and moving of the body, yet no sign of blood or paraffin on the clothes, boots or shoes of the accused man; the second, the agreement of independent explanations given by both husband and wife to the police before they had the opportunity of consulting; the third, that piece of cloth on the bottle, which was undoubtedly hacked in some way from the clothes of the murderer, but which was certainly not hacked from any clothes that the prisoner possessed.

Yet probably the most important and effective argument Mr Wild marshalled was one of those easily overlooked opening passages of formality in which counsel remind jurors of their oaths and duties. Defence counsel nearly always stress the 'reasonable doubt' that must be surpassed (Mr Wild did). They plead their own inadequacy for the responsibility they bear (Mr Wild did). But he added one more vital directive:

> I need hardly point out that the verdict you give is not a
> collective but an individual verdict. It is not like a
> misdemeanour, for each of you is sworn separately to make a
> deliverance between our Sovereign Lord the King and the
> prisoner. I appeal to any man, if he believes that the prisoner is
> innocent, to let no consideration blind his eyes to the fact that
> he has individual responsibility.

Whether it was owing to Mr Wild's appeal or not, just such a consideration was to save Gardiner's life.

Mr Dickens, by contrast, was far more restrained, as became a prosecutor. He complimented Mr Wild, drily pointing out, however, that his appeal had not been as purely to reason as he had claimed.

His own chain of reasoning was splendidly demonstrated as he took up Wild's suggestion that someone else had committed the murder and left clues pointing to Gardiner.

> What conditions must be fulfilled in order to make the unknown
> man fit in with the circumstances of the case? He must have
> been the man who wrote the letter 'A' [the assignation note],
> who, according to the defence, wrote in a handwriting
> extraordinarily like the prisoner at the bar; who on that night
> wore indiarubber shoes and walked to and fro between the
> prisoner's house and Providence House; a man who had a knife
> similar to the kind of knife found in possession of the prisoner;
> who was curiously brought into connection with a medicine
> bottle bearing the words, 'Mrs Gardiner's children'; who got
> hold of those buff envelopes in order to write that letter making
> the assignation; who had the same reason to get rid of the
> woman as we have been able to prove the prisoner had; who
> must have been on the look-out for the light in the window at
> ten o'clock, in the way that the prisoner was; he must have been
> a man of such position that it was imperative for him to conceal
> his shame, as we say the prisoner's position was. It is my painful
> duty to point out these facts. Are all these coincidences? Is it
> probable that this unknown man who committed the murder
> must fulfil all the conditions which in every case point to the
> prisoner at the bar?

Look at the other side of the case. The prisoner lives at Peasenhall, the prisoner writes remarkably like the letter 'A'; he has indiarubber shoes corresponding to the marks of the footprints going to and fro on that terrible night, he has a knife which fulfils the conditions which you would expect the knife to show by which that crime was committed, he is brought into natural communication with the medicine bottle because it is brought from his own house. The prisoner has access to the buff envelopes. The prisoner has reason to get rid of Rose Harsent, if you believe the witnesses. The prisoner looked out for the light just at ten o' clock because, from his own evidence and the evidence of his family, he was in a position in which exposure would be fatal.

All other books on the case give Mr Wild the forensic triumph. But in fact there is no passage of sustained argument in his closing speech to match Mr Dickens's excellent outline of the case against Gardiner.

In responding to Mr Wild's three logical points, Mr Dickens was not quite so persuasive. The little scrap of blue cloth forced him back on to the hypotheses that either it came from clothing the police had not found because they never really searched Alma Cottage, or, alternatively, from clothing that Gardiner burned in the washhouse fire. Alternating hypotheses were unhappily reminiscent of some of Mr Wild's own substitutes for clear argument.

To the fair point that the Gardiners' statements to the police tallied even before they could have consulted each other, Mr Dickens presented a couple of niggles. Georgianna had said once that William woke up and offered to fetch the brandy for her, and another time that he slept through that excursion. And she had not told the police that she was sleepless all night until the trial itself.

These were very trivial deviations from a single story. Indeed, had they not been made, one suspects that Mr Dickens might well have complained that the Gardiners' narrative of the night's events was too pat, and must have been prepared and rehearsed.

Finally, how did Dickens tackle the really strong point that no blood had been found on any of Gardiner's clothing or footwear? First, by the somewhat strained suggestion that, since there were no bloody footprints in the vinery or on the path around the house, the murderer, whoever he was, must have taken his shoes off to commit the murder!

And second, in a way which cannot now be described. He performed a small, discreet mime to show the jury exactly how, in his submission, a murderer might have inflicted the wounds on Rose without being touched by her blood. We should love to have seen it. We find it very difficult to imagine, since there was quite definite evidence that blood had spurted a distance of twenty-four inches beyond Rose's feet. On the whole, we think that we should not have found it the most persuasive part of Mr Dickens's speech.

Mr Dickens's persuasiveness, however, now faded into insignificance. Sir William Grantham gave his judicial summing up. And, to Gardiner's visible dejection, it proved to be a far more damning prosecution speech than Mr Dickens's. Point by point, he described the defence case, and expressed his own disbelief in it.

First he indulged in a characteristic aside. He criticized Mr Crisp for having 'acted the part rather of a coward'. If he had followed his wife's instincts and accompanied her downstairs they might have discovered the murderer or prevented the murder.

Then he turned to two secondary issues. The first was the Doctor's Chapel incident. He dismissed the Sibton chapel inquiry completely as prejudiced. The fact that Mr Guy gave Gardiner 'a good dressing down' suggested that he did not think Gardiner had been exonerated. It was not incumbent on the jury to decide whether Wright and Skinner's story was true, though if they did believe it they must regard it as 'a very strong piece of additional evidence'.

The second irrelevant issue was Davis's alleged paternity of Rose's child. There was 'not a tittle of evidence' to support this.

Gardiner's appearance of innocence on learning of Rose's death weighed against him in Mr Justice Grantham's mind. He thought it was most unnatural if he really was innocent. His 'normal' response fitted a murderer showing no remorse. (This tends to suggest that the Sibton Methodist congregation jointly killed Rose, as Mr Fidler had been quite explicit about Gardiner: 'He was affected with the news of what was thought to be a suicide as we all were.')

Rouse was an injured innocent in the judge's eyes. He could not believe that he would wickedly perjure himself. The jury, he thought, would be obliged to come to the conclusion that they must believe Rouse. Likewise Morris would not have lied to hang a man. It had been said that the road was too sloppy for footprints to remain, and the judge could understand that. But Morris said he saw them so they must have been there.

In tackling Mrs Crisp and the time of the murder, Sir William gave a most remarkable instance of that lack of intelligence said to characterize him. He believed that the scream Mrs Crisp heard marked the time of the murder. But he thought that Mrs Dickinson's, Mrs Gardiner's and Mrs Pepper's testimony that Gardiner was nowhere near Providence House until at least half past one was utterly irrelevant, because Dr Lay had estimated from the rigor mortis that death occurred about four hours before he saw the body. Therefore Rose died at five o'clock in the morning, after Mrs Gardiner had fallen asleep and long after the storm, so that Gardiner's footprints would be quite plain for Morris to observe. The judge was very pleased with this Holmesian deduction.

This crass suggestion was uniquely his own, and has never been given a moment's credence by anybody else. Apart from the extraordinary unlikelihood of Rose's sitting patiently on her bed for five hours, Mrs Crisp, whose testimony the judge was accepting, said plainly that it was dark when she heard the scream. Not only was it broad daylight by five, Mr Justice Grantham's preposterous flight of fancy almost allowed for the murderer to wave cheerfully to James Morris as he approached along The Street. Read in cold print, it completely discredits the judge's whole thinking on the case and exposes him as the stupidest lawyer connected with the case at any point.

He went on to say (perfectly correctly) that the jury did not have to establish a motive to find anyone guilty of murder. But he thought the evidence pointed to a relationship between Rose and Gardiner which gave him a motive to desire that the child should never be born.

He told the jury to pay no attention to the copy of the *East Anglian Daily Times* under Rose's head. That journal's readership was so wide that it could not point to any particular suspect. This was the only point in Gardiner's favour which he left unchallenged.

He noted that Rose was said to have received a medicine bottle from the Gardiner household, so that if the one in the kitchen were the same, it ceased to be evidence against Gardiner. But given that it was full of paraffin before it was broken, he did not think it could be suggested that Rose brought it there. So the murderer must have brought it. And it had come from Gardiner's house.

Mrs Gardiner's evidence must be weighed against the fact that her husband's life depended on it. If Stammers was right in saying the washhouse fire was alight at half past seven, then her evidence was not true, as she said they had not arisen till eight.

The knife was important. The handwriting was very important. Mr Larkin was an even more damaging witness than Mr Gurrin, for he, from the defence side, conceded so great a similarity between Gardiner's hand and the assignation note that he thought the writer must have been imitating Gardiner. Mr Bird's evidence was worthless, for he did not think the two hands were similar, and the judge did.

His conclusion was a clear invitation to the jury to return a verdict of guilty. The full words he probably used are completely fair and correct as reported in the *East Anglian Daily Times* (which thought his summing up balanced and perspicacious):

> If they believed the evidence of the prosecution that there were relationships between these two of an immoral character, if they found this letter making an assignation for that very night was written by him, and that she was murdered that night, there could be no suggestion of anybody else having committed that murder, however foul, however deliberate, well thought out, and however incredible it might seem that anybody like the prisoner could have done it. If, on the other hand, they thought the evidence was not conclusive, that there was a loophole anywhere, or any doubt, it would not only be their duty, but their privilege and their pleasure to say that they were not convinced, and to find him not guilty.

But the effect of his tone is brought out in the *Eastern Morning Gazette* (which noted that the summing up was biased against the prisoner):

> However incredible it might seem for Gardiner to have done the deed yet all these facts pointed to the one conclusion that he must have done it, and if the jury thought so, it would be their duty to say so. If, on the other hand, they thought the evidence was not conclusive it would be their duty to give the prisoner the benefit of the doubt.

No wonder, when the lights were lit as the evening shadows fell, it was seen that Gardiner, who had begun the day looking firm, plump and determined, now seemed to have shrunk into himself, his eyes staring desperately out of a pale and sunken face. Only a miracle, it seemed, could persuade the jury to disregard such pointed direction.

At a quarter past four the jury filed out. At half past six they returned, with the first hint that such a miracle might occur. They asked an intelligent question that the judge had not covered in his summing up: what weight should they give to the absence of blood on Gardiner's clothes and the lack of evidence that he had destroyed any clothing?

Mr Grantham said as far as they went, these facts were in the prisoner's favour, but they were not conclusive.

The jury filed out again. At twenty to nine they returned. They could not agree. The judge asked if he could help by answering any questions. One juror stood up and said there were no questions he wanted to ask. The judge correctly identified him as the one man holding out, and asked if more time might be of value to him. The juror replied that he had not made up his mind not to agree if he was convinced the prisoner was guilty, but he had not heard anything to convince him that he was guilty. There was applause in court.

The jury was dismissed. Gardiner was recommitted for trial at the next Assizes, and was helped out of the dock in a fainting condition. He had been so sure of his conviction after the summing up, that he was visibly relieved when the foreman said the jury had not reached a verdict.

The independent-minded juror was quickly identified. Superintendent Andrews recorded this in his *Work Journal*, where, since the opening of the trial he had been misrecording the month as October:

MONDAY 10 OCT
IPSWICH ASSIZE. At 8.45 PM the Jury being unable to agree upon their verdict were discharged there being 11 against Prisoner. The Juror for him was Mr Evan Edwards of Felixstowe who was and is against Capital Punishment.

This interpretation of Mr Edwards's stance was so widely reported that the juror wrote to the *East Anglian Daily Times* denying it at the end of Gardiner's second trial.

A more likely ground predisposing Mr Edwards to favour Gardiner's case was religious sympathy. He was himself an active evangelical Christian, and one who had shown himself both charismatic and courageous in opposing popular feeling. When General Booth, founder of the Salvation Army, first visited Ipswich, he suffered the very hostile reception which often greeted the opening of missions in new places. Mr Edwards immediately offered to accompany the general through the streets personally the following day if he would hold another rally. And as he had anticipated, he himself commanded such widespread respect that no more eggs and fruit were thrown, and the general was able to march and preach unhindered. Thereafter the general remained a friend, and always stayed with Mr Edwards when he visited East Anglia.

Evan Edwards was a good target to heed Wild's repeated suggestion that Gardiner was victimized as a man of religion. And Mr Edwards was an individualist who would have no difficulty in holding out against eleven opponents if he believed he was right and a man's life was at stake. His obstinacy had its reward. If any one man can be said to have saved William Gardiner from the gallows, it has to be Evan Edwards.

SEVEN

The Second Trial

The hung jury now turned public opinion strongly in Gardiner's favour. The feeling prior to the trial had been that Gardiner was guilty. When somebody in the crowd awaiting the jury's return raised three cheers for the prisoner, it was seen as remarkable, and a rival faction groaned the cheers down.

But now all was changed. Gardiner would have spent nearly eight months in gaol before he finally knew his fate. The instant identification of Mr Evan Edwards, and the knowledge that eleven other jurors had found him guilty, suggested that his next trial might be seriously prejudiced. And the *Eastern Morning Gazette*'s editor was willing to acknowledge that the victim herself was not quite the innocent maiden of waxwork melodrama.

> Rose Harsent herself had not worn the white flower of a
> blameless life. She appears to have revelled in the filthy verses
> whose author received a well-deserved castigation from the
> bench.

The inference was apparent. Gardiner need not have been the only man in Rose's sex life.

The *East Anglian Daily Times* opened a defence fund. Georgianna was living on charity, and had written to *The Times* of London asking for aid as she was 'penniless and heartbroken'. Evan Edwards was a wealthy man, and he inaugurated the fund with a generous donation of £20. Two days later another £9.5s.0d had been added by other sympathizers. Within a week this had risen to £53.17s.6d. The newspaper printed collecting sheets and kept the fund going until the end of the trial by which time £360.8s.10d had been collected: about £50,000 at today's values.

Georgianna went to stay with her sister in Ipswich. This enabled her to visit her husband in prison. Not surprisingly his health had suffered a good deal from the continued confinement and anxiety.

Meanwhile there was turmoil in the Wangford Primitive Methodist Circuit. The murder was deeply divisive. Both victim and accused were members of the congregation: Gardiner highly esteemed, and Rose the sole Methodist in a family of Anglicans. The Harsent family made no secret of their belief in Gardiner's guilt, and the scandal was hard for the Nonconformists to live with.

Sibton chapel was not united. William Tripp, a Yoxford shoemaker, had been assistant class leader under Gardiner prior to the Doctor's Chapel scandal. By the time Gardiner allowed his leadership to lapse, Tripp had moved to Halesworth and become an insurance agent. Brother Powell became Sibton class leader on Gardiner's resignation, with none other than Henry Rouse as his assistant. Tripp had been with Abraham Goddard when Mr Guy allegedly declared his belief that the scandal was trumped up. Rouse had joined the Anglicans in pointing the finger of suspicion at Gardiner.

Nor was this dissension easily quelled from above. When Mr Guy left the Circuit and the District in the normal way in July 1902, his place was taken by a rather young and inexperienced superintendent minister: the 29-year-old Reverend Joseph Roxby. He was only to last one year, and in that year, Wangford changed its previous practice, and sent a layman instead of the superintendent minister as their delegate to Norwich District Committee. That layman was Mr Abraham Goddard.

Mr Goddard was too weighty for the affront offered by Mr Guy to be passed over. Wangford Circuit protested that Mr Guy's unexpected and (in their opinion) untrue testimony had caused Mr Goddard and, to a lesser extent Mr Fidler and Mr Tripp to be brought into disrepute before the public. They demanded that disciplinary action be taken against Mr Guy, wherever he might now be.

District Committee discreetly replied that since no verdict had been reached, the case was still *sub judice*. To admonish Mr Guy in any way could be contempt of court, and nothing should be done until the hearing was over. No doubt District Committee hoped that tempers would die down given the passage of time. But this particular dispute simply went underground for the length of the second trial.

The lawyers had a couple of months to strengthen their respective cases. Mr Wild visited Peasenhall personally, escorted by Mr Leighton. They went to Providence House, where Mrs Crisp let them walk around the building, and Mr Wild familiarized himself with the peculiar layout which effectively cut Rose's attic off from the Crisps' bedroom and parlour.

Mr Leighton continued his general search for gossip to discredit hostile witnesses and managed to find out a good deal about Henry Rouse.

The prosecution, too, went looking for new witnesses. On 24 November (again, misdated October in his *Work Journal*) Superintendent Andrews went to Sibton where he and Eli Nunn met with Rouse. The police wanted to be sure that the feet-in-the-lap would have been visible to a large number of people, and hoped to interview some to support Rouse's story.

Rouse pointed one out immediately. Mr Thomas Hunt, a wheelwright and ironmonger, was the father-in-law of one of the trustees and lived in a cottage next to the chapel. Andrews hoped Hunt would help them. He did not. Andrews noted with disgust, 'Conferred with Mr Hunt whose word I found was not to be trusted re Gardiner. He being anxious to screen the Murderer at the expense of Justice.'

Somebody – possibly Rouse – also tried unsuccessfully to enlist a Miss Walker's support for the prosecution contention that Gardiner misbehaved in chapel. She was a member of the choir, and in a position to see the alleged misbehaviour during the sermon. She also happened to be the daughter of Mrs Martha Walker, a willing defence witness – indeed, she would eventually marry Gardiner's son Ernest – and the approach was duly reported back to the defence lawyers.

In the end, the only new witnesses Mr Ridley and Mr Dickens called were a professional architect to supplement Superintendent Andrews's account of the houses and neighbourhood, and two prison officers to identify documents broadening the base from which Mr Gurrin drew his conclusions. Otherwise Mr Dickens contented himself with tightening up the arguments in the case he had already presented.

This intelligent reappraisal emerged in minute details of Mr Dickens's opening speech, given before the new trial judge, Mr Justice Lawrance, and a jury on Wednesday 21 January 1903. He predicted that Stammers would say the 'fire in the copper' (actually the grate beside the copper) was lit 'unusually early'. He alleged that the death was believed to be suicide for so long that 'from Saturday [*sic*] till Tuesday morning the police had taken no steps whatever', and in consequence it was impossible for the prosecution to say whether all Gardiner's clothes had been handed over to be tested for blood and paraffin. He reverted to his earlier suggestion that the murderer took his shoes off before committing the murder, tempering it this time with the alternative that he was 'so careful in what he was doing as not to trample in the blood'.

He suggested that the motive was to get rid of the girl, and, if possible, burn her body so as to destroy the evidence of pregnancy. He appears to have recalled Mr Wild's being jocular about the tight cork in the medicine bottle, and jesting that the murderer would have had to ask Rose for a corkscrew with which to get at the paraffin to burn her. Mr Dickens now put forward a very plausible explanation for the tight cork.

> For that purpose, we suggest, he took with him the bottle filled with paraffin oil, but in putting the cork in, with a view of putting it in in such a way that it was not likely to come out, he put it in so tightly that when the murderer took the bottle from his pocket he could not move the cork.

And, perhaps most sensible of all, he simply conceded that the prosecution could not say at what time of night the murder took place.

The Ipswich architect, Mr W.H. Brown, was the prosecution's first witness. In laborious cross-examination, Mr Wild showed how thoroughly he now grasped the layout of Providence House, and we may hope that the jury was enlightened rather than bored.

When Wild came to cross-examine Bill Wright, who essentially repeated his previous testimony, he discovered what was to be the biggest difference between the first trial and the second. Sir John Compton Lawrance would tolerate no extravagant sallies eliciting laughter.

Wright – possibly directed by Mr Ridley or Mr Rickards – had checked up on the reproof for bad work Gardiner had suggested as his motive for malice. Smyths' recorded formal reprimands, and this one, administered to Wright and his immediate overseer, a man called Mayhew, had actually taken place some weeks after the Doctor's Chapel incident. Wild tried to establish some earlier unrecorded ticking-off:

Wild:	Were you found fault with in your work?
Wright:	No; not by Mr Smyth.
Wild:	Mr Gardiner?
Wright:	No, I don't think I was.
Wild:	You don't know one way or the other?
Wright:	I feel perfectly sure.
Wild:	You feel a little surer as you go on? (*Laughter.*)
Judge:	If there is anything like laughter, I will have the gallery cleared. People must remember what it is at which they are present.

Mr Wild took the hint. There were no more of his witty sallies, and he never quite came to dominate this trial as he had the first. Indeed, Wright won an exchange with him handsomely when it seemed that he inadvertently admitted to having been coached in his evidence since the magistrates' hearing:

Wild:	Did you leave out about hearing Rose Harsent say, 'Oh, oh!' and hearing the rustling noise?
Wright:	Yes, I left that out.
Wild:	Why?
Wright:	Because it did not come into my mind; there was a long time between.
Wild:	But there is a longer time between now?
Wright:	I have been over it since.
Wild:	Oh! Who have you been over it with?
Wright:	I have with you.

The public had taken its warning as well as Mr Wild. There was no laughter.

Only one new point emerged from Wright and Skinner's evidence. Skinner said positively that when Gardiner sent for the eavesdroppers after the incident, he tried at first to deny that he had been at the Doctor's Chapel at all.

Mr Guy repeated his evidence and gave a fresh example of his poorish memory. He denied that Noah Etheridge had been present at the Quarterly Meeting which heard his unminuted oral account of the Sibton Chapel inquiry. He was wrong.

The first fireworks of the new trial came during Wild's cross-examination of Henry Rouse. The old road-mender had to deny or explain away a whole host of accusations culled from local gossip. He had laid information against a lad called Turrell whom he accused of setting fire to a barn at Wrentham, and the magistrates had dismissed the case.

He had employed a horsehandler called Gooch and in some way made over a sow to him. Rouse used to go over to Gooch's cottage when Gooch was away. Gossip said he was pretending to visit his sow, but was really up to hanky-panky with Mrs Gooch. Rouse said he was going to visit Gooch who had become 'a God-fearing man', and it was sheer accident that he might occasionally have visited when Gooch was out.

Gossip said that Rouse had misbehaved with a lady whose name started with B. Rouse denied it.

Rouse had given evidence at a previous murder trial; that of Edna Carter. (She had suffocated her two-year-old child in woods near

Wrentham in 1884, and Rouse, working in fields nearby, had heard a child's cries and unsuccessfully gone to investigate.) Wild believed that on this occasion, too, Rouse had thrust himself forward suddenly at the Assize Court. Rouse insisted that he had appeared before Halesworth Magistrates.

Rouse denied that he had accused two daughters of a Brampton labourer called Snelling of immorality. He had not told Mr Curtis, the vicar of Brampton, that Snelling was effectively keeping a bawdy-house. Snelling had not charged him with this malice to his face in the presence of one of the Redgrifts. Nor, while he was steward for a farmer called Nash, had he tried to appropriate the labourers' pay increase until Snelling threatened to complain to the master.

He said that he did not have a reputation for going about laying traps to try and lure people into thieving. And he had not tried to get Miss Walker to back him up in his story about Gardiner's feet on Rose Harsent's lap.

Rouse was admitting to an awful lot of smoke in denying the fire of these various rumours. He left the witness-box to some extent discredited, and few jurors can have liked his sanctimoniousness. Mr Wild accused him of preaching and delivering sermonettes in his answers. There was certainly something very distasteful about a damaging prosecution witness in a capital case saying of the prisoner, 'I love his soul, but I do not like his ways.'

Seventeen-year-old Harry Harsent was less satisfactory to the defence than he had been previously. He now said he had taken two or three letters from Gardiner to Rose in 1901 and another one or two in 1902. He listlessly contradicted himself in cross-examination, however, and struck the *Eastern Morning Gazette* as stupid, so he probably did little harm to Gardiner.

Mrs Crisp was willing to agree with Wild that the Doctor's Chapel door had been painted since the scandal. She again laughed nervously in answering, and Wild again reproved her, saying, 'You seem to think it is a great joke.'

'I am not joking, Mr Wild,' she said.

'Would you mind not addressing me by name?' said Wild coldly. 'Just answer the questions, please.'

Mrs Crisp did not understand this court-room formality nor why she should be bullied by a man she had entertained. As she explained to the judge, 'My lord, Mr Wild and Mr Leighton came to my house yesterday three weeks.' And, turning back to Wild, 'I have given you every opportunity to come to our house, and I do not know why you should doubt my word.'

Her appeal to the court was in vain. Mr Wild was not raising unseemly mirth in His Lordship's presence; he was merely being very rude to an amiable if scatterbrained lady. There was no reason for the judge to make a lawyer behave like a gentleman, and Wild was allowed to snap at Mrs Crisp on the two other occasions when she forgot that he was supposed to be anonymous once encased in his wig and gown.

'Old Tailor' Crisp created a mild sensation when he saw his wife being tormented again about the times at which she had come downstairs. He was in one of the seats beside the bench, and he rose to his feet, saying, 'May I speak?'

'Sit down! Be quiet!' ordered Sir John Lawrance, and thereafter he prohibited anybody except magistrates from sitting on the raised seats beside the bench.

The following day there was a rather smaller public attendance at court. Mr Justice Lawrance's conduct of the proceedings made for less entertainment than Sir William Grantham's had.

The prosecution team was strengthened for the first time by the presence of the Treasury Solicitor, Mr Sims, who had travelled from London especially for the case.

Harry Burgess came and went. Mr Wild did not even bother to ask him if he had frequently seen a light in Rose's room at ten o'clock.

Mrs Dickinson came and went. James Morris came and went. The defence had picked up a rumour that he went out and looked for the footprints again at midday on the Sunday after hearing of the murder, but was unable to find them. Morris denied it.

Herbert Stammers brought out the important aspect of his testimony at the outset: the fire in the washhouse was unusually large and unusually early.

Mr Rickards made it clear that Wright's immediate superior, Mayhew, was the man really responsible for the faulty workmanship for which Wright had been reprimanded. Interestingly, Skinner had told the previous trial that Mayhew was one of the people who had been regaled with the story of Gardiner and Rose getting up to no good in the Doctor's Chapel.

When old William Harsent came to tell the distressing tale of finding his daughter's body for the fourth time, Mr Wild made a merciful stipulation. He invited Mr Dickens to save the witness time and pain by putting leading questions. This is normally forbidden in direct examination. But it meant that Mr Dickens could, for example, ask 'Had her throat been cut?' instead of forcing Mr Harsent to say it himself.

Eli Nunn's appearance led to another exchange which showed Sir John Lawrance's determination to tolerate no gibing from Mr Wild, and no expressions of approval from the public, even if they were reacting to the judge's own words. Wild took Nunn over the experiment with Wright and Skinner at the Doctor's Chapel, and asked sarcastically:

Wild:	They succeeded in making you hear?
Nunn:	Certainly they did; so could anybody else.
Wild:	Please answer me properly; don't answer in that way.
Judge:	I do not think you ought to complain of him, Mr Wild. You draw an answer of that kind. You ask him did he succeed, and it is a matter of observation afterwards. I am sure you will allow me to say this. It will make any witness turn round.
Wild:	I did not mean to do anything of the kind, my lord.
Judge:	I am quite sure you did not, but you put it offensively to him, and then blow him up if he makes an observation. It is not fair to any witness. (*Applause from the public gallery.*) Silence!

Mr Justice Lawrance further proved his capability when Nunn's notebook with the disputed entry about Mrs Gardiner and the camphorated oil bottle was handed up to him. Sir John declared that the erased original entry was, 'I gave my sister a bottle of camphorated oil'. This didn't really help anybody, as it was not in question that Mrs Gardiner had both said so and done so.

Superintendent Staunton's evidence produced the most startling new material of the second trial. It was introduced by Mr Wild in cross-examination. Had Mr Staunton, he asked, made inquiries at the Triple Plea public house, about eight miles from Peasenhall, where a traveller (Mr Wild called him a tramp, but the Superintendent demurred) called for breakfast on 1 June 1902, saying he had walked from Peasenhall? The Superintendent had made inquiries, found that the man was in Halesworth for the rest of the day, but failed to trace him.

And had the Superintendent seen an anonymous confession sent to the *East Anglian Daily Times*?

Mr Dickens objected at once, but Mr Wild declared that he proposed to submit the letter and ask the handwriting experts if it was not similar to the assignation note.

It was one of three anonymous confessions that had been found. The other two were a notebook leaf picked up in a Devon lane, and a letter posted from London to Eli Nunn. Both of the other two were believed to be irrelevant hoaxes (see *Appendix A*). But the judge insisted that if one was to be read all three must be.

The letter obtained from the *East Anglian Daily Times* was read out first. Three short indecent phrases were omitted in the press, but the court was informed of the remarkable mis-spelling and punctuation of the document. It ran as follows:

From My darling Rose Ann Harsent['s] deveoted true lover[.] but she has deceived me God only [k]no[ws] both with Gardiner and Davis[.] God only knows as davis was the farther off her child as my own darling rose told me the night before i comitted this horrowble murder[.] but i hope she is at rest[,] bless her[!] but i feel i cannot rest night nor day as she is haunting me every night & every min[u]te[.] but God is the farther of them both now[.] and i shall sertinly swing for that – [dash in original] davice [Davis] for deceiving me as i [k]no[w] she was not so [i.e. pregnant] by me[.] and now i must confess as G[ardiner] is not the murder[er] of my darling rose as i am[.] but i am not a superer [superior? supervisor?] nor a counter jumper but i am a mal[t]ster chap and have a mother to keep[.] but sir i must comfess as i am to[o] sharp for you all[.] you ar[e] all deleribliy [deliberately?] liers about G[ardiner] we[a]ring barred glossours [galoshes.] they was my malting shoes with barres across and i must comfess that i filled both shoes full of stones as they was all blood[,] and tied a brick and but [put] them in the water so as no traces could you get on them[.] and i must confess that i had them on and went from Peasenhall in my old malted shoes [from/to?] Crisp['s] house so as you would think G[ardiner] had done it but he is as incionint as Mr Justice Grantham[.] i am laughing in my sleves to think you can not fined me[.] there is t[w]o of us who was there and B was watching while I did it[.] my darling Rrose Gave me 5£ for a last token[.] i am sorrow for for [sc. her?] poor Dad now[.] as for old woman Crisp she is nothing but a nasty – lier and that is swe[a]ring to say that she came down staires at 12 o'clock[.] She did not as i was in the house at that time[.] and i did write the letter to my pet lamb to tell her to put the light in the window for me as it was not the first time i had been there at that time[.] as i can go so far as to say i have had my darling in my arms all night [words omitted]

and was on the sofer the night i did the murder[.] but i can
swe[a]r as rose told me she had been unfaithful to me with
D[avis] and if a man can stand that[,] tell me[,] all through
[although?] we was on the rug to Gether befor i killed her[.]
and as for the medesin bottle rose Gave me some whiskey in it
the night before and I took the parafin in it from my own home
at Suffock[.] And you must fined out the rest as i have been had
[at?] malting to day and i cannot send you my name but shall
committe sueside before long[.] when we come back we shall
Put old Crisp and his old woman through the mill worse than
my rose[.] and as for her [Mrs Crisp] saying she heard a noise
she did not as i filled her [Rose's] mouth full off my mufflur as i
did [it] in a cool blood[,] not hot[,] as i know she would be
deceiving me this [malting] season while i was away like last[.]
but it was Harsent that said my only love had been unfaithful to
me by going with Gardiner[.] and now i must confess that no
one will act immorall with her again as [words omitted] before i
killed her[.] and G[ardine]r must thank God they [he and
Davis?] was not served the same fate[,] but they will do [be.]
even my trou[s]e[r]s and shirt was drowned [thrown in the
water] with brick end inside them[.] but [i] shall not say
w[h]ere[.] find out[.] i have to take lodnum [laudanum] to inset
[induce? for the onset of?] sleep as i cannot rest without my
own darling pet[.] had i not have took all my letters out of
rose['s] box i should be w[h]ere G[ardiner] is and had the rope
now[.] but go on[,] let G[ardiner] have it[,] or else D[avis.] he is
the corse of this[.] he is been the ruin of my young life[.] and
now i must conclude by saying it will be a good job done with.
from H B the murder[er] of my own darling lover[.] i could not
think of her having [words omitted] by that – Davis[.] i shall put
a bullet straight through them as i shall be coming back in six
months[.] now i am a murderer

False confessions are common in sensational crime cases, and this
missive bears all the external marks of being written by someone who
had read details of the first trial and become unpleasantly obsessed with
a fantasy of seducing and killing Rose Harsent.

But Mr Wild had noted that it seemed curiously well informed for
someone whose writing suggested such poor literacy that he could
hardly have struggled through the tiny print of contemporary newspaper
reports. He thought he detected indications that the illiteracy was faked,

and believed that there were similarities to the handwriting of the assignation note. He had, in fact, decided to make this letter the linchpin of his preferred strategy of suggesting an alternative murderer. It was less risky than pillorying Davis, since there was no visible suspect to impress the jury with his apparent innocence, or hold in reserve a strong alibi.

Certainly Mr Wild was right in suggesting that the letter showed a closer knowledge of Peasenhall than could have been acquired from the press. It was postmarked Burton upon Trent, 1 December. Since 1879 there had been a seasonal movement of young Suffolk migrant workers to Burton where they lived in bachelor accommodation and found employment in Bass the brewers' malting sheds. They earned good wages, and spent them freely on beer and smart suits to impress the lads and lasses back home at the end of the season. The Suffolk maltsters were, on the whole, lively, hard-working, cocky and confident Jack-the-lads.

From start to finish, Peasenhall contributed a regular component to this migrant labour force. And there can be no doubt that the false confession was written by somebody who either was a Peasenhall maltster or associated with them. He certainly knew the odd thing that had not appeared in the papers: notably, that Rose's eldest brother William was a seasonal maltster. He used the epithet 'old Crisp' which was reminiscent of the village boys' name 'Old Tailor Crisp'.

The police had discovered that only one maltster from the Peasenhall district could be described even loosely as having 'a mother to keep'. This was illegitimate Albert Goodchild of Badingham (the parish adjacent to Peasenhall on the west). He supported his maternal grandmother Rachel who had brought him up as if she were his mother. Moreover, Goodchild had come home to Peasenhall on the weekend of the murder and he had travelled from Burton with young William Harsent.

But Goodchild could not have been the murderer, in Staunton's opinion, as he had been in Burton or on the train at the times during which the assignation note was put in the post at Peasenhall on Friday night or Saturday morning. And the confession letter claimed that the murderer had seen Rose the night before she was killed ('as my own darling rose told me the night before i comitted this horrowble murder'). Goodchild had not arrived at Badingham until 7.00 p.m. on Saturday.

Moreover, Staunton had established that Goodchild's malting shoes were flat-soled and not barred. He was a scrupulously honest witness, always conceding points that seemed to tell against his position, so it must have been genuine error on his part when he misled the court with the suggestion that malting shoes were always flat-soled.

In fact, some of them were quite strikingly barred. They were special shoes worn on the malting floor to minimise bruising the grain and protect the maltsters' feet from heat. Some, like Goodchild's, had flat soles, often made of canvas (though Goodchild's were said to be leather). Others had heavy clog-like soles on which pegs or bars lifted most of the foot almost an inch off the ground.

Staunton had also secured an example of Goodchild's handwriting and satisfied himself that it was not like that of the letter.

The defence had pounced on the letter as soon as it reached the *East Anglian Daily Times*. When Staunton heard of their investigations from Mr Leighton, and tried to obtain the original on 10 January, Wild had already advised Leighton to send it on to the Treasury.

Wild played the same rather dubious game he had played with Davis in the first trial. He questioned Staunton in such a way as to cast suspicion on Goodchild, while subsequently claiming that he believed him to be innocent of the murder in fact.

Wild: Have you ascertained that that man was in Peasenhall on the night of the murder?
Staunton: I have not ascertained that.
Wild: I suggest to you that that is the case?
Staunton: I do not know.
Wild: And that he got home to Badingham on Sunday morning?
Staunton: He went to Wickham Market that night.
Wild: Haven't you heard that he went out again after he got home between 11 and 12 o'clock and did not return until 7 or 8 o'clock on Sunday morning?
Staunton: No.

Sir John Lawrance was noticeably quick to defend policemen from hectoring, in contrast to his failure to help Mrs Crisp. Now he became irritable when Wild insinuated that Staunton had been remiss in not calling Goodchild before the court or producing his malting shoes in evidence:

He could not pursue everything. . . . You are speaking as if he was wanting in his duty. He would be wanting in his duty if he followed up these suggestions in this anonymous letter.

Undeterred, Wild went on to ask about the sofa mentioned in the letter. Was there one in the kitchen or Rose's attic? Or the Crisps' part of the house?

'You don't suggest that the girl would go into Mrs Crisp's room?' interjected an exasperated Mr Dickens, bringing this line of questioning to a halt. Yet Mr Dickens's rhetorical question was misplaced. By Mrs Crisp's own account, Rose had been into her room and purloined the Scotch shawl from the chest in the parlour where it had been on the Saturday morning before the murder.

The other two anonymous confessions were read out to the court. Then followed the medical evidence. Dr Richardson, Dr Lay and Dr Stevenson repeated the evidence they had given at the first trial.

Dr Richardson was recalled to the witness-box when one of the jurors asked whether Rose had been standing up when she was killed. Richardson was certain she had been lying down when her throat was cut, and the murderer had been on the right side of the body. The blood from Rose's jugular vein was all to her left. The implication was that it would not spurt over him as he crouched at the right-hand side of the body and drew his knife across the throat toward him. But the upward stab might well have been inflicted while she was standing. Dr Richardson stated that the more serious wound must have caused more violent spurting, but it is hard to see how the blood that had spurted twenty-four inches beyond Rose's feet could have come from any wound inflicted after she was lying down. Richardson stated that the upward wound was forceful enough to have knocked her backwards to the ground.

Dr Richardson was further interrogated by the judge on something his lordship had noticed in the confession letter. Since the *News of the World* (the only paper known to report this exchange) did so very obliquely, it evidently referred to something all the others considered 'unfit to print'. Dr Richardson said he had suspicions which, if verified, would have confirmed the statement in the letter, 'but he was unable to say definitely that anything of the kind had taken place'.

Now, two of the omitted passages in the confession letter are clearly stating that the murderer enjoyed sexual intercourse with Rose shortly before he killed her. ('i have had my darling in my arms all night . . . and was on the sofer the night i did the murder,' and 'no one will act immorall with her again as . . . before i killed her'). This suggestion was strikingly supported in 1952 when Alderman F. Jenkins of Southwold, who, as a young man, had been employed by the police to photograph the murder scene, told crime historian Dorothy Erskine Muir that evidence in the kitchen left no doubt that Rose had enjoyed sexual intercourse there with a man that night.

Richardson's evidence, then, was that he did indeed see something that led him to suspect that intercourse had taken place shortly before death,

Mr Ernest Wild

Mr Justice Lawrance

Mr Justice Grantham

Ipswich Shirehall exterior in 1905

Spy cartoon of Henry Fielding Dickens five years before the trials

Mr Evan Edwards, 'The juror who disagreed'

Mr Arthur Leighton

Scenes from the trial, and witnesses: Mrs Gardiner; William Harsent; Henry Rouse; Revd John Guy; Fred Davis (centre) photographed in later life; James Morris, photographed earlier in his life and PC Eli Nunn: note Rose's actual lamp shade and candlestick in the drawing of Nunn

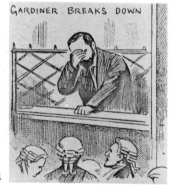

6

MR HENRY ROUSE

7

THE REV. JOHN GUY

8

10

WHG
IPSWICH
'02-1-05

9

The Gardiner family, left to right:
Ida; Annie (or Dora); Georgianna;
Ettie; Bertie; William; Dora (or
Annie); Ernest

Gardiner's letter to the *Star*,
written with a broad-nibbed
pen. Note the difference from
the assignation letter

A photo believed to be of Gardiner (front, centre) with
Mr Leighton (extreme right) and possibly Evan
Edwards (at Gardiner's right) at the time of his
discharge from custody

Southall Green as known to the Gardiner family in the 1920s

but either he decided against testing for it, or he saw the body too late to take swabs to establish definite semen traces.

Davis followed the doctors into the witness-box, and was again roundly abused by Mr Wild. He said little that was new. With striking honesty he did not cling to his previous claim that he had given Rose the contraceptive leaflet in September: he only insisted that he would swear it was not later than December. He described an aspect of the leaflet which casts a very odd light on Victorian marital problems: 'There were some useful recipes in it. . . . It told how to cure chilblained feet and sweaty feet.' And he revealed that Rose knew about the leaflet before he gave it to her: 'She knew another fellow had it.' Wild still insisted that Davis was obviously the father of Rose's unborn child. Davis still insisted that he was not.

But Wild allowed himself one dubious little exchange with Mr Dickens. He was still, apparently, willing that the jury should believe Davis to be the murderer if they chose, provided he was not actually accusing him outright:

Dickens: I presume my friend, Mr Wild, takes the same line as before, and does not suggest Davis had any part in the murder.

Wild: I know nothing about it.

Dickens: You said in terms that you did not impute it to him in the slightest degree!

Wild: I should not be so wicked as to make any such suggestion.

Moses Dummer, a former warder at Ipswich Gaol, identified the letter Gardiner had written to Georgianna, and then Mr Gurrin reappeared to take the second jury through his photographic chart of words and characters. Mr Wild tried to object that this was the wrong way of going about comparisons: the original documents should be used. Mr Dickens said wearily that it would take six times as long, and pointed out that the originals could always be consulted in any case of doubt.

Again Mr Gurrin expressed the view that the assignation note was perhaps not in a diguised hand, but certainly very carefully written: while its envelope was somewhat disguised. He did not describe the features that led him to think it was disguised. He suggested that the broader nib and better ink used in the assignation note explained the major differences between its calligraphy and that of Gardiner's Paris letters. The great difference between the two hands was the upright formation of letters in the assignation note, compared with Gardiner's copy-book slope, and the evenness and regular spacing of words in the assignation note, which suggested greater habituation to writing.

The anonymous confession letter from Burton upon Trent struck him as very illiterate and quite unlike Gardiner's acknowledged hand or the assignation note. He would not accept Mr Wild's suggestion that the spelling 'davice' by a man who elsewhere wrote 'Davis' correctly was a mark of deliberate disguise. Sir John Lawrance refused to let Mr Wild pursue the question of spelling mistakes (which occur in all Gardiner's letters that can be checked today, but not in the assignation note). Taken over all, the strongest point of similarity Mr Gurrin seemed to establish was that both Gardiner and the writer of the assignation note tended to capitalize words beginning with P in the middle of sentences.

This should have ended the prosecution case, and the court adjourned for the night.

When it reconvened the following morning, public interest was seen to have revived, probably in anticipation of Gardiner's evidence.

Before Mr Wild opened his case, Mr Dickens was given permission to introduce another prison warder, John Shepard, who identified a letter Gardiner had written to his solicitor from prison. This seemed closer to the linear regularity and even spacing of the assignation note.

Mr Wild's opening speech was less dramatic than that in the first trial, and less inclined to play on the pathos of Gardiner's situation. Yet that made it all the more effective: probably the most effective of all his four speeches in Gardiner's defence.

He allowed himself to dwell on Gardiner's long ordeal in prison. He touched on his own feeling of responsibility and strain. But he promised to try to present the story 'logically, without any attempt at rhetoric'. He enjoyed a few bursts of his old sarcasm, particularly directing them against Rouse. Putting one's legs on a girl's lap was: 'a curious way of making love. I don't know that one ever heard of it before. It is at all events a novelty that has been reserved to Mr Rouse to invent.'

What was Rouse preaching on? The Ninth Commandment? Gardiner had 'the comforting reflection that Henry Rouse loves his soul, if that can do him any good!' Even the prosecution, at one point, was accused of promulgating a hypocritical theory, 'worthy of Rouse'!

One of Mr Wild's sallies was regrettably misplaced. In commenting on Mr Dickens's admittedly extraordinary suggestion that the murderer took off his shoes in anticipation of the blood-covered floor, Wild observed: 'That is mere theory – the histrionic ability my friend possesses from heredity and personality. It is the sort of thing that would do in a novel, but not in a murder case.'

It was really very bad manners to impute to Dickens a forensic style tainted by imaginative heightening inherited from his famous father. Henry Fielding Dickens, though he was proud of his father, was fully entitled to expect that colleagues would judge his work at the bar on its own merits, as it was entirely his own. His presentation of the case had been consistently reasonable and unromantic, and not in the least (Charles) Dickensian.

Mr Wild had no new witnesses as to the facts and no new hard evidence to offer. He really had his old case from the last trial to go over, and, like Mr Dickens, tighten.

He did this well. He brought out strongly, on this occasion, the dilemma Mrs Dickinson's evidence created for the prosecution, and suggested that Mrs Crisp's varying recollection of the times at which she came downstairs and heard the scream bore a sinister relation to the original police presumption that the murder took place soon after midnight, and their subsequent realization that Gardiner could not have committed it before half past one.

He brought out the potential importance of the scrap of blue cloth, and pointed out what damning evidence it would have been if it had come from Gardiner's clothing: there would be no question, if that were the case, of Mr Dickens airily dismissing it as too small to be of any consequence!

He made a full and justifiable point of the absence of blood on Gardiner's clothes and shoes. His junior tugged his sleeve to remind him that Gardiner's rubber-soled shoes had canvas uppers which would inevitably have retained blood in the fibres, no matter how carefully they were washed.

He made an excellent point about the fire that Stammers saw, which produced instant nods of agreement from the jury and stayed usefully in their minds:

> What did he burn? Did he burn the india-rubber shoes, the clothes he wore on Saturday, his boots, his underclothing? He burned nothing, and if he did, what a smell it would have made, as you jurymen evidently know. Nothing was suggested to Gardiner about burning anything at the last trial, and if he had burned anything the nose of Mr Stammers would smell what the eyes couldn't see. There would have been evidence of it, too. When the police looked they would have found remnants of burning.

(Mr Wild had been cautious, however, when Stammers gave evidence. He had not asked him whether he smelt anything like burning clothes. He dared not run the risk that Stammers, like Morris, might produce an unexpected and unwanted answer and stick to it!)

With regard to the medicine bottle, Mr Wild was misled (as Mr Dickens may himself have been) by the police suggestion that they did not suspect murder for one or two days. So he overlooked the fact that they originally thought the label must have read 'Mrs Culham'. He never knew that Andrews and Nunn had suspected Gardiner from the day the body was found. He assumed that the bottle was their key clue, and he was scathing:

> But for [the bottle] Gardiner would never have been accused in this case. But the police in Peasenhall had got the bottle, and they said to themselves: 'Gardiner did this murder, and he has left his card. Out of consideration for us, in order not to tax our brains too heavily, Gardiner has considerately brought a labelled bottle with his name on it – and, of course, he did the murder.' If this were not a murder case, it would make us laugh.

For all his sarcasm, Wild knew that this was such a damning piece of circumstantial evidence against his client that he must go further and suggest some alternative way in which it could have got there. He put forward a theory, admitting it was only a theory, that Rose, a slightly slovenly servant, kept the medicine bottle in the kitchen with paraffin in it for starting the fire and topping up the lamp.

> In all probability the bottle was on that shelf which was broken, because you remember the shelf was standing above the side of the door and the bottle fell down, and the pieces were found just on the left of the girl's head. It would be exactly where they would be found if they fell off the shelf. The very fact of this paraffin falling in the scuffle that must have ensued made the [murderer] suddenly think: 'I will try to burn the body.' So he at once went to get the paraffin out of the lamp, and in his hurry neglected to hide the bottle.

Mr Wild's logic shook a little. No murderer except Gardiner had any need to hide the bottle. And Gardiner would not know he needed to if he had not brought it with him and it was simply a broken bottle with an illegible label that had fallen off the shelf. But the suggestion fitted the layout of the kitchen perfectly, though the bottle would have had to stand well to the edge of the shelf. For the broken bracket was one of the thick segments of wood commonly used in rows to support shelving in Suffolk. It was in the middle of a row, and its damage did not cause the shelf itself to fall out of alignment. On the other hand, the bracket must have received a very powerful blow in order to break it, which would have jarred the shelf.

Mr Wild's wholly new argument related to the confession letter. It became rather contorted, as he tried to insist that it was not incumbent on him to produce a suspect, nor did he want to cast false suspicion on anyone. So he put himself into a very awkward posture. First he fitted Goodchild into the frame of suspicion:

> It is remarkable that there was a man answering the description
> of that letter, who came home that night, a man who had
> walking shoes, who came home in the company of young
> Harsent, and who lives at Badingham, and keeps his mother.

Then he tried to take him and Gardiner out again together:

> It is possible that the man who wrote that letter committed that
> murder. Let us assume that for the moment, and that he knows
> Gardiner is unjustly accused. It is conceivable that he is now
> trying to throw the blame on an innocent man, Goodchild, to
> ease his own conscience and to prevent Gardiner from being
> hanged, because he knows Gardiner can prove his innocence.

Mr Wild's ingenuity had got the better of his sense of logic again. If Gardiner could prove his own innocence there was no earthly reason for any guilty murderer to try and embroil yet another person in suspicion. What is more, Wild was still clinging to the preposterous suggestion that the murderer carefully put on shoes with barred soles and walked deliberately from Alma Cottage to Providence House and back, all in the hope that someone like Morris would come along and accuse Gardiner of sinister nocturnal perambulation! Henry Fielding Dickens might justifiably have protested that even in his most strained and melodramatic moments, his father would never have dreamed of such an improbable plot!

Mr Wild anticipated having a second means of discrediting Morris. He hoped Leighton and Aldous were going to produce a witness who would swear to Morris's unsuccessful search for the footprints at midday. They failed to do so.

Nor was Davis absolutely exonerated by these new suggestions. Mr Wild still thought, 'it is obvious that the real paternity of the child rests at the door of Davis'. He had a perfectly fair and permissible parallel to establish between Gardiner and Davis, starting from the hypothesis that Davis might, although innocent, have found himself on trial. It strains belief, however, that Mr Wild genuinely expected his words to convey Davis's unblemished innocence to the jury:

> I want you just to consider; supposing Davis were in the dock, what a case a man who is, as far as we know, innocent of this murder, would have had against him. I make no suggestion, and have not made any throughout the case, except the one that he is the father of this child. But I ask you to consider this. Supposing a case were attempted to be made against Davis, what a case my friend, with his imagination, with his ability, could make of it. . . . There is the motive; the man who gives the girl a medical work, the girl who is *enceinte*. Whom does she go to for a book? That is as far as it could be taken in my judgement. Assuming Davis were there instead of Gardiner, what a case with these letters and means of access! What could be said on the other side? All he could say was this; he could call his father to prove an alibi, just as I can call Mrs Gardiner to prove an alibi, and I ask you to extend the same consideration to Mrs Gardiner as you would to him if he were unjustly accused.

In his peroration Mr Wild cautiously introduced religion, and then rose to the declamatory climax of asserting that 'William Gardiner, unjustly accused of the murder of Rose Harsent, has had a greater power than his own to rely upon, or he would not be alive today.' He came very close to the serious forensic impropriety of declaring his own belief in his client's innocence. Wild normally tried to stay within the limits of propriety; 'submitting' that Gardiner was innocent; asserting that this or that question of his guilt was 'for the jury to decide'. But there is no doubt that what made his speech so impressive was the ringing, powerful personal conviction of Gardiner's innocence which informed it from beginning to end. No one could question that Mr Wild believed his own statements and was committed, heart and soul, to the case he was making. This stood out in the court-room of quieter, more conventional lawyers, aware that innocent men might have to forgo trained counsel if juries ever came to expect that they must be persuaded that advocates personally believe the cases they submit. Still, many laymen may feel that Gardiner was fully entitled to have the jury perceive how deeply his counsel believed in his innocence, regardless of the fact that not all prisoners at the bar can enjoy the same advantage.

After this resounding speech, which lasted two and a half hours, the defence witnesses had nothing strikingly new to offer. Mr Wild left the court-room for a moment to rest. Claughton Scott, his junior, tried to examine a Dr Elliston who was expected to testify that the wounds in Rose's throat must have spurted blood over the murderer, and that the body had been moved after death, so that the murderer would have been bloodstained again. Mr Dickens promptly quashed this testimony as improper. Dr Elliston had not personally seen the body, so he was not a witness to the medical facts.

Mr Wild returned to take Georgianna through her testimony. She really had nothing new of substance to add, except that Mrs Pepper's kettle, as well as the Gardiners', had been boiled on the washhouse fire on 1 June.

What made her appearance memorable was her physical condition. She was close to collapse from start to finish, and Gardiner was reduced to tears on seeing how ill she looked. She had to use Mr Wild's ever-present smelling salts to get through the examination on Nunn's visits to Alma Cottage. She fainted as the court rose for lunch shortly before two o'clock and was taken out in hysterics. Her moans could be heard from the public areas of the Shire Hall throughout the break. Mr Wild suggested that she was in no state to face cross-examination, and was given permission to call his next witness after the break. Gergianna remained hysterical for the next four hours.

Sir John Lawrance had noted Wild's device of calling Gardiner last of the material witnesses in the first trial, and did not allow it to happen again. He pointed out that Mrs Gardiner might testify before her husband (because, as a *femme couverte*, her statements could not be used against Gardiner), but the prisoner must precede all the other witnesses. Mr Dickens observed that he had spotted the irregularity, but deliberately refrained from protesting.

Gardiner was in the witness-box for a long time. He was thinner, paler and more strained than he had been previously. But he still gave his evidence firmly and confidently. It added nothing new to what had gone before.

Mrs Pepper, too, repeated her earlier performance, even to the length of asserting again that she had recognized Mrs Gardiner's footsteps on the stairs, and again being shaken by Mr Dickens's production of her signed statement made to Staunton.

Mrs Walker again testified that Rose had received camphorated oil from Mrs Gardiner which cured her cold. She also added that her daughter Eve, who sang in the Sibton choir, had never seen Gardiner behave improperly in chapel, where almost the entire congregation would have seen it if he had put his legs on Rose's lap.

Accountant James Fairbank and chief bank clerk Herbert Bayliss did not believe that the same hand wrote the Paris letters and the assignation note. James Hart repeated his description of his walk up Heveningham Road in hob-nailed boots. Mr Leighton again described his experiments at the Doctor's Chapel, and remarked that the door had been repainted since he first went there. He now revealed that when he first visited the chapel he had noticed that the edge of the door was planed down.

Abraham Goddard, William Tripp, Noah Etheridge, Samuel Goddard and George Fidler all came to overturn Mr Guy's claim that he had never reported Gardiner's innocence to Quarterly Meeting, nor privately called the scandal 'trumped up' and 'fabricated.' Mr Etheridge stated (as did Abraham Goddard) that Gardiner would have been suspended had the case against him been upheld.

After this sequence of witnesses, Mr Wild was ready to rest his case, waiting only for Mrs Gardiner to recover sufficiently for her cross-examination. A sharp little exchange before the court adjourned for the night showed that Mr Justice Lawrance was displeased with the reckless blackening of Goodchild's name. The Badingham maltster had been fetched from Burton upon Trent and kept waiting around the court all day, and Mr Dickens asked that he should, in all fairness, be invited to give evidence if he was wanted. The judge revealed that he had ordered the police to fetch him to give him the opportunity to answer any inculpatory suggestions made about him. Mr Wild rapidly said that he hoped that he had not said anything out of place. The judge made no more direct response than a grim, 'If you do, he will be called; if you don't say anything, he will not be called. His name was mentioned, and it is very unfortunate.'

Wild hastened to fix the blame for naming Goodchild on Staunton (though it was an indiscretion he had happily exploited at the time) and again expressed the hope that he had said nothing improper. The judge's silence was eloquent.

The last day of the trial saw Noah Etheridge telling the court that Mrs Gardiner was still in no state to face cross-examination. Mr Justice Lawrance and Mr Wild agreed that she should appear in any case, with a doctor in attendance if necessary, and when she arrived, Mr Dickens questioned her very gently. The cross-examination passed off without incident.

Mr Wild's last speech on behalf of Gardiner was, once again, less effective than his opening. He returned to his emotional mode, and his client spent a good deal of the time sobbing in the dock. He permitted himself a feeble attempt at his old gibing jokes, saying that Superintendent Staunton was interested in a capital P for Policy because no doubt he had a very large insurance policy. Through sheer ignorance, he said a couple of things that were undoubtedly false: that it was virtually impossible for a husband to leave his sleeping wife's bed without her hearing; and that only a stranger to the village would have addressed the envelope of the assignation note to 'Peasenhall, Saxmundham'. (In fact this is and was the correct postal form as every villager would have known.) He said one thing that was almost certainly true: if the jury convicted Gardiner they were also convicting Georgianna, since he could not have committed the murder without her knowledge. And he invited the jury to put the assignation note next to the samples of Gardiner's handwriting, and ask themselves whether they looked at all similar. He had always shown an encouraging tendency to think that the jurors could reach a sensible conclusion on this question from their own observation, without needing to rely too heavily on the experts' detailed comparisons.

But perhaps the passages that best exhibited Wild's dramatic flair were his account of the Wangford Primitive Methodists, and his account of Gardiner's little daughter asleep in her father's arms. He compared Mr Fidler, Mr Tripp, Mr Etheridge and the two Goddards favourably with Henry Rouse, and visibly astonished those worthies, who sat in a row behind him, by describing them as: 'these fathers of their Primitive Church; these men imbued with the principles of Christianity; these men who we know are fair examples probably of their Huguenot ancestors who settled in East Anglia, and in their rough and ready way serve their God.'

His account of Gardiner waking up to find his little daughter in his arms was a tear-jerker:

> Gentlemen, pretty well the last thing the poor man did before
> he was locked up for eight months was to be in bed with his

little infant; and the child worked its way, nestled up to its father – that father whom you are asked to say is a murderer – and the wife noticed the arm around the little girl.

For the third time in the course of the speech, Gardiner was convulsed with sobbing.

Mr Dickens's closing speech was, predictably, a far cooler affair. He repeated, almost word for word, the very effective catalogue of circumstantial evidence that pointed so precisely to Gardiner. He pointed out that there was not a breath of evidence to support Wild's statement that Gardiner was unpopular in Peasenhall, and asked what motive, then, the range of hostile witnesses – Wright, Skinner, Rouse, Burgess, Morris, Stammers, even Mr Guy – could have for swearing a man's life away. He omitted his little mime, possibly deterred by Mr Wild's impertinent reference to his father. But he pointed out that the blood from the throat had spurted to the left, and would not have stained a murderer standing on Rose's right.

He made only one blatantly obvious error, and that was in trying to explain why the anonymous confession must be false. He offered three completely unacceptable reasons for claiming that it could not have been written by the murderer. It mentioned a sofa, and there was none in the kitchen. But it was only Mr Dickens's own interruption which had ruled out the possibility that the letter referred to a sofa in the dining-room or the hall or the parlour: only Mr Dickens's personal and erroneous belief that Rose, who purloined the shawl, would not dare go into the Crisps' part of the house without permission.

The letter also claimed that the writer had worn his maltster's shoes, but, Mr Dickens wrongly averred, these would have been flat-soled and not barred. Here he cannot be blamed for being wrong: he had been innocently misled by Staunton and by the fact that Goodchild's malting shoes were flat-soled.

Finally, the writer said that his shoes were awash with blood, yet, Mr Dickens claimed, if one thing was certain about the murder it was that the murderer had got no blood on his shoes. Mr Dickens was now seriously begging a question. His case against Gardiner was in considerable difficulty if it were supposed that the murderer had got blood on his shoes. But it was the defence's contention that he must have done, because there was so much blood in the kitchen. It was only Mr Dickens's personal theory that he could not have done, because he did not trail it out of the conservatory and over the path. And Mr Dickens could not be cross-examined, or he might have been asked why anybody should have noticed this presumed blood trail if, as they claimed, the police believed for two days that they were dealing with a case of suicide.

Mr Justice Lawrance was in some ways surprisingly similar to Mr Justice Grantham. He was another Tory traditionalist, whose political prejudices were felt to vitiate his judgment occasionally. Both men had provoked some surprise in the legal profession by their elevation to the bench. Lawrance was noted for his courtesy: it will already have been apparent that he was extremely polite, even when putting Mr Wild down strongly. His obituary in *The Times*, however, commented unfavourably on his intellectual capacity to see his way through difficult cases or disentangle complicated parliamentary legal drafting.

His summing up was not nearly such a piece of biased condemnation as Grantham's had been. Its tenor was undoubtedly against Gardiner, but not in such a way as to make one wonder where the defence case had gone. It contained no ridiculous speculations; no attempt to find a way of showing that Gardiner did it which the prosecution had missed. And in general it seems a better and more balanced judicial appraisal of the case.

But it contained an amazing number of sheer errors, compounded by a quite extraordinary insistence that they must not be challenged.

His first blatant error came when he remarked, 'It is said there had been scandal about this girl and him, and that there had been reports before the scandal on May 1st.'

Dickens and Wild, both leaped to their feet in protest, Wild saying, 'My lord, I don't think there were any reports before the chapel incident.'

'I have looked at my notes,' responded Sir John severely, 'and am very careful about it; I can prove to you both about that, if necessary, that there had been.'

It was true that Lawrance had taken voluminous notes and studied them carefully during breaks in the proceedings. But he was absolutely and categorically wrong in this instance.

Next he showed that he had not understood the evidence of the Methodists.

> These gentlemen come here to contradict Mr Guy, and to contradict each other, I am bound to say, in an important matter, for some said Mr Guy said he would rather believe two in the church than two out – and that does not show a very judicial spirit – whilst two said he said it was a fabrication of lies.

Here again the judge was wrong. Both Goddards and Noah Etheridge had been at Quarterly Meeting. All three reported that Mr Guy said the scandal was a trumped up fabrication. The Goddards also confirmed that Guy had made the 'two witnesses inside the Connexion, two out' remark to the meeting, though Samuel Goddard had to be reminded of it. Noah Etheridge did not remember it, but thought it might very well have been said. William Tripp had not been at the meeting and had never heard the 'two in, two out' argument. He had been with Mr Goddard subsequently when Mr Guy mentioned in conversation that the affair was 'pure fabrication'. Fidler had been at the Sibton inquiry, but not Quarterly Meeting. He had heard the words 'trumped up' used by Guy a week after the inquiry. He also clearly distinguished between the 'two in, two out' argument, which he had heard at a later date, and the inquiry at which, he said, Mr Guy was perfectly satisfied of Gardiner's innocence.

Taken all together, the Methodist laymen did not contradict one another in the slightest: they told a unanimous story of Mr Guy's being completely convinced of Gardiner's innocence at the inquiry; acknowledging that there were two hostile witnesses from outside at Quarterly Meeting, though he discounted them; and subsequently starting to hedge without giving his laity any hint that he was shifting from the certainty he had put before them.

But the judge showed distinct anti-Methodist bias in some sarcasm worthy of Mr Wild:

> I do not like to make observations, but I think the accused must
> have been extremely unfortunate in the church to which he
> belongs. There is Mr Guy, the superintendent of the circuit, not
> to be believed, and Rouse, who led an infamous life, according
> to the questions put in cross-examination.

Next, the judge revealed himself less attentive than the jury to what had passed. According to him, 'Mr Guy averred that he spoke to the accused about it afterwards, and the accused promised him that there should be no more scandal between him and Rose Harsent.'

'Would it not be Rouse?' asked a juryman.

'No,' said the judge, 'Mr Guy.' And he read out the relevant portion of evidence:

Guy: He promised he would be careful in relation to
        young people in general, and he promised to keep
        clear of Rose Harsent. . . .

Wild:	. . . are you sure he said those words of keeping clear of Rose Harsent?
Guy:	Of course he did, I am not imagining them.

But Mr Wild had spotted the danger of these answers at the time, and had cross-examined to make it clear that Gardiner's promise had not entailed any concession of justified scandal:

Wild:	He never for a moment admitted he was guilty of the conduct imputed to him?
Guy:	Oh, no.
Wild:	He always denied that he had been in the chapel at all?
Guy:	He did.
Wild:	With regard to going home with her, he admitted walking with her?
Guy:	Yes.
Wild:	There is nothing very wrong in that?
Guy:	No.
Wild:	That was the amount of indiscretion he admitted?
Guy:	Yes.

Naturally, Mr Wild was pleased that one juror at least had seen how well he brought out the difference between Guy's testimony that Gardiner promised to avoid future trivial indiscretion, and Rouse's evidence that he subsequently promised to stop his scandalous conduct. He asked the judge to read the cross-examination, and received a pained reproof:

> Please don't, Mr Wild; my troubles are quite enough. I hope I
> have the whole thing in my grasp. I was very careful when
> counsel were speaking not to interrupt them. I have a certain
> course to pursue, not the easiest task to impose upon anybody.
> I was going to read the rest of the evidence.

If he did actually read out Wild's questions and Guy's answers, he must have revealed that the juror's query was well founded.

Next the judge protested that he could not imagine why James Hart the poultryman had been called. It is hard to blame him. Mr Wild was always better with emotion and wit than with pure reason. Hart's evidence became a jumble of sloppy roads and where he'd walked and what he hadn't himself seen. His own failure to notice the footprints outside Providence House was no proof that they did not exist.

But the fact that Morris had walked for half a mile in a narrow lane beside Hart's footprints before he finally noticed them did strongly suggest that Morris's insistence that the Providence House footprints started from Alma Cottage might be unreliable. There was no reason to doubt that Morris saw a double track of footprints as he said, and no reason to doubt that the turning point, which he had inspected carefully, was the gate of Providence House. Looking back down The Street from the gate, he would not have been able to see precisely how far they ran. By his own admission, he had not made a close inspection of the Alma Cottage end of the trail. It was therefore legitimate to question whether his impression that the trail began from Alma Cottage was not wrong, just as any impression he might have offered as to where Hart's footprints started might well have been wrong. Hart was a logical witness, except that Mr Wild did not bring the point out clearly. Whether he was a legally admissible witness is quite another matter.

One juror had a good question for the judge when he invited them to ask for any clarification. Had there been a smell of burning cloth at the fire Stammers saw? Correctly, Mr Justice Lawrance said there was no evidence on the point, and they must argue it among themselves. Another juror noted that Stammers had not been asked, and the judge gave an exemplary direction:

> The question might not have been put by accident or intentionally. Your duty is to deal with the evidence, and you can only deal with what they have put before you. If there is something not put that you think ought to have been, then you can draw your own inference from it.

This direction is particularly good, because it does not spell out any possibilities, and so cannot bias the jury. But did they understand it? Did they realize that if they thought Wild had deliberately refrained from asking Stammers about the cloth, it meant the defence feared there was such a smell, in which case Gardiner's crucial claim to possess no blood- or paraffin-stained cloth went up, literally, in smoke. Conversely, if Mr Dickens deliberately withheld the question on redirect examination, it meant that the prosecution seriously doubted whether there would have been any smell of burning clothes, in which case there was a strong presumption of Gardiner's innocence since all his clothes were untainted by blood.

The judge nearly ended his summing up with an outstanding error. 'I think I have gone through the whole facts of the case,' he remarked, complacently. 'I do not remember one I have missed.' Mr Dickens hastily reminded him of the scrap of blue cloth. Sir John made a perfunctory observation about it: 'There is a very tiny piece of cloth of some kind. I do not know whether it is woollen cloth or not. Take it and examine it. It is said to come from some clothing, but no clothing to which it corresponds has been discovered.'

This seems to mark a turning-point in the summation. Hitherto, Mr Justice Lawrance had allowed telling points for the defence to emerge and stand, even if rather brusquely, but from now on, he offered no comfort to the prisoner. The points to be made about the cloth were that the prosecution offered it as factually present at the murder scene, and it was impossible to link it to any clothes they had found. The defence said this exonerated Gardiner, as it must have come from the murderer's clothing. The judge let it pass.

He did bring out the great arithmetical mystery of the shirts, asking how a man with only two shirts could have had a clean one for Sunday morning when he was already supposedly wearing one and with one in the wash.

He also made a question-begging statement of Gardiner's guilty association with Rose over a long period of time in what seems very like a clear invitation to the jury to find him guilty:

> Whether he is the father of the child or not does not so much
> matter. It appears to me that the matter of importance is
> whether he was having immoral relations with the girl. . . .
> [H]ere is a man who knew this girl was six months *enceinte*, and
> had had immoral relations with her for a considerable time, and
> who, whether he was the father or not, was pretty sure to have
> the credit of being the father. You have been rightly told . . .
> that if you have a reasonable doubt, the accused is entitled to
> the benefit of it. But the doubt in a case of this kind must be
> fair and reasonable, and not a trivial doubt, such as the
> speculative ingenuity of counsel might suggest.

It was a surprisingly hostile coda. It suggests to us that Mr Wild's tactics had offended the judge: that it seemed to him that the defence promiscuously mingled extravagant emotional appeals, contradictory arguments, far-fetched hypotheses, dubiously admissible testimony, innuendoes against Goodchild and Davis, and furious personal attacks on the integrity of prosecution witnesses. He must have felt that the impropriety of such tactics might have made an excessive impact on the jury. It seems likely that Mr Justice Lawrance thought he was necessarily redressing a balance which had been improperly tilted against the prosecution as he sent the jury away to consider their verdict.

Two and a quarter hours later they returned. They, too, were unable to agree. This sensational case, already drawing national attention, would have to be heard for a third time at the next Assizes at Bury St Edmunds.

EIGHT

The Aftermath

G ardiner left the dock in a daze. He had been sure that the trial was moving in his favour since Mr Wild's opening speech. Now he had another six months in prison looming up – another six months before he would know his fate. Everything seemed unreal as he steadied himself against the walls of the stairs leading down to the cells.

Georgianna went into hysterics and spent the next day completely prostrate in her lodgings.

The crowd awaiting the result outside the court-room was stunned. For the rest of the night, the Peasenhall murder was the only topic of conversation around Ipswich.

The next day, the whole country was given the news and was equally stunned. The first trial had been sufficiently fully covered by the national press that the GPO in London had sent congratulations to the Ipswich postmaster on his efficient handling of the journalists' telegrams. The second had promised so much more excitement that the GPO prudently sent down a team of specialist Morse telegraph operators who usually concentrated on rushing out the racing results. Between them they handled an average of sixty thousand words a day for the week of the trial, and nobody in England could have glanced at a newspaper without noticing something about it.

The press unanimously condemned the injustice of leaving Gardiner to languish in gaol for a further six months. They proposed three alternatives. His case could be transferred to London Sessions, where it could be heard again at the Old Bailey on 9 February. This would have the further advantage, some thought, of obviating local prejudice against him. Others thought that feeling in Suffolk and the rest of the country was pretty similar, and mostly in favour of Gardiner after his long ordeal. The Suffolk local papers were not happy about this proposal as it would increase the already high costs of the prosecution, and the expense would still be charged to the county.

An alternative suggestion was that Gardiner could be brought up in court again immediately, for the Crown to announce that it would bring no evidence against him, and a jury could be directed to deliver a verdict of Not Guilty. The final suggestion was that Gardiner should be released on bail for six months to enjoy the directed verdict of Not Guilty at Bury St Edmunds in June.

Most commentators at the time thought that Gardiner would be the first Briton ever to face three consecutive trials for the same murder, but they were wrong. In 1873, a bank sub-inspector named Montgomery was convicted of the murder of a teller named Glasse in Ulster, after two previous juries had disagreed. He confessed after his conviction and was hanged.

The lawyers were busy. Leighton consulted with Wild. Dickens consulted with the Treasury Solicitors. The judge summoned both counsel for consultation. Nobody knew what the outcome of these deliberations might be.

In fact, Mr Wild was making his second attempt to take a minor role in future proceedings. After the first trial, he had felt acutely that his own inexperience had failed an innocent man, and he approached the eminent KC Charles Gill, asking him to lead for Gardiner in the second trial with Wild as his junior. Gill studied the brief and returned it, saying that Wild was better informed than anybody else about the complex case, and should continue. Now Wild was making renewed efforts to persuade Gill or Sir Edward Clarke to lead in future proceedings. It was a touchingly modest reaction to an achievement that was hailed on all sides as a forensic triumph.

The *East Anglian Daily Times* reopened its appeal fund for Gardiner. Mr Evan Edwards once again contributed the first £20. By the end of the week it had accumulated £67.5s.1d.

The *Sun* – a London paper run by Horatio Bottomley and completely unconnected with the journal of that name today – inaugurated a petition for Gardiner's release which gathered six thousand signatures in two days. They also opened a 'Shilling Fund' for Gardiner's family. When Gardiner wrote from prison thanking them, they proudly printed facsimiles of his letters on their front pages.

It is unlikely, however, that much of their fund ever reached the Gardiners. Bottomley was notorious for pocketing the proceeds of his journals' appeals and competitions!

On Tuesday 27 January, Georgianna began to plan her return from Ipswich to Peasenhall. She had sent the children to Alma Cottage where her mother was looking after them. Earlier in the proceedings, when the family's resources were at a low ebb, Gardiner and Cady relatives had taken over caring for them. Ettie, the eldest, had gone to William's sister and brother-in-law, Mr and Mrs George Batten in Ealing. Ida went to cousins of Georgianna's in Lowestoft; Ernest to her sister in Battersea. The twins stayed with Mrs Cady in Walberswick, while Georgianna kept little Bertie with her. His health gave rise to continuing anxiety.

But now she felt she could not do without all her children around her. She made one attempt on Wednesday to visit her husband in gaol, but her cab was mobbed as she tried to leave her lodgings, and she retreated indoors and took to her bed in hysterics. On Thursday she went back to the village, supported by her brother-in-law, Mr George Batten. Although, as she said, it wasn't easy, and people 'looked hard' at her in Peasenhall, for her and the children, it was still home.

So she didn't see Thursday's special slip edition of the *Sun*, predicting that Gardiner would be released under a *nolle prosequi* in the very near future.

Sure enough, on Friday the *Sun* was crowing. Exactly as it had promised, official denials notwithstanding, Gardiner had been released at half past eight the previous evening.

Gardiner's only comment when he was told he was to be freed was, 'I always knew I should be acquitted'. And that seems to be what he assumed had happened, although the *nolle prosequi* – a decision to proceed no further – implied no opinion whatsoever on his actual guilt or innocence.

Mr Leighton and his assistant Horace Bullen met him at the prison door with a cab. The streets were empty and nobody noticed Gardiner, who was wearing a grey lounge suit but had not troubled to put on a collar and tie. In the privacy of the obscure house where his solicitor took him he had his beard shaved off, leaving a heavy moustache: a style he would retain in later years.

He was very grateful to those who had supported him. The *East Anglian Daily Times*, which had done so much for him and his family, was allowed to send a reporter, and Gardiner gave his first exclusive interview.

'I don't know how to thank the paper for what it has done,' he began, in a slightly tremulous voice. 'Had it not been for the fund you started, my defence at the second trial could not have been conducted with such vigour as it was by Mr Wild. I am heartily thankful to you and all the papers that have taken up my case.'

He expressed equal gratitude to the prison governor and warders, who had behaved kindly to him, and heartfelt, lifelong gratitude to

Mr Leighton. His one regret was that Georgianna would not hear the good news till seven o' clock the next morning: the earliest telegram delivery time was no quicker than the mail.

The reporter asked him tentatively about Rose Harsent.

'Well,' said Gardiner, 'she was really more of a friend of my wife's than mine. She used to do little odd sewing jobs for my wife, and was so occupied at my cottage on the night of the murder. I didn't see her that night, though, as she was gone when I returned home. . . . My relations with the girl were only as a friend at a chapel.'

The press was about to boost the legend of 'Gardiner, the man of iron nerve'; the defendant whose terrible ordeal in two trials made no mark on him. It has already been seen that this seriously misrepresents a sensitive and perhaps mildly hysterical personality: frequently tearful; occasionally fainting; and only the more impressive in his inner strength which braced him for cross-examination. But Gardiner encouraged the misrepresentation by expressing no surprise when hailed for his courage, complacently agreeing, 'Yes, my strength has served me well.'

The key moments of the two trials, for him, were Mr Justice Grantham's summing up in the first, and Mr Wild's speech for the defence in the second. The speech was, 'a masterpiece, and much better than the one he made at the first trial'. The summation was full of 'the most audacious statements, some of which were not entirely accurate'.

He offered no explanation for the hostility to him in Peasenhall, but recognized that it meant he would not be able to live there in future. He did not intend to go abroad, however. England was his home, and he would look for carpentering work in some other part of the country.

After the interview, the reporter heard the conference that followed between Gardiner and Leighton. A couple of lecture organizers and a theatre manager had tried to contract Gardiner for immediate appearances. The theatre manager was willing to pay him £20 a week for the next six months – a fortune for a man in Gardiner's position – merely to walk on the stage every night. Decisions about these offers were deferred, though Leighton's fear that they might be indiscreet probably only reinforced Gardiner's natural inclination for privacy and dignity.

It was decided that Gardiner should travel to London overnight, and take obscure lodgings out of reach of the throng of reporters.

Georgianna was in bed the following morning when a letter or card arrived at seven o'clock. The Post Office at Yoxford knew the contents and the glad tidings were told to George Batten before the message was read. The children were thrilled, laughing and crying. Little Bertie thought it meant his father was on the way home already, and rushed into the road to look out for him. Then they all remembered their mother, and charged up the tiny staircase, yelling, 'Dada's coming home! Dada's coming home!'

Georgianna was too overcome to leave her room for a couple of hours. By the end of the morning, however, she had recovered, and after giving a brief interview to the *Eastern Morning Gazette* and making her farewells to friends who had been especially kind – Mrs Hart, Mrs Dickinson and Mrs Pepper – she went to Darsham with Mr Batten and caught the train to Ipswich. Mr Leighton met her there, and took her to his office, where she gave another interview to the *East Anglian Daily Times*. She was as grateful as her husband for their efforts, and less certain than he that it would be necessary to leave the village.

'Georgie' (as her husband called her) wanted everyone to know of his uncomplaining thoughtfulness in adversity. When her sudden poverty meant that relatives pooled resources to help her, they also started sending food to him in prison. This was agreeable to the regulations for remand prisoners, and still more agreeable to him, as the unremitting diet of small brown loaves, suet pudding and fatty cocoa was not especially digestible. But the regulations also said that once outsiders were sending in food, the prison should supply nothing else but cold water and Gardiner dearly loved his cup of tea. But he resolutely refused to let his family know that he was deprived of it, feeling that he had occasioned enough trouble and expense as it was.

Telegrams and messages of congratulation poured into Leighton's office all day. Mr Evan Edwards was one of the first to step over and express his delight at the outcome. The general feeling across the nation was one of pleasure at the end of Gardiner's tribulations.

Except in Peasenhall. Reporters found that the news was greeted there in sullen silence. Murmurs of 'Gardiner had better not come back to Peasenhall!' could be heard. Workers at the drill works were particularly angry that their former outside manager had not been hanged.

The local gentry were not very pleased by the adverse publicity, either. Mr Smyth was appalled that the whole nation knew Gardiner's weekly wage had been a mere twenty-six shilllings. This was scandalously low for such a skilled craftsman, and like other employers, Mr Smyth didn't like the world to hear how little he paid his hands. He urged the *East Anglian Daily Times* to print the fact that the men received 'premiums' on work completed, so that Gardiner's usual take-home pay had been thirty-six shillings.

He was also uncomfortable when asked whether or not he would take Gardiner back. Here one can sympathize with him. However unjust it might be to dismiss a man who had not been found guilty of any crime, he would have had serious problems on the shopfloor if he tried to impose a high-minded sense of justice on Gardiner's fellow-workers. Mr Smyth temporized. He couldn't really say. He had held the position open for Gardiner for three months after his arrest, but then really had to replace him, so the old post was not available.

Strangely enough, the man who replaced William Gardiner was another William Gardiner. Stranger still, when the Gardiner family finally left the village, the new William Gardiner took over Alma Cottage. Today, the second William Gardiner's daughter-in-law still lives there, and so the little dwelling that was nationally known in 1902 is still 'Mrs Gardiner's cottage in Peasenhall'.

Mr Cooke, the vicar, also had a reputation to defend. He was responsible for the morals of a village which was now widely believed to enjoy shocking sexual freedom. Mr Cooke had made his own investigations, and reported that it was not true. The only traces of 'corruption' in Peasenhall were confined to 'a little knot' of three or four 'lads' centring on Davis. The rest of his flock, he believed, led unblemished lives.

This was utter rubbish. The village had a high bastardy rate, like most rural areas. Rose was pregnant. She and Davis both knew of a third person who would lend information on contraception to the unmarried. Mr Ludbrook's malarkey with several women was common gossip. Mrs Crisp's wedding night was the subject of local hilarity. Harry Burgess's daughter 'went wrong', and presented him with two illegitimate grandchildren to bring up. Mrs Newberry's two daughters came to sad ends. One committed suicide; the other died of 'drink and meths'. 'Doris,' said the village severely, 'was oversexed'. By the Victorian standards proposed at the trial and respected by Mr Cooke, Peasenhall was happily immoral.

On a higher ethical plane, the vicar was concerned to clear his neighbours of the charge of a lack of charity. He denied that Georgianna had ever been destitute; insisted that villagers had always helped her; and instanced the local butcher who, he said, had sent a free joint of meat to the family every week when their plight became known.

This doesn't quite jibe with Georgianna's own view that many people in Peasenhall who sympathized with her dared not say so. There were tiny indications that some of Mr Cooke's Anglican congregation in particular were foremost in fuelling anti-Gardiner indignation. It may or may not be significant that Mrs Gardiner's friend Mrs Dickinson, who ran the hardware stores and supplied oil to St Michael's church as her husband had done for years before her, stopped doing so very shortly after the trials.

Back in Mr Leighton's office, Mrs Gardiner and Mr Batten debated the possibility of taking a slow train to Bethnal Green, in case reporters were waiting for the fast trains. In the end they decided to risk it and travel to Liverpool Street.

While they did so, Gardiner was giving another interview, this time to the *Daily Express*. It described him as so muscular that he looked more like the 'village blacksmith' than the 'village carpenter'. It is, perhaps, worth stressing that this giant wodwose, though fit and stocky, was of average height.

The reporter was interested that he only mentioned religion once; that it was in reply to a direct question; and that his manner in responding was entirely free from unction or cant.

Gardiner was by now in high good spirits. A merciful amnesia blotted out the lack of appetite and sleepless nights that had dogged his days of trial. Now he scouted the idea that it had been a terrible ordeal, and laughed frankly as he admitted that some of Mr Dickens's loaded questions had perplexed him.

He was still angry about Grantham's 'damnable summing up' at the first trial, and had been told that up to that point, nine out of twelve jurors were for acquitting him. Since he had been in touch with the *East Anglian Daily Times*, which was in touch with Mr Evan Edwards, this information may be absolutely correct.

The *Star*, too, was accorded an interview. There was little new for Gardiner to say, but he showed a keen appreciation of the central point indicating his innocence: 'On the evidence of [Mrs Crisp and Mrs Dickinson] nobody could have convicted me.' He explained Peasenhall's hostility to him, partly with sound sense, and partly with an unsupported version of the legend that he was seen as a 'Holy Willy':

> The explanation is that a very bad murder was committed there, that nobody knew who it was, and when the police said they had got the man, most of the villagers accepted the situation. There would have been just the same feeling against any other man the police charged with the murder.
>
> But you must remember, also, that a foreman can never be very popular if he does his duty. . . .

> I was never a man to go to the public house or in that class of society where a man becomes popular, but those who know me – the thinking part of the people – believed in me and do so still.
>
> I had worked my way up from the bottom of the ladder, and there were several men there who had been there years before me, and when I was made foreman that caused jealousy.
>
> Then I went to Paris for the firm, and that made things worse.

He also assured the paper that with the exception of Mr Guy and Mr Rouse, the entire Wangford Primitive Methodist Circuit was behind him. He could offer no explanation for Rouse and Guy's hostility.

Nor could the rest of the circuit. Quarterly Meeting made a renewed appeal to District Committee to discipline Mr Guy for 'making statements . . . which were directly contrary to what he had said both publicly & privately thereby causing much discomfort to a large number of the officials of this Station'. District Committee advised them that Mr Guy had moved to another station and it would be a long and laborious task, falling into someone else's hands, to decide on a reprimand. They informed 'the Wangford Circuit Authorities that, in our opinion, the wisest course is for them to take no further action in the matter.'

The circuit contented itself with suspending Henry Rouse from all his offices for three months. The reason was sound: not that he had contradicted the opinion of weighty members of the Connexion, but that he had written an anonymous letter. This was and is something completely at variance with the integrity expected of Methodists.

The row rumbled on in Sibton, where Mr Roxby was quite unable to restore order. William Tripp tried to resign all his offices; the brethren refused to accept his resignation, and tried to reason with him. Harmony was not restored until Mr Roxby was replaced by an older and extremely successful circuit superintendent, the Revd Joshua Biggs of Buckingham. He healed the breaches in the community, increased the numbers in the flock, and was resoundingly invited to serve for a fourth year in Wangford after he had completed the normal three.

The Revd Mr Cooke had one devoted Anglican parishioner who gave the lie to his suggestion of neighbourliness. On 4 February, Mr Green, the Yoxford postmaster, and Frederick Mann, a detective-clerk sent down from the GPO, set a trap for someone who appeared to be tampering with Georgianna's mail. They marked two letters addressed to her, and counted the number of items addressed to Alma Cottage given to Brewer for delivery and re-sorting in Peasenhall. Brewer gave sub-postmaster Hurren and his 33-year-old spinster daughter, Christianna, a bundle of letters that included seven for Georgianna and one for Ettie. When he came back to pick up his village deliveries, there was only the one for Ettie.

Green and Mann went to Peasenhall Post Office with Police Inspector Fowler and found Miss Hurren behind the counter. They asked her about the missing letters, and she replied, 'I know nothing about it.' Mann said they had definitely been posted, and the office would have to be searched. At that Miss Hurren produced seven letters for Georgianna from the next room. They had all been opened, but their contents had not been removed.

Fowler then told her that complaints suggested another thirty-nine letters were missing, and cautioned her. She went upstairs with him and produced thirty-eight of them. Thirty-six contained postal orders to a total value of £9.18s.0d. Since she had made no attempt to cash the orders, Mann asked her why she had held them back.

'I had a mind to look into them,' said Miss Hurren. 'I have had a lot of trouble over Gardiner, Sundays and all. He does not deserve the money. He ought to be hung. The Post Office don't pay us too much money.'

While Inspector Berry's wife was searching her at Yoxford, she repeated, 'This is all through the Gardiners I'm here. I've been working all morning and late at night and on Sundays and the Post Office does not give me any extra money. That's why I've taken Mrs Gardiner's letters and postal orders, and you would have done the same.'

She was evidently a very disturbed woman. She had used young Herbert Denny to deliver the Gardiners' letters when she didn't want Brewer to see the marks of her tampering. Her father lost his sub-postmastership because of her malefaction, and used his bricklaying skills to remove the letter-box to the wall of Emmett's Store at the other end of the village. In view of the fact that she didn't actually steal any money, the Post Office was anxious to prosecute Christianna no more rigorously than necessary.

The magistrates had to send her on to the Assizes. Interfering with the mails was and is a very serious offence. She had hysterics in court, and pleaded guilty to detaining letters. She was given a deferred sentence – effectively equivalent to a conditional discharge. Everyone agreed that her motive was not dishonesty, but irrational malice. Mr Cooke appeared as a character witness on her behalf, testifying that she was a devout and regular Anglican communicant.

The final accounts of the *East Anglian Daily Times* fund showed that £460.9s.8d had been collected. Of this only £10 had been given to

Georgianna, but £400 had gone to Leighton and Aldous for their costs. And Gardiner received the last £50.9s.8d in March 1903. Clearly, charitable villagers, independent donors sending postal orders, and family support had played the major part in maintaining Gardiner's wife and children during his incarceration.

But around the village, rumours grew that he would have been hanged as he ought to have been, 'if only . . .'. If only Alfonso Skinner had told *all* he knew, instead of deliberately keeping back evidence that would have hanged Gardiner. If only the village band had told the strange story of their return from a recital at Leiston on 31 May. As they drove back to Peasenhall, they heard the familiar sprightly clip-clop of Smyths' black mare approaching them from behind. When it came into view, Gardiner was driving. As soon as he saw the villagers he slowed down, pulled back, and drove home via Rendham, hoping he hadn't been seen. Now why did he do that? Because, as Mrs Driver knew, and told the bandsmen, he had been to Leiston to arrange with a woman in Valley Road for Rose to have her baby there in secret. If only Mrs Driver had come forward at the trial. . . .

The steady drip of innuendo affected some of Gardiner's erstwhile supporters. Mr Fidler is said to have come to believe in his guilt. Others stayed firm for his innocence, however. Mrs Pepper's grandson, Mr Harold Mills told us, 'My mother was a Pepper, and she would never hear anyone say Gardiner was guilty.'

All this had little effect on the Gardiners. Herbert Denny saw them pay one more visit to Peasenhall, in a closed taxicab. Gardiner stayed in it, while his wife went in for tea with Mrs Newberry. And the Gardiner family disappeared off into welcome obscurity in South London.

The Peasenhall murder briefly resurfaced in the press in August 1904 when a Suffolk soldier serving a prison sentence for desertion in Dover made a false confession to the governor. He claimed to have been walking through the village at night, and to have selected Providence House as suitable for burglary. So he went round to the back, where he saw a man – apparently Gardiner – talking to a maid with a candle in her hand at the door. He waited till the man left with the words, 'Then God help you,' before breaking into the back kitchen through the window. The maid came back, and he killed her with a kitchen knife and made good his escape to Ipswich.

The Gardiners' first response on hearing of the confession was to thank God, and say they had been sure the truth would come out, but it quickly became apparent that this was not the truth. William Taylor, the soldier, knew about the case from what he had read in the newspapers.

He did not know the internal or external layout of Providence House, nor did he know what Rose had been wearing when she was killed. His story broke down very quickly when Staunton interviewed him.

The people involved in the case moved away or passed away. Football-playing eavesdropper Bill Wright died first. He collapsed in the road in 1904, and died of dropsy and kidney trouble. Henry Rouse died the following year. Rheumatic arthritis carried him off, restored to good terms with his chapel. Young Harry Harsent, Gardiner and Rose's go-between, died of phthisis (inflammation of the lungs) in 1906. His father died four years later. After Bertie Gardiner's chronic 'trouble with his head', he too died young. Polio carried him off aged fifteen in 1912. The family believed the prime cause was a serious accident at a children's party, damaging his foot, which had to be amputated.

Alfonso Skinner survived until 1960, when he died near Basingstoke. He married in 1903, and soon gave up working at Smyths'. He became a gamekeeper, as his father had been before him, and moved from place to place, earning a reputation for throwing up jobs if ever he felt put upon. Alf Skinner (we know of no evidence that he was ever nicknamed 'Fonso' as one writer claims) quoted the Bible a lot, 'always to his own advantage', in his family's cynical view. He never talked about the case. His son was grown up when he heard a description of it on the radio, and learned for the first time of his family connection with a notorious mystery.

Fred Davis, the young man held up to public notoriety, went to the Home Counties and stayed in the retail trade where he enjoyed remarkable success. He worked for many years in a furniture store near Luton and married in 1910. In 1921 he moved to Tunbridge Wells to manage the furniture department of Waymarks' Department Store. He was a director of the company and a churchwarden by the time he retired in the 1950s. Despite his traumatic experience at Ipswich, he frequently revisited Peasenhall in the days of his prosperity, and was much loved by those who had worked with him or succeeded him at Emmett's Store. Miss Gertie Rose remembers the pleasure with which they all looked forward to his visits and the promise they held of drives and picnics in his motorcar. He died in 1965, and his employees at Waymarks', who remembered a somewhat fussy and punctilious organizer with a kindly outgoing personality and a cheerful sense of humour would, one hopes, have been outraged by his treatment at Mr Wild's hands as a young man.

Ernest Wild went from strength to strength. He entered Parliament, but never held one of the great law offices of state because he committed himself to the Lloyd George Coalitionists, a group that hoped to perpetuate non-partisan government after the end of the First World War. They were relegated to the political margin after Lloyd George fell in 1922, and Wild was dead before Winston Churchill became Prime Minister and elevated some of his early associates.

Again in 1922, Wild and Dickens clashed. Dickens had been Common Serjeant of the City of London since 1910: the second judicial figure in the City Courts and chief assistant to the recorder. In 1922 the recordership fell vacant. It was a prestigious position, and a large group of distinguished lawyers presented themselves as candidates. It was one of the few judicial posts that was not in the gift of the Lord Chancellor. The recorder was elected by the aldermen of the City of London.

Mr Dickens had long hoped to succeed to the recordership. This led his most prominent challenger, Edward Marshall Hall, to withdraw his candidacy at considerable sacrifice, as Marshall Hall was unpopular with the Lord Chancellor's office, and the City bench offered his only chance of gaining judicial prominence.

Ernest Wild became the leading contender against Henry Dickens. Wild's victory in the close-fought election was controversial, as it was said that he had persuaded two of Dickens's committed supporters to absent themselves from the final vote. There were letters in *The Times*, and many lawyers argued that this post should not be left in the gift of laymen.

Dickens himself believed that Wild had intrigued against him. Sir Henry's memoirs showed that the wound was still open at the end of his life. The old man dismissed the Peasenhall trial in three sentences. And in a book which described almost all the notable lawyers he knew, there was no mention of Sir Ernest Wild, despite the fact that the two men worked together as Recorder and Common Serjeant for years after Wild's election.

In the years of his prosperity, Wild remained a personal friend of the Gardiner family. He had urged them to emigrate to Canada for a new life, but visited them regularly when they refused. His chauffeured Rolls Royce made quite an impression on Hartington Road, the suburban street in Southall where they lived, and the children knew him as Uncle Ernest.

Mr Guy died at his home near Reading in 1924. His obituary remarked that 'He was quiet in disposition, and his ministry was marked by spirituality rather than energy.'

The policemen in the case all came to good ends. George Andrews retired in 1903 and received a gold watch from Jasper Mayne. He lived until 1931, the same year that Eli Nunn died.

George Staunton was highly commended for his active investigation of the case, receiving an engraved silver matchbox as a testimonial from the coroner. Possibly inspired by this, he made a premature and unsuccessful application for appointment as Chief Constable of Norfolk in 1909. Thereafter he resigned himself to holding increasingly senior positions with the Suffolk Constabulary, rising to become its chief constable thirty years later, and managing a force whose professional priorities had greatly improved since the days when Jasper Mayne's delight was to hire the band of the Scots Guards to play at the Police Sports Day.

Brewer the postman was awarded the Imperial Service Medal for meritorious conduct on his retirement in 1924, and his behaviour in 1902 and 1903 suggests that he richly deserved it.

After their warm and tearful reunion in London, Willie and Georgie Gardiner went to stay with the Battens while they looked around for employment and accommodation. They took the corner-shop at 63 Hartington Road, Southall Green, Norwood, a confectioners, tobacconists and general stores. They uncompromisingly painted the name 'Gardiner' over the door and lived there for the rest of their lives. Very occasionally William served behind the counter in his carpenter's white apron.

Two more children were born to the couple in Hartington Road. They lived through the transition of Southall village from an offshoot of Norwood into a borough in its own right. William's carpentering skills made a substantial contribution to the town's growth as he worked for A. & B. Hanson, Builders and Undertakers.

His pride in his workmanship, his good neighbourliness and his appearance remained. He always wore a collar and tie, even when in his working apron. He always wore smart and perfectly cleaned shoes.

He did not keep up his membership of the Methodist Connexion. He seems to have felt it would be embarrassing to the church. Instead, he took his children for walks and serious conversation on Sunday mornings. And he loved to have family and neighbours in for weekly hymn-singing around the harmonium in the parlour.

That harmonium itself supplied his intimates with their most marked memory of his fine workmanship. It was ornately decorated with Victorian Gothic turrets and arches, and Gardiner designed and constructed a mantelpiece which exactly matched it to the larger scale.

Neighbours remembered Georgianna as being the dominant partner in the marriage. She was strong and possessive; he was comparatively shy and retiring. Their description was far removed from Peasenhall's man of iron nerve with the massive muscular frame and the great black beard. It also seems to accord better with his conduct at the trial, always allowing for the inner resources that really did bear him up through the ordeal.

The couple made no secret of the past, but they did not stress it. Some of their children and grandchildren knew nothing about the murder and the trials until they were grown up. Some grandchildren probably know nothing of it to this day. The immediate family were counselled to say nothing about their affairs to others, lest their friends fall under the shadow of the murder. In the late 1930s Willie and Georgie destroyed all their family letters and photographs so that they might never fall into the hands of the press. We have been specifically asked not to name people, including the world-famous, whose association and friendship with Gardiner had no direct connection with the trial.

Georgianna established a reputation in the neighbourhood as a friend and counsellor to young women; something that may cast light on Rose Harsent's 'friendship' with her, and the frequently-alleged visit Rose paid to Alma Cottage on the evening before she was murdered. The family saw her counselling as harmless gossip, but remembered that she would never hear a word said against Rose, always insisting that it was 'the man's' fault.

Despite the immense shock the Doctor's Chapel scandal occasioned Georgie, neither she nor her husband seems to have fallen into the puritanical error of thinking his sexual lapse with Rose was a serious sin. Georgie always maintained that even at that traumatic time, she knew she came first with Willie as she had done every minute of her life since she was seventeen years old. William believed his own great sin in Peasenhall was pride.

A neighbour remembered him as 'the greatest gentleman he knew'. The act that particularly impressed him was Gardiner's constant and willing mathematical assistance when he found book-keeping difficult and the tax calculations impossible to understand.

The Gardiner family was recognized by all who knew them as warm and close. They enjoyed family parties to which cousins and nephews and nieces came. William adored and protected his children; perhaps especially his daughters. He would carry them long distances when they were tired; wrap them in his coat and walk in shirt-sleeves to protect them from the weather. He gave up an afternoon to making two of his his grandsons a perfect spliced-handled willow cricket bat. Mr Wild's highly emotive picture of his little daughter nestling in his arm after the thunderstorm really does describe the man whom Wild himself came to love.

But his life was overshadowed by the murder. Never a day went by without his feeling that people remembered it and looked askance at him. Still, he accepted this as just punishment for his pride. 'God hates pride more than any other sin', he told his daughters. 'There was once a very proud man, and God humbled him.'

In 1941 William Gardiner died. With his hospital bed screened as the end approached, he astonished the entire ward by suddenly bursting into a firm rendering of 'Jesu, lover of my soul.' He sang it like a fit young man of thirty. Then, saying twice, 'It is over,' he passed with relief from the mortal punishment for pride he believed God had inflicted on him to the divine eternity of forgiveness which he had never doubted would be his.

Georgianna survived him for seven years, living alone in a room above the shop which was carried on by their daughter. There are no Gardiner descendants in Southall now.

NINE

Gardiner: The Conclusions

I n our view the juries' indecision in both trials was the correct
historical verdict on the evidence and arguments put before them.
Legally, perhaps, they should have given Gardiner the benefit of the
doubt. The circumstances were highly suspicious. But the evidence that
Mrs Crisp heard the murder during the storm left Gardiner with an
uncontradicted alibi. Any proposed alternative later hour of murder left
Rose implausibly sitting up awaiting her lover for an hour and a half.

Mr Wild, on the other hand, did fail to clear away the rest of the
prosecution case. The two largest pieces of circumstantial evidence were
substantially unchallenged. There was no proof that the medicine bottle
really was the one Georgianna had given to Rose; only supposition.
There was only Mr Wild's ingenious theorizing to explain its presence
on the floor beside her. Nobody asked Mrs Crisp, for example, whether
any bottles normally stood on the shelf above the kitchen door. If
anything else pointed to Gardiner's presence in the kitchen that night,
then he was surely the likeliest source for the medicine bottle.

And the footprints did point strongly toward his presence. They
didn't go away simply because Mr Wild said that the road was too sloppy
for Morris to see them. He also suggested its surface was too hard to
take footprints – a suggestion we have found to be absolutely false. How
could Gardiner be innocent – etymologically 'unknowing' – if footprints
ran from his door to Providence House and back?

There were other points Mr Wild had failed to bring round to his
client's favour. Where was his third shirt? How could he possess only
two, given Georgianna's testimony? Why should so many people come
forward with evidence that told against Gardiner?

The blood in the clasp-knife might be inconclusive, but it pointed in
Gardiner's direction. Why had somebody taken the trouble to scrape out the
inside of the clasp? Who could this have been, since Gardiner denied it?

Finally, Wild had completely failed to shake the suggested motive. Wright and Skinner had never seriously contradicted themselves, and the only reason for disbelieving them would be because a belief in Gardiner's innocence of the murder blotted out the rest of the testimony against him.

A close scrutiny of Wright and Skinner's testimony suggests that it is true. Indeed, in our opinion the most likely sequence of events is that hinted at by Mr Dickens but never followed up: Gardiner met Rose and helped her with the chapel door exactly as Gardiner himself described, but at half past seven when he first came away from the works; not after he had been home for tea. (The best lie follows the truth as far as possible.) Rose did not walk down the hill to Church Street with him. He went home alone, and she walked up the hill to await his return after he had eaten. And so Bill Wright saw nothing of that original meeting. He first saw her coming down the hill alone – not, as might have been expected, up from Providence House – to go to the chapel and wait for Gardiner. Wright then erroneously recollected seeing Gardiner go briefly to and from the drill works. After that, events were much as the young men described.

Mr Wild's weak case has led most writers to assume that Gardiner was guilty of the murder, though none was able to put forward a convincing account of how and when he did it, until, in 1987, Stewart Evans of the Suffolk Police turned his attention to the case (see his full timetable in *Appendix B*).

As an experienced policeman, Stewart was immediately persuaded by the strong chain of circumstantial evidence that Mr Dickens put forward. With a case like that, no serious police force would spend time looking for an alternative suspect.

Stewart also noticed that Gardiner's defence was essentially that of a typical guilty man. Whatever the evidence against him, he claimed that the witnesses were mistaken or lying. Wright and Skinner were lying. Rouse was lying. Mr Guy was lying. Stammers was lying. Morris was either mistaken or lying. Only Mrs Crisp and Mrs Dickinson were telling the truth: prosecution witnesses who fortuitously made a case that suited Gardiner.

And when inanimate circumstantial evidence told against him, Gardiner simply had no explanation. He didn't know how the medicine bottle got into the kitchen. He didn't know who had scraped out the inside of the knife. He didn't know why footprints ran from his house to Rose's and back. He didn't know how many shirts he had or what his wife did with them when he wasn't wearing them. Classic guilty dumb ignorance, to a police mind.

Nevertheless, Stewart would not have wanted to present a case in court with a whacking great alibi slicing through the middle. He wouldn't have liked to suggest that Gardiner left the footprints after the thunderstorm if it also meant suggesting that Rose sat up two hours for him.

There was, however, one more feature of Mr Dickens's case that did not match modern expectation. The notion that Gardiner deliberately went out with malice aforethought to kill Rose and burn her body was bizarre. While husbands, wives and lovers comprise 30 per cent of all murderers, they are most likely to use poison or some staged 'accident' if they deliberately pre-plan their killing. Rose's injuries bore all the marks of the typical lovers' quarrel that ends in unexpected tragedy: a bruise on the face suggesting a first blow; then the knife-wound above her collarbone knocking her backward; then the panic-stricken throat-cutting to stop her screaming and fetching the Crisps downstairs.

But if the murder was unpremeditated, why on earth was Gardiner carrying a bottle of paraffin in his pocket? And with that question, it all suddenly fell into place.

The prosecution's error, Stewart realized, lay in suggesting that the murder and the burning of the body were part and parcel of one deliberate action. In fact, he proposed, they were entirely separate. Gardiner visited Rose and unpremeditatedly killed her. He fled from the crime, returning later with paraffin to destroy – not the pregnant body – but the scene of the crime. In effect, the murder took place before, or at the very beginning of the storm: the paraffin blaze was started after the storm was over. The footprints indicated Gardiner's second visit. All traces of the first visit, when he met Rose waiting for him as prearranged, were washed out.

What was more, Stewart noticed two gaps in the evidence, allowing Gardiner time to make his two visits. The mutually supporting tale Willie and Georgie originally told Staunton placed their visit to Mrs Dickinson very soon after eleven o'clock, and stated that they went *together*. It was only when Mrs Dickinson contradicted this that they introduced the story of Willie's stopping behind to see that the children were all right.

This seemed uncharacteristic. Gardiner, the man at whose approach young Herbert Denny had to be hustled out of the house with a slice of fruitcake, now emerging as a post-feminist, child-minding father?

Moreover, the Gardiners continued throughout every hearing to try to strain at the start of Mrs Dickinson's timing. Mrs Dickinson consistently said Georgianna came over at around half past eleven, and

William followed about half an hour later. The Gardiners tried to hold Georgianna's arrival between eleven and half past, with William following in a very few minutes. The Gardiners, it seemed, were determined to provide an alibi for the critical half-hour before midnight. Stewart believes Gardiner almost confessed in a Freudian slip as Mr Wild examined him:

Wild:	Do you remember what time you went into Mrs Dickinson's?
Gardiner:	Half past twelve.
Wild:	Half past what?
Gardiner:	Half past eleven, I mean.

Sometime between half past eleven and midnight, Stewart suggests, is when William kept his appointment with Rose. This is when he killed her, and fled in horror from the deed. Then he took off his bloodstained clothing and shoes and hid them in his empty kitchen, hastily donning dry clothes and carpet slippers to slip across the alley and establish an alibi with Mrs Dickinson.

But all the time he sat there in neighbourly composure, his mind was racing over the horrific event. Had he left some trace of his presence? Wouldn't people think he had something to do with it when Rose was found murdered? (A reasonable fear: Eli Nunn, as we have seen, immediately jumped to that conclusion.) As he sat there, a plan formed in his mind. He would set light to the kitchen. Everything, including Rose's body, would be destroyed in the blaze. And with any luck, people would think it had been an accident.

But when did he find time to do this without Georgianna knowing? Again, Stewart spotted the gap in the testimony. Gardiner, Georgianna and Mrs Dickinson all agreed that the Gardiners went home at half past one. According to Georgianna, they undressed together and went to bed at two o'clock. Half an hour to undress? Surely this was improbable?

Stewart is persuaded by the testimony of almost everyone who knew her that Georgianna was a lady who would never have connived at or assisted in the murder. But how could Gardiner have gone out again and set the fire unless she was a co-conspirator?

The answer would be obvious to anyone who thought beyond the decorous bounds permitted in detective fiction. Would not the Gardiners have gone to the lavatory before going to bed? It was located at the bottom of the garden. Leaving Georgianna to go first, Gardiner could then have pretended to make a lengthy visit to the privy. In fact, he quickly seized a medicine bottle from the cupboard and filled it with paraffin, driving the cork home so that it should not spill in his pocket. He snatched up the *East Anglian Daily Times* for tinder before hastening back to Providence House. (The 208 yards can be covered in less than two minutes at a fast walk.)

In the kitchen of Providence House, he found he had rammed the cork in so tightly that he could not open his bottle. He took the kitchen lamp apart, hoping to take the paraffin from its well, but in his nervous state could not unscrew the burner. So he smashed the medicine bottle, sprinkled his paraffin over the body, struck a light, and hurried home, satisfied that the impressive 'Whoomph!' of flame as the paraffin went up meant that an impenetrable tragic mystery would remain.

Of course, the paraffin and newspaper were not sufficient to start a funeral pyre. After damaging the combustible nightdress and part of the tablecloth, the flames sank down and went out. Rose's body remained. And the label on the bottle, which Gardiner had not considered, remained, too, to pin the guilt on him.

Gardiner quickly returned home, rinsed any blood or paraffin off his hands, and hurried upstairs to undress with Georgianna. He was aware of the need to dispose of his bloodstained clothing, and the opportunity came early the next morning. After her bad night, Georgie was deeply asleep between six and eight o'clock. Gardiner arose and built the mighty fire in the washhouse before seven, piling his clothes and shoes on it. Stammers said he saw a good blaze at seven. He also saw Gardiner sneaking back out at half past seven to make sure everything was consumed. At half past eight, of course, Gardiner could go out and restart it, or start another small fire for the kettles.

This is Stewart Evans's brilliant reconstruction of the murder. He is only forced to contradict one piece of relatively hard evidence: Mrs Crisp's original testimony that it was at or shortly after midnight when she and her husband went downstairs, 'must have been' wrong. She can't have heard the clock chiming as the coroner's juror suggested. She must have been remembering more accurately later when she declared that she didn't really know at what times she had come downstairs and heard the scream and thud. And, in fact, according to Stewart, she and Mr Crisp must have come downstairs between eleven and twelve, before Gardiner had arrived: the scream and thud must have happened at or just after midnight.

If this elaborate correction of Mrs Crisp looks strained, we must point out that it is well within the bounds of possibility. True crime historians are sadly familiar with the unreliability of evidence about time in the days before everybody wore watches and expected to know the right time accurately.

Stewart's reconstruction has convinced the distinguished East Anglian crime *aficionado* and collector, Mr Ray Cole. So we are aware of our temerity in questioning it. And the first few points we make in Gardiner's defence have to be considered, but would not, in our view, finally refute it.

We don't like Stammers's evidence. It really does come forward suspiciously late in the day; suspiciously fitting an urgent prosecution need. We do not have any proof that he, like Morris, was already telling his story so close to the time of the murder that his memory cannot be faulted. We are suspicious of precise timing and dating remembered over a long period. Once Gardiner had been identified as the murderer by the village, it would be very easy for Stammers to misremember a morning when there had been an extremely large fire remarkably early in Gardiner's washhouse as being the morning after the murder. If his first claim to remember it really did come four months after the event, then we would dismiss the accurate memory of time and date as incredible. (Of course, there is no evidence that he had not told neighbours of the fire earlier.)

We think that Morris's testimony was honest, but that he really did not know where the footprints started, any more than he knew where Hart's footprints first crossed his path. We think that on seeing that they led to and from Providence House he remembered *noticing* them as he passed Alma Cottage, but we think that his tendency to insist more and more strongly that they led from its doorstep was irritable bloody-mindedness (not consciously dishonest), as Mr Wild's pressure intensified his resistance to being told what to think. We note that all Morris's discussion of the Alma Cottage end of the trail relates to the doorstep, although, as Stewart postulates, Gardiner would more probably have used the alley from the kitchen door.

We don't think Georgianna's complete innocence is compatible with Stewart's reconstruction. (He agrees that she may have had later suspicions, but sympathetically notes that it would have spelled ruin for her not to support her husband.) We think that a man returning from the conflagration would have smelt too strongly of paraffin for his wife to miss it in bed. Stewart argues that oil-lit cottages all stank of paraffin in any case. One of us shares with him the childhood experience of sleeping in oil-lit houses, and disagrees that this would disguise Gardiner's activities from Georgianna. On this we can only differ.

If, as Stewart believes, Gardiner did own a third shirt, and the washhouse fire was its destiny, then Georgianna certainly perjured herself. But how could he have owned only two?

The complex arithmetic was explained in 1955, with confused dates, by the East Anglian poet Cecil Lay, who had once spoken to Gardiner and may have been a young relative of Dr Lay. One of Gardiner's shirts was washed every two weeks. After it had been washed on Monday, it was put away clean, until he wore it to chapel on Sunday. It was then put away as 'clean' once again, and worn again the following Sunday, thereupon taking the everyday-wear place of the dirty shirt which was washed the following day and put aside for Sunday. A shirt that had received only one day's wear was definitely 'clean' by the standards of a man who wore one shirt, night and day, for two weeks!

Now, Mrs Gardiner's evidence was that Monday 2 June was not her washing-day. She would next be washing on 9 June. She also said that on Tuesday 3 June she gave Eli Nunn her husband's 'dirty' shirt along with a coat and vest. By Cecil Lay's rationale, 'dirty' must have meant 'clean, but worn once'. On the day when he was arrested, Gardiner must have been wearing the shirt he had worn on Saturday night. For Gardiner's acknowledged 'dirty' shirt was only discarded on the day before washing-day, and only spent Sunday in the dirty linen before it was washed. Either Mrs Gardiner described the shirt she handed over inaccurately by the standards of her household as 'dirty', or she was deliberately lying to the police.

We believe the 'dirty' shirt given to Nunn was in fact 'clean but worn once'. Stewart thinks there was more probably a third shirt, and this would be the first point at which Mrs Gardiner realized that some prevarication would be demanded of her to save her husband's life. Her persistent hysterics throughout the trials might, of course, be taken as evidence of guilty suspicion or knowledge.

Somewhat unhappily, we take the position of the second trial jury over the medicine bottle. We think the defence more or less got it right. It was the one Georgianna gave Rose and it had been used for spare kitchen paraffin. It did fall off the shelf when the bracket was broken (its position in the kitchen was absolutely compatible with that theory). We don't like depending on a mere theory dreamed up by Mr Wild during the second trial, but we think it makes more sense than any other explanation.

But we note with interest that the bottle may well not have broken when it fell, or been smashed by the murderer or anyone else. Dr Stevenson's opinion was clear and unreserved: 'The glass was apparently fractured by the heat, the broken edges being quite clear and free of blood.' Now, it is true that he was being asked essentially to refute the improbable suggestion that Rose's throat might have been cut with the broken glass. But he was absolutely decisive in saying that the glass appeared to have been fractured by the heat. This was never challenged. (Nor, typically, did Wild even notice it.) Stevenson was the Home Office expert. And his testimony strongly suggests that the glass fell on the floor, disregarded by the murderer, and exploded when his pathetic fire reached it. If the bottle was broken by the heat and not the murderer, the whole motive for bringing it into the kitchen disappears.

None of the above seems to us to refute Stewart's reconstruction; only to put forward interesting problems for his consideration. We feel we are on much stronger ground with our next point.

It is inherent to Stewart's case that Gardiner was a man of 'iron nerve', capable of sitting out an hour and a half at Mrs Dickinson's without the least sign of discomposure. We frankly think this is incredible.

We do not share the contemporary opinion that no Methodist could have sat through a thunderstorm without trembling at the Voice of God condemning his murderous plots. Methodism is a religion, not a superstition. But we do not believe for one moment that the man who who wept and fainted during the trials, who climbed up the gantry and took the afternoon off work on hearing that the police wanted him, could possibly have committed murder and then conducted himself throughout Sunday in such a way that no one suspected anything out of the ordinary. The only evidence supporting such an interpretation of Gardiner's character is his self-possession at the Sibton chapel inquiry. But there, as Mr Justice Lawrance noted, he was among friends who were committed to believing him in preference to his accusers. The rest of the legend of 'Gardiner, the man of iron nerve' is transparent newspaper dramatization, albeit accepted by Gardiner himself.

Stewart objects that this is mere psychological theorizing. We should stay with the facts and the circumstantial evidence, he demands. We counter that it is the manifest duty of the historian to explain human conduct in terms of the human personalities involved, and our reading of Gardiner's personality is a reading of the evidence about him.

Yet even that point would merely disincline us to accept Stewart's reconstruction as conclusive. The reason we do not believe Gardiner murdered Rose Harsent is because we are quite sure he did not write the assignation letter.

Until Stewart Evans, Dennis Jaques, Wilfrid Goodman and John Gleeson started work on the case, nobody writing about it after about

1920 had seen a sample of Gardiner's handwriting. Everybody was dependent on the words of the experts, and Gardiner's own admission that there was 'some similarity' between the writing in the assignation note and his writing in his letters to Rose. There was a small, but unimportant, mystery in the fact that the prosecution did not use these letters for comparison purposes. But with no known surviving handwriting of Gardiner's to go on at all, the general evidence that there must have been a striking similarity gained currency. One 'graphologist' has even reproduced the assignation note with what purports to be an 'analysis' of Gardiner's personality based upon it.

When the new generation of crime historians using scholarly methods tackled the case, they quickly unearthed Gardiner's facsimile letters in the *Sun*. And they were immediately confronted with the problem that there was no very obvious similarity at all.

But these letters were written with a fine nibbed pen. And Gurrin had suggested that the difference between a fine nib and a broad nib probably explained the difference between the Paris letters and the assignation note. Since then, we have found the letter written to the *Star* using a broad-nibbed pen. And taking that, together with Mr Gurrin's own document, we feel quite certain Gardiner did not write the assignation note.

Some of Gurrin's character-by-character comparisons do, indeed, look like percipient recognition of unusual formations. But in every single case we have now found examples of the same formations somewhere in other East Suffolk hands of the period.

Some of Gurrin's strongest points, like the capital Ps in mid-sentence, are clearly wrong. Gardiner's are always formed with a single sweeping loop curling around a separately drawn stem. The assignation note offers something like a small p enlarged in the word 'Place'.

And Gurrin's own reputation must also be held against him. Although he pioneered the whole business of handwriting comparison, he is better known for his failures than his successes. For it was Gurrin who assured *The Times* that Charles Stewart Parnell wrote the notorious letter bearing his signature that approved of the Phoenix Park murders. The blackmailer Pigott confessed to that forgery before he shot himself. It was Gurrin who declared that Adolph Beck had written letters that were the work of the swindler 'John Smith'. An innocent man spent years in gaol for that notorious miscarriage of justice. Gurrin confidently declared that Osborne cadet George Archer-Shee had forged his classmate's signature on a stolen postal order in a case which led to the Royal Navy's humiliation in court; the original case behind Terence Rattigan's *The Winslow Boy*.

And Gurrin gave evidence against George Edalji, wrongfully accused of mutilating animals and writing anonymous letters in the village where he and his Parsee father were victims of racial prejudice. Sir Arthur Conan Doyle corrected that injustice to the satisfaction of posterity, though he was unable to secure the compensation Edalji deserved.

Gurrin must have had successes, or he would not have been able to establish the business that his son carried on for many years. But he was resoundingly wrong in the major criminal cases where he appeared for the prosecution. His testimony is worth no more than the comparison of your own eyes. We do not believe that the two writings are by the same hand.

Stewart Evans' answer to this objection is that Gardiner was too clever not to have disguised his hand. He had gone out of his way to make his assignation through the discreet and extraordinary route of a letter in the mail. He would certainly make sure that nobody subsequently spotted that he was writing to Rose.

Naturally, Stewart concludes, Gardiner would have made sure that none of his handwriting thereafter resembled the widely publicized assignation note.

Again, we note that this argument has persuaded Mr Ray Cole, which is very strong support. But we remain completely unconvinced. We have studied some of the acknowledged disguised handwriting of Madeleine Smith, noting the absolutely consistent recurrence of similarly formed letters and equal height ratios between capitals and lower case letters on envelopes which superficially do appear to be in quite different hands. We do not find similar consistencies in Gardiner's hand and the assignation note. We do not believe that Gardiner or anybody else in Rose's social circle would have been a sufficiently accomplished penman to produce consistent and convincing disguised handwriting for the length of a letter, and to match it convincingly on an envelope. We note that a similar disguise would have to be assumed in the buff envelope letters to Rose preceding the disputed note. Alternatively, his handwriting would have to change from the moment of his arrest, without anybody noticing the new disguise. We do not believe that anyone but the most experienced calligrapher would ever be able to produce a disguised hand which suggested *greater* habituation to penmanship than his normal writing. We believe that the assignation note was written in its author's normal hand, with some extra care over the envelope to make sure it did not miscarry in any way.

We do not think that author could possibly have been William Gardiner. Taking that in conjunction with the other pointers to his innocence, we are convinced that he did not murder Rose Harsent.

TEN

The Murderer

All of us who think William Gardiner was no murderer share a few
points in common. We are forced to accept something like Ernest
Wild's theory to explain away the medicine bottle. We have to dismiss
James Morris's footprints as fabricated or wrongly described. We must
put down the similarity of Gardiner's knife to the murder weapon as
coincidence; its extraordinary cleansing inside the clasp as irrelevant, or
(less probably) erroneously detected by Dr Stevenson. The case against
Gardiner is still inviting, firmly though we reject it.

And most published alternative solutions have been very weak: an
impossible accident in which Rose falls downstairs, cutting her own
throat on the breaking bottle; frivolous speculations about Dr Lay or
'Old Tailor' Crisp or Morris as geriatric lovers and murderers; a novel
with a narrator based on Evan Edwards shielding a relative; another
which postulates a conspiracy of Peasenhall wives to assassinate Rose
for conceiving.

Again, years after the case, an equally amazing rumour actually
circulated. The late Mrs R.J. Meads of Southall was a school friend of
Gardiner's twin daughters. According to Mr Meads, his wife said that
'the family' believed Georgianna committed the murder. It was said that
she was pregnant at the time, and lost the child between the trials, which
accounted for her state of mind. There is a genuine family tradition that
Georgianna had a babe at the breast which stopped suckling when its
mother received the shock of seeing her husband arrested, and died
shortly afterwards. In fact, the records show that Daisy May, the
short-lived Gardiner baby, died immediately after the Doctor's Chapel
scandal, which family tradition also holds was the most traumatic shock
Mrs Gardiner remembered.

Many of Mr Meads's recollections of his wife's stories of the Gardiners are demonstrably erroneous. And in any case, we must reject out
of hand the suggestion that Georgianna committed the murder. The
violent knifing was self-evidently a man's crime and the footprints were
a man's footprints.

Our own serious search for an alternative murderer did not begin until we had completely satisfied ourselves that William Gardiner must be innocent. Since we felt sure the author of the assignation note had kept the tryst that ended in tragedy, and probably at least believed himself to be the father of her unborn child, we were looking for a man who could have been Rose's lover.

The first name to suggest itself was that of Bob Kerridge. Next to nothing was known about him. His surname had never been made public. He was thought to have broken off his engagement at around the time of the Doctor's Chapel scandal. But had he? Could he have continued to see Rose, and killed her in a fit of rage or jealousy when the meeting at midnight ended in a quarrel? He certainly moved to Uggeshall very quickly and kept out of the way during the trial, only returning to Peasenhall and Sibton to live when it was all over.

Enquiries around Peasenhall swiftly pushed Bob out of the frame. He was remembered as a widely loved and respected Methodist local preacher. He was 'a dear old boy'. 'He couldn't have killed a bloody fly!' said Mr Denny. Photographs of Bob in old age supported this impression: a wonderfully peaceful, bucolic figure.

Bob remained a farm-worker all his life. In 1905 he married Frances Lizzie Hunt, daughter of an illiterate labourer. His courtship may have hindered his religious studies, for while he was a ploughman in Uggeshall he kept up his ties with Sibton chapel and within a year of the murder, he began preparations to be appointed a local preacher. But he took longer to finish the homework than the circuit expected. After he had held the prescribed books and papers for over a year, Quarterly Meeting minuted a request that he return them if he was not going to present himself for consideration. He completed the test, however, and became a chapel trustee before he was out of his twenties.

This religious activity seemed improbable for a man who had just committed a secret murder, as did the universal admiration for his sincere Christianity. When we found a copy of his signature, we knew he was as innocent as his blameless life would suggest. He could not possibly have written the assignation letter.

In middle life he became the sexton of Sibton. When his wife died he remarried in old age. His second wife was felt not to have cared for him as well as he deserved. But on his death in 1957 the worst thing that anyone could find to say about him was that he tended to frighten his children when he told them gloomy stories and prophecies from the Bible. Rose Harsent was a silly girl to look for a man with 'more life' than Bob Kerridge.

Only one other man's name had been associated with hers – that of Fred Davis.

It certainly seemed that Mr Wild suspected him at the time of the first trial. His alibi was stronger than Gardiner's inasmuch as he had two sleepers to pass – his brother and father – before he could get to Providence House. But its weakness was that he had no wide-awake witness like Mrs Dickinson to cover him for the most likely time of the tryst.

His published love letter suggested that he had not enjoyed inter-course with Rose. Not yet. By his own account, his letters dated back to the time before she conceived. The Gardiners said that he went out with Rose. There was only his own word for it that she had nothing more to do with him once she had obtained the contraceptive leaflet.

What was more, Davis had been involved in a violent altercation with two women early in 1902. Despite his generally quiet demeanour, he could be roused. He appeared at Halesworth Petty Sessions on 11 Feb-ruary, and the *Halesworth Times* gave the following description of the case. (Like several newspapers at the time of Gardiner's trials, it misspelled his name.)

> Frederick Davies and Harry Smith were charged with assaulting Alice Spoor, at Peasenhall, on the 19th of January. Mr H.A. Mullens appeared for the defendants. Prosecutrix said she was out in the evening with her mother for a walk, and saw Harry Smith, who said her hat was not paid for, and threw stones at her. She had a stick in her hand and went to hit Smith with it. Davies came up and told Smith to let her have it. Davies smacked her head against the wall, and seized her throat with his left hand. A lad, named Lambert, came up and held her by the shoulder, and Davies took the stick out of her hand and kept it. In cross-examination she admitted the stick was loaded with lead, but her mother did not have a stick, and she did not strike Smith, who went into an allotment and ran away, and she met him at another gate, but did not hit him, although she tried to do so. Mrs Spoor gave corroborative evidence, but contradicted herself and her daughter in cross-examination in several particulars. Mr Mullens for the defence said that defendant [sc. complainant] started all the trouble. Hy. Smith was standing in the street when complainant's mother made a disgusting remark to him, and complainant struck him with a loaded stick, and followed him and struck at him again.

Evidence in support of this statement was given by each of the defendants, and by Arthur Lambert. PC Eli Nunn gave defendants a good character, and the Bench dismissed the case.

Now that was an interesting little story! In Harry Smith it seemed that we had found the lad called Smith who knew the dirty poems Davis sent to Rose, and went into the army before the trials. Perhaps he and Lambert formed the nucleus of Mr Cooke's corrupt 'knot' around Davis.

Not that this led us any closer to Rose's murderer. Sixteen-year-old Harry was too young to be a probable lover for Rose. (And the name is so common that it has not been possible to discover anything more about him except that he was probably born in Hoxne.)

But Davis's reaction when infuriated was very interesting. First he smacked Alice Spoor's head against a wall. Then he went for her throat. First Rose's murderer hit her, bruising her face and knocking her against the door. Then he stabbed her and cut her throat.

Careful consideration of Davis drew attention to another peculiar point about Rose Harsent's murder. Assuming Burgess's testimony that there was usually a light in her room around ten o'clock to be true, her signal was extraordinarily unreliable. And since she was saying, 'Good-night', to Mrs Crisp at a quarter past ten, it probably was true. How on earth was anyone outside Gardiner's house to know that the light was a signal and not just Rose going to bed normally? Even if Gardiner waited for the light to disappear after ten or fifteen minutes, he could not be sure that it had been deliberately removed, and not just extinguished as Rose went to sleep.

Moreover, as Wilfrid Goodman had long observed, the wording of the assignation note made it a reasonable inference that this signal had been used before, though sometimes the light might have been shown at the more useful time of midnight. How, otherwise, did Gardiner explain his sudden peregrinations into the road just before bedtime? He couldn't have anticipated that threatening weather would always bring him outside plausibly.

There was only one way in which the signal could be absolutely reliable. If the whole point was that the candle was in the window and not somewhere else inside the room, then it could be observed by Rose's lover and he would know that the coast was clear. A candle anywhere else in the room would mean danger, as clearly as no light at all.

But could you tell the difference from as far away as Gardiner's house? We carried out tests at a house outside the possibly confusing range of street lamps. We found that a candle flame seen through a window at night is visible for an enormous distance. From any distance you can distinguish between a visible flame and a lit candle out of your line of vision. But from beyond about fifty yards away, it becomes increasingly difficult to tell whether a candle flame is actually in the window or somewhere else in the room. From the 208 yards to Gardiner's house it would only be possible to say that there was a candle flame clearly visible in the room. And Rose's window was wide enough in relation to the walls of her room and set low enough to the floor to make it probable that a candle set on a table or dresser would be visible at the shallow angle from the road opposite Alma Cottage.

But anyone standing immediately outside Providence House would know at a glance whether Rose's candle was in her window or set even a few inches back from it. He would clearly see the candle itself, the candlestick, anybody holding it, or any furniture on which it stood, and anything else in the room, unless his rather acute line of vision allowed him to see little but the candle flame, wall and ceiling.

Fred Davis was bound to pass the window at ten o'clock. That was the time he finished work at Emmett's. By his own account he stayed outside until about half past ten. Certainly Fred was a more plausible observer for the 'light in the window' than Gardiner, who would have been more safely signalled by, for example, opening the window for a short time.

And the assignation note specified *not* replacing the signal at midnight. Why not, if the writer intended to approach the house at that time? In Fred's case, the answer would be obvious. As Mr Wild suggested, he would travel from his back door to Rose's if he had previously gone home, and would not see Rose's window at all.

If that was evidence which seemed to incriminate Fred, was there anything to exculpate him? The shawl over the kitchen window was ambiguous. It would cut out any light which might have shown Fred creeping across the back gardens. But the writer of the assignation note had apparently seen light anticipating his arrival in the past. So why should Fred want to approach total darkness when he specified an arrival at the back door?

The handwriting experts confidently declared that Fred's writing was nothing like that of the assignation note, but how much trust could one place in men who thought that Gardiner's *was* similar? Why, if the letters were so dissimilar, had Staunton admitted that he was very anxious to find their author at the time of the magistrates' hearing?

Morris's footprints were a serious problem, on the other hand. Despite Mr Wild's best efforts to suggest that Davis owned rubber soled shoes before he left Peasenhall, we could not believe his insinuation that young Davis deliberately padded down to Alma Cottage and back leaving a trail to incriminate Gardiner. Of course, if he had done so, his address eliminated one obvious problem. When Fred came back to Providence House, he would naturally follow the gravel path around the back, and return home the way he had come, leaving no further footprints on the soft road surface.

But pursuing Davis as a suspect is a journey up the garden path. We have found his signature, and we are quite certain that he was as blameless as his subsequent life suggests. He was not the writer of the assignation note. Nevertheless, giving serious consideration to his case undoubtedly cast new light on the murderer's signalling system with Rose.

If we were impressed by Mr Wild's first alternative suspect, Wilfrid Goodman was impressed by his second. Examining the confession letter in the *East Anglian Daily Times* carefully, he became the first person since Mr Wild to notice that its writer seemed rather better informed than might have been expected of a mere crank.

If the information in the letter (see pages 100–11) is compared with the demonstrable facts of the case, it can be seen that the writer makes one statement that is untrue, another that seems improbable, and he appears to contradict himself once. Yet these failings seem to be outweighed by the possible truth of everything else he says, and his pointing to one likely fact that had never been mentioned in the newspapers, nor, so far as we know, in court.

The 'confession' says, 'i did rite the letter to my pet lamb to tell her to put the light in the window for me'. A glance at the two documents shows that this is untrue. Wild's attempt to prove it had the merit of suggesting that the 'disguised' hand was the less literate of the two, but in every other respect it made Mr Gurrin's attempt to pin the assignation note on Gardiner seem a model of convincing scientific demonstration.

'[H]ad i not took my letters out of rose box i should be were G is', said the anonymous letter writer. One can only ask why Rose saved his letters in her box, and not in her drawer with the rest of her correspondence, and how he came to overlook the one which still lay on top of the box with its envelope when Nunn and Dr Lay searched her room?

And the writer apparently claimed to have had intercourse with Rose 'on the sofer' before killing her, later changing the venue to 'on the rug'. The latter position would have been seriously inconvenienced by the table, if he meant the rug in the kitchen. But it is not absolutely certain that he meant to imply that it was the site of sexual activity.

What is impressive is the fact that he claims to have enjoyed sexual intercourse with Rose at all that night. It had barely been hinted in reports of the murder and the various hearings. As far as we know, it was only vaguely brought out when Mr Justice Lawrance re-examined Dr Richardson, evidently expecting that he would disprove the claim. Instead of which, Richardson came very near to upholding it!

The letter claimed that two people were present. 'B' watched while 'H.B.', the writer, 'did it'. The letter might conceivably have been written by either: it might be a false confession by someone who had witnessed the true events, and roughly described them, to exonerate Gardiner. And that would explain why the writing did not match the assignation note.

The interval for love-making would also help to explain the gap of an hour or more in Mrs Crisp's original estimated timing between midnight and the scream.

It took Wilfrid Goodman little investigation to determine that the police had dismissed the letter rather too cavalierly. He found photographs of maltsters' shoes and proved that they could be strikingly barred. He noted that the police had found that William Harsent the younger was working in Burton as a maltster at the time of the murder, and was most probably the 'Harsent' mentioned in the letter. He also discovered that Suffolk maltsters normally returned home at the weekends on special trains run for them between Burton upon Trent and Ipswich. He speculated that the writer's two references to the night before the murder might actually mean the night when he last visited Rose. He felt that such details as the £5 she was said to have given the writer rang true.

He had noticed, like us, that the signal of a light in Rose's room was unreliable if directed at any permanent resident of Peasenhall. But he reflected that it might be a very good signal indeed for occasional nights only: the nights when a migrant worker, not perhaps hailing from Peasenhall itself, might arrange to come through the village at a given hour. Rose would then be especially careful to *extinguish* her light after ten minutes or so if she did *not* want her lover to visit her. This would seem especially convenient if the nights in question were those on which he had returned from Burton and was travelling from the railway to some village near Peasenhall.

Wilfrid Goodman is cautious. He does not suggest that the letter *is* a true description; only that it cannot be ruled out. He is even more cautious when it comes to naming the writer, but suggests that Albert Goodchild should not be dismissed prematurely.

Wilfrid began with a deep suspicion of the police, since he had early noted Nunn's evasiveness over his notebook entry on Georgianna and the medicine bottle, and Staunton's improbable claim that he still believed the death might be suicide two days after the body was found. His suspicion was intensified when Stewart Evans was shown Andrews's *Work Journal* and told us that murder had been assumed from the outset. Wilfrid took it that the police were unscrupulous in eliminating any evidence that conflicted with their decision to charge Gardiner.

They certainly did not draw any hasty conclusions from the fact that the letter writer referred to a Harsent, and the only maltster they had found who approximated to the writer's self-description had travelled from Burton on the day of the murder with a Harsent.

We may wonder whether the two travelled together out of choice or necessity, however. They changed trains and split up at Wickham Market. Harsent stayed on the Great Eastern Main Line to Darsham; Goodchild went along the Framlingham Branch Line. Peasenhall and Badingham were adjacent villages. Peasenhall was just under six miles from Darsham: Badingham was the same distance from Framlingham in the opposite direction. Either young man could have chosen to travel with the other, giving himself company for the first five or so miles of the final walk home at the cost of something like two miles of additional walking. For anyone accustomed to serious walking, as such young men were at that time, the extra distance would be a small price to pay for company over the greater part of the journey. From this there is no reason to suppose that Harsent and Goodchild liked each other.

If the 'B' who watched was Bill Harsent, it would seem certain that he only watched the love-making. We cannot believe that Rose's brother would conceal her murderer's guilt and allow the rest of the family to continue to believe Gardiner had killed her. Wilfrid Goodman never contemplated his signing the letter with his initials reversed; a device too literary for a man whose parents both made their mark in lieu of a signature.

Wilfrid examined the lists of migrant workers compiled by Dr Colin Owen of Stafford before Messrs Bass destroyed the records. The relevant year, 1902, was already missing when Dr Owen carried out his research. In the remaining years, several workers had the initials HB, but none seemed likely to be involved with Peasenhall.

Bearing all Wilfrid's caveats in mind, we still conclude that this confession, like the other published confessions to the murder (see *Appendix A*), was the work of a fantasist, albeit one who was probably a Suffolk maltster. The only significant piece of special knowledge is so probable a part of such a fantasy that the completely false confession posted from London to Eli Nunn also postulates an attempted rape before the murder:

> I curse the day when I first knew many men would visit Rose
> Harsent, and their intimacy with her. Oh! that terrible night.
> Rose would never let me have improper relations. I was
> desperate. Rose said she would scream. What could I do?

It seems to us that the crucial revelation emerging from Wilfrid Goodman's investigation of the confession letter is the probability that the tragic meeting included a sexual episode before the quarrel.

The most time-consuming area of research was in examining as many contemporary manuscript documents from the Peasenhall district as we could find, looking for handwriting similar to that on the assignation letter. But we also kept up our contact with the old people of the village, and in one conversation with Mr Herbert Denny, we suddenly noticed a remark introducing a new name into the story.

'Of course', said Mr Denny, 'it was Fred Grice that put Davis up to writing the letter. He knew that he lived next door to her, and so he got him to write to her.'

Fred Grice? Who was he? Why was he distancing himself from direct correspondence with Rose?

Fred Grice worked in Emmett's Store. He was twenty-five years old in 1902, and according to Mr Denny he was 'different from the rest of them'. He liked to 'pull people to pieces'. He was a mischief-maker.

Miss Gertie Rose, too, seemed to evince less warmth about Grice than she did over other employees at Emmett's. Like Mr Denny, she remembered Grice making an offensive remark to a woman who he felt was talking too much.

It was a surprise to hear that Davis needed any encouragement to write to Rose, given the floridity of his one known letter. But at the first trial he had given Grice a rather different role. It was a man called Grice, Davis said, who had lent him the contraceptive leaflet.

There is not much to go on there. A young man in a shop might easily have shown off his adult information to impress the apprentice. But in the second trial, without mentioning the name Grice, Davis revealed something else which escaped everyone's notice. Rose asked him for the leaflet *because 'she knew another fellow had it'*. Davis's implication is quite clear. He was merely a go-between.

Was Grice, then, the mysterious father of Rose's child? Did he make the assignation because his contraceptive information had failed? Like Davis, he was well placed to see the signal in her window when he came off work at ten o'clock.

As a matter of fact, however, we can be quite certain he was innocent. His signature, while a little more clerkly than that of a craftsman or a labourer, was quite unlike the writing of the assignation note. But the information about Grice casts important new light on the murder.

To start with, it confirms that Rose was not the innocent victim of Gardiner's sole lust that her stoutest defenders would make her. Not one, but two young men were let into the secret that she wanted to know how to avoid pregnancy without preserving celibacy. And Grice was no innocent puppy-lover next door; he was two years older than Rose.

Secondly, it suggests that she was consciously manipulative in her exploitation of Davis. He had not given Rose the leaflet off his own bat in the hope that she would try out its suggestions with him, as Mr Wild insinuated. She had asked him to get it for her, after which (and why should we doubt him?) she dropped him. And she told him the source from which he was to obtain it. He was only the delivery boy.

Could the same be true of Grice? Was he the actual owner of the leaflet? Davis never specifically said so. Did Rose know someone else who owned it, living with or close to Grice? Was there a chain of two people between the so-called 'dirty book' and the recipient who knew 'the fellow' that had it? For Grice lived in Sibton, and anyone travelling from and to his lodgings could have been the one who left the incriminating footprints.

Anyone coming from Sibton or Yoxford to work in Peasenhall would also pass the Hurrens' Post Office and the letter-box quite naturally. This stood at the eastern end of the village in those days, near the Wesleyan chapel. Anyone living in The Street, The Causeway or the Hackney Road area and working at (say) Smyths', would have made a striking little ramble away from the normal workplace and the main shops if he went to post a letter to Rose. Would someone who dared not attract attention by dropping the letter in Providence House by hand have risked this?

We don't know exactly where Fred Grice lived. We don't know whether he lived with his family (originally from Blyford), or whether he was in bachelor lodgings. But Mr Denny is quite clear that Fred Grice lived in Sibton before his marriage in 1904, after which he lived in Hackney Road, Peasenhall for some time, before moving back to Sibton where he opened a small shop of his own. Some time around the end of the First World War, he and his family left the district. We have heard Colchester and Ipswich variously suggested as their immediate destination. All we know is that he died in Dorking in 1961 where he had owned a fish and chip shop for some years.

A resident of Sibton, or the Sibton end of Peasenhall, was topographically well placed to be the murderer. This was the crucial clue to emerge from the investigation of Fred Grice.

A further suspect emerged from the investigations made by the late Mr Dennis Jaques. He learned from Mr Eric Godward of Felixstowe that Mr Godward's late brother-in-law, wheelwright and blacksmith William Goddard of Peasenhall, had always believed the murderer to be a farmer's boy who ran away to Australia by the train from Darsham after the murder. Mr Goddard's parents had disagreed, stoutly following the village belief in Gardiner's guilt. But after their death, some time in the 1940s or early 1950s, Mr Goddard was shown a letter from the farmer's boy who had run away to Australia. The letter amounted to a confession, and Mr Goddard was able to borrow it from the customer who received it, and showed it to Mr Godward. Mr Godward clearly remembered seeing it, but he did not remember any details. He is not himself a Peasenhall man, and the murder had had less impact in his mind than in his brother-in-law's.

Nor did Mr Goddard's surviving daughter know anything about her father's beliefs in this matter. The letter seemed unlikely to have survived in her father's possession, and certainly she had never seen or heard of it.

The farmer's boy who ran away after the murder gave us a good deal of trouble. Nobody we spoke to could remember him in those terms. Mr Herbert Denny remembered a steward of the Levett-Scriveners called Tom White who ran away to Canada after he had accidentally killed a boy with a riding crop. This had evidently been the biggest scandal in the village prior to the murder, but it is now completely forgotten except in Mr Denny's memory, and he says it happened before his time. The directories show that Thomas Girling White, steward to the Levett-Scriveners, left Sibton and Peasenhall between 1898 and 1900, and could not have had anything to do with Rose Harsent's death.

But when we simply asked about a farmer's boy who ran away to Australia, making no mention of the murder, Mr Billy Rowe placed him at once. He couldn't remember his name, but he came from Sibton where his father kept the shop in Poys Street by the chapel. He hadn't run away in 1902 but in 1906. And the reason was well known. He had got a girl who worked in the shop in the family way. She continued to live in and around the village with her 'youngster' for some time. She was herself some relative of the shop-owner.

Armed with this clue, we returned to Sibton and sounded out Mr Hubert Aldridge, who now lives next to the old Primitive Methodist chapel, and is a fund of information on the Methodist community of East Suffolk. He had heard Mr Jaques's 'farmer's boy' theory, but had never connected it in his mind with this very familiar tale of a man he had actually met. 'Why, you're talking about Tom Hunt!' he said. Everybody knew Tom Hunt had run away when he got a girl pregnant. Everybody knew that the happy conjunction of the pair had taken place in a wheelbarrow. Tom Hunt was the son of Thomas Hunt, that very chapel steward whose refusal to confirm Rouse's story about Gardiner's feet in Rose's lap had so exasperated Superintendent Andrews. Mr Aldridge now lives in their former home. And at the end of his life, Tom Hunt had come back to Suffolk and settled in Ipswich with his daughter. He had visited his old house and been shown around by Mr Aldridge.

Immediately opposite Mr Hunt's shop stood Mr William Goddard's forge. The wheelwright and blacksmith was, from a Peasenhall point of view, a Sibton man, though understandably his brother-in-law in Felixstowe didn't make the precise discrimination along the wandering parish boundaries that villages followed. After all, to most of the world Rose Harsent is simply a Peasenhall girl.

Mr William Goddard's lone suspicion of Tom Hunt was self-explanatory. He had linked the two greatest scandals on his own doorstep in his mind. The letter he saw from Tom Hunt might well have confessed that he ran away 'because of that girl I got into trouble'. Tom was preparing to return to England at the time when it was written, and would quite probably have sounded out the sort of reception he might expect. He could not have killed Rose Harsent. He was only sixteen in 1902. He was twenty when he went to Australia.

Our scrutiny thus far has, we think, covered all the useful areas indicated by evidence produced at the trials and hearings and in local gossip, and cleared the men whose names emerge from that search. In the light of the evidence, it remains for us to describe the kind of person the murderer must have been.

A modern police psychological profile would start by saying, 'Male, white'. White, because there was no black community in rural Suffolk. Male, because the violent blow to the face and stab over the collarbone suggest masculine anger and violence. The possession of a knife carried on the person points equally to a man. So, of course, does the tentative suggestion that Rose participated in a heterosexual act shortly before she died.

It has been proposed that a jealous woman might have followed Rose's lover, and, driven to frenzy by what she saw, waited until he had left, and killed her rival. But a woman would be unlikely to carry a knife with her in anticipation of being stirred to a *crime passionnel.* And none of Mrs Crisp's kitchen knives was missing.

The murderer was alone in perpetrating the deed. There was no bruising anywhere except on Rose's face: no marks where an accomplice held her. The unsuccessful first bruise and stab, together with the cuts across the hands where Rose tried to ward off the knife, all point to a single assailant.

The murderer was Rose's lover – or one of them. We incline definitely to the view that Rose had more than one, while accepting that this is an unproven suspicion.

We do not think that Gardiner was still her lover in 1902. We do not think that a man with such a demonstrable affection for his family would have continued the liaison after the scandal which was felt to have caused Daisy May's death. The Gardiners discussed and retained Rouse's anonymous letter so that Georgianna was able to bring it forward while William was in prison. Had its accusations been well founded, we do not think it would have survived Gardiner's guilt or Georgianna's anger to be available for the defence almost a year later.

We make no suggestion as to whether Rose had more than one lover concurrently. But we do not think her age and background are compatible with her knowingly making love to one man while another watched or stayed within earshot, as the confession letter from Burton upon Trent suggested.

We cannot believe that another man came into the house after her lover had left. We believe she was killed by the man she had arranged to meet at midnight after they had passed an hour or so, possibly in love-making; and probably in tense discussion of her pregnancy, culminating in a quarrel.

Rose showed in her treatment of Davis and her explanation of the ending of her engagement that she was selective. She liked her men to have vitality ('life'). She was not interested in the romantic adoration of her juniors. Gardiner was a handsome man in the prime of life, and it would not be surprising if she continued to find rather older men attractive.

Men who were very significantly older, on the other hand, would probably have to have had serious attractions of status or wealth to secure her. Moreover, any sexual act which took place in the kitchen, as Dr Richardson and Mr Jenkins suggested, would have taken place under uncomfortable circumstances: on or leaning against the table; on the rug or the brick floor; or leaning against the wall.

While this testifies to her lover's lusty determination, it probably rules out someone of middle age, who would more likely insist on retiring to her attic bed. Or it could be an indication of her murderer's lack of nerve that they did not go there. He could have been too young, too humble or too nervous a man to venture far into the Crisps' house. Conversely he might have felt his dignity and reputation to be at risk if he left any distance between himself and the kitchen door through which he could escape from discovery *in flagrante delicto*.

He certainly felt a need for extreme discretion, since he went to the length of posting letters to her in the village. This might have been simply because he was married. The Doctor's Chapel incident shows that Rose was not scrupulous about taking a married lover, even if she was friendly with his wife.

The assignation note shows that her murderer was a better and swifter penman than the generality of labourers and petty craftsmen in the village. Its even, confident writing with sharp regular minims and accurately dotted 'i's is markedly superior to the laboriously rounded letters we have met repeatedly in marriage certificates and Primitive Methodist documents. On the other hand, it does not have the assured sweep and continuity of magistrates' signatures, or the decisive regularity and clarity of Dr Lay's hand or the hands of Methodist ministers. Its persistent mispunctuation confirms that the writer was not of the 'educated' classes. A superior young artisan, rising toward a social equality with Tailor Crisp or his shoemaker brother might fit, or perhaps a small farmer or farm bailiff. William Gardiner, Fred Davis and Fred Grice are all round about the social and educational level the handwriting suggests, even though their individual hands are markedly different.

We feel that the writing is definitely more confident than that of Gardiner. But several of the other points made so far about the murderer's personality fit him very well. Most of the evidence ruling him out is specific to him. We think that Rose probably continued a pattern of selecting lovers a cut above the village lads and devout labourers who might satisfy her peers, and this led to her death.

The topographical evidence is also rather interesting. The murderer certainly lived or stayed within walking distance of Providence House: quite likely in Peasenhall, since he posted his letter there. He might, on the other hand, have come into Peasenhall to work and posted it on the way before ten o'clock on Saturday morning.

The footprints came from the east, and started far enough down The Street to be out of sight of Providence House. Yet the murderer had to be within reasonable distance of Rose's window at ten o'clock in order to see her signal. A worker at Emmett's would have attracted no attention. A worker at the drill works would have had to go and work on his own at that time in the evening. We know Gardiner sometimes did this, but he was a foreman and possibly privileged. An ordinary worker risked attracting attention. A manager like Mr Rickards would have been perfectly placed to come in and go over the books in the evening. But he would not have capitalized words in mid-sentence.

A murderer from Hackney Road or further west is effectively ruled out by the absence of footprints leading west. On the other hand, given that a murderer from the Sibton or Yoxford end of the village has been suggested, we want to know how he saw the signal. The Swan Inn was within sight of Providence House, and might have supplied a base from which a murderer who was not a Methodist could look out.

Why can't the murderer be traced from among the young men of Peasenhall, Sibton and Yoxford? A few statistics and examples will demonstrate the impenetrable haystack in which this needle is hidden. The aggregate population of the three villages was 2,333, according to the 1900 directories. This is a definite underestimate, resting on census returns almost ten years out of date. Taking account of later marriage, higher infant mortality rates and shorter life-spans than today, we may calculate that around five hundred of those would have been able-bodied adult males under middle age. A number of them will have remained unmarried. Bachelors of the class of Rose Harsent's probable murderer are unlikely to have left any surviving sample of their handwriting.

Those who married will have signed the register. But could they all be traced? Identical names have given us some difficulties even in following up men like Mr Fidler of High House Farm and Bob Kerridge. There are two High House Farms on the old large-scale maps of west Peasenhall. There were two Methodist brothers called Fidler who farmed in the village. There were two Robert Kerridges in Sibton. And these are men about whom we knew enough to be certain, in the end, that we were consistently describing the right ones.

Now consider the cases of two other men whose names have emerged in our study. Harry Smith, we have seen, was too young to have been Rose's lover. But suppose we were not convinced of this? There were ten Harry Smiths born in England and Wales in the same year that he was born in Hoxne. According to Davis, his friend joined the army before June 1902, and thus moved out of the district. Any of the ten whose fathers held the same rather common occupation of labourer would be indistinguishable from him on their marriage certificates – unless, by great good fortune, our Harry stayed in the army until his wedding.

Another man's name is fleetingly mentioned in both trials. At the first, Alfonso Skinner remarked that 'a man called Mayhew' was one of the people he and Wright told about the Doctor's Chapel incident. At the second, Mr Rickards said that Wright's immediate boss, Mayhew, was really responsible for the bad workmanship which brought down a reprimand on Wright. It is probable (though not certain) that the same man is being described in each case. There is nothing, of course, to associate him with Rose Harsent. But suppose we wanted to trace him?

Nobody who remembers Smyths' Drill Works can remember any man called Mayhew working there in any capacity. The only individual named Mayhew remembered in the neighbourhood today is a gamekeeper who once lived at Bruisyard. Yet in 1902 this must have been one of the commonest names in the area. There were three families named Mayhew living on Sibton Green, and between 1871 and 1880 no less than forty-nine male infants with that surname were registered in Blything and neighbouring Hoxne! Christian names seem to have been followed fashionably from time to time, so that often we find identically-named Mayhews being born in the same year, or even the same quarter. Any one of these men aged between twenty-two and thirty-one might have been Wright and Skinner's acquaintance. Or any other Mayhew up to four or five years older. And he had certainly left Smyths' by the time Mr Herbert Denny began his apprenticeship in 1910. How could he possibly be identified today?

Multiply the problems of Mayhew and Harry Smith by, say, two hundred, and it becomes clear why the murderer of Rose Harsent cannot be named. The premature suspicion and sensational trials of William Gardiner provided a smokescreen under which he escaped attention. If his family ever suspected him, they kept it well to themselves. Not a whisper against him has survived. Our own experience with the Gardiner family has shown that a Suffolk tradition of preferring to say nothing at all to outsiders – even outsiders who are convinced of a relative's innocence – is amazingly strong.

There are those in Peasenhall who don't like the continuing search for Rose Harsent's murderer. They think it morbid. Several times we were asked, 'Why don't you leave that poor girl to rest in peace?'

The answer is because factual uncertainty is a nagging irritant, and published falsehood gives us genuine distress. There are far too many books and articles purveying unsubstantiated portraits of Gardiner the pious and hypocritical brute; of Rose, the striking village beauty, seduced by her calculating elder. We are first and foremost interested in establishing the truth.

We shall not be outraged if many readers disagree with us that Gardiner's handwriting and personality eliminate him from the case, and give Stewart Evans the palm for finally proving how Gardiner did it. We should have been happy to present his argument as the truth, supported and garnished by the subsidiary data our researches uncovered, if we genuinely believed it. And we had by no means made up our minds finally against Gardiner's supposed guilt when we encountered Stewart's theory: we had to do a good deal of searching before we were fully persuaded that Mr Gurrin hadn't seen something that eluded our inexpert eyes.

The fact remains that, in our view, Gardiner's innocence is incontrovertible. The case remains unsolved and insoluble. The murder of Rose Harsent is still the mystery of Peasenhall.

Appendix A

The note written on a leaf from a pocket-book which the police found in Devon ran as follows:

> Dear wife,
> Can you see me at Stone Challenger [sc. ?Challenor] tonight. I find the police has got Gardiner, who I said killed the servant, when it was me. Excuse me for breaking news of that sort. Please not tell anyone of the crime.
>
> > I am, your loving husband.

The text is taken from the *Eastern Morning Gazette* of 23 January, 1903; a more reliable source than the familiar *Notable British Trials*.

The other letter was posted from London to PC Nunn. The following text is collated from *Notable British Trials: the Trial of William Gardiner* and *Eastern Morning Gazette*, 23 January 1903. They have both probably garbled the final references to the sea and seeing Gardiner; we include all possibilities, but doubt whether more than two phrases included the words 'sea' or 'see'.

> London.
> I cannot keep silent no longer. My thoughts are all of that terrible night when I visited the one I love. Oh! miserable time. I curse the day when first I knew many men would visit Rose Harsent, and their intimacy with her. Oh! that terrible night. Rose would never let me have improper relations. I was desperate. Rose said she would scream. What could I do? Where did the knife come from? I was sorry afterwards. I put Rose's nightdress over her head to stop the blood. I lifted her up but she fell. I got the lamp to see if Rose was dead. Down

went the lamp. Did I put the flame out? I walked out of Providence House, down the street to the bend of the road. My rubber shoes which Rose admired so much is worn out, like myself. Rose, I shall never rub your knees with oil again. I cannot rest. No peace. I cannot work now. My mind is never at rest. Oh! [words possibly omitted] Brother Gardiner, I never thought you would be charged with the murder of Rose Harsent. Rose said you was her best friend. No beastly talk from you, innocent Bro. Gardiner. Must I give myself up to the law? I cannot. My beard is grown like Bro. Gardiner's. I must wander on the sea. Let me die, Rose, dear. Kill me. Oh! Rose, I shall see you before Gardiner. I was tired. Good-bye, I can walk to the sea. Good-bye, I cannot write.

Appendix B

TIME-CHART OF THE EVENTS OF MAY 31–JUNE 1

by Stewart P. Evans

9.00 p.m.	Rose calls at Gardiner's back door. Family out.
9.30 p.m.	Gardiner comes home.
	Children put to bed.
	Rose places light in window, then goes downstairs.
9.55 p.m.	Burgess sees Gardiner at front door.
10.00 p.m.	Burgess chatting with Gardiner.
	Light seen in Providence House.
10.05 p.m.	Storm brewing. Wind easterly.
10.10 p.m.	Burgess leaves Gardiner.
10.15 p.m.	Mrs Crisp sees Rose in hall.
	(Rose sits on bed, waiting.)
11.00 p.m.	Thunder and heavy rain.
	Crisps go downstairs.
11.30 p.m.	Mrs Gardiner goes into Mrs Dickinson's.
	Rose goes into kitchen.
12.00	Rose in kitchen for assignation.
	Gardiner arrives.
	Quarrel and murder.
	Mrs Crisp hears scream.
12.00+	Gardiner joins wife in Mrs Dickinson's
12.30 a.m.	Gardiner testifies 'joined wife at 12.30' – slip by Gardiner!
1.00 a.m.	Gardiners chatting with Mrs Dickinson.
1.30 a.m.	Storm abates.
	Gardiners go home. Check children.
	Gardiner purports to visit privy?
	Gardiner starts fire in Providence House?
2.00 a.m.	Gardiners undress and go to bed.
	Mrs Gardiner cannot sleep.

S
T
O
R
M

2.20 a.m.	Bertie wakes up. Mrs Gardiner goes to him.
	Mrs Gardiner returns to bed. Gardiner still in bed.
	Mrs Gardiner rises again for brandy.
3.00 a.m.	Dawn around this time.
3.30 a.m.	Twins wake up. (Time uncertain.)
	Mrs Gardiner puts one with big sister.
	Brings other into bed with Gardiner.
4.00 a.m.	Hart passes along Hackney Road and Heveningham Long Lane.
5.00 a.m.	Mrs Gardiner falls asleep for the first time.
	Morris sees footprints.
6.30 a.m.	Gardiner lights fire and burns clothes.
7.00 a.m.	Stammers sees fire.
7.30 a.m.	Stammers sees Gardiner coming away from washhouse.
8.00 a.m.	Gardiners get up.
	William Harsent finds body at Providence House.
8.30 a.m.	Gardiner makes fire for kettle.
8.40 a.m.	PC Nunn arrives at scene of murder.

Notes and Sources

ONE: THE MURDER

The thunderstorm: *East Anglian Daily Times* (henceforth *EADT*) 2 June 1902; *The Peasenhall Murder. Graphic Story of the Trial. Reprinted from . . . the Eastern Morning Gazette*, East of England Newspaper Co., Norwich, 1902, collated with *Eastern Morning Gazette* (henceforth *EMG*), 7, 8, 10, 11 Nov 1902, and Stewart Evans, full MS transcript of all reports of trial from *EADT*, (collation henceforth *1st Trial*) – evidence of Harry Burgess.

Peasenhall village, fear of flooding and Burgess's movements: *1st Trial* – evidence of Harry Burgess; *Trial of William Gardiner*, ed. William Henderson, *Notable British Trials* series, Hodge, Edinburgh, 1934 (henceforth *NBT*), collated with *EMG*, 22, 23, 24, 26, 27 Jan 1903 and Wilfrid Goodman, MS notes and observations on sources and shorthand errors in above (collation henceforth *2nd Trial*. Mr Goodman demonstrates convincingly that *NBT* is essentially a reproduction of the *EADT* reports) – evidence of Harry Burgess and William Gardiner; information Mr Billy Rowe, conversation with the authors, 5 May 1989.

Movements of Mr and Mrs William Crisp and Rose Harsent, and layout of Providence House: *EADT*, 4, 20 June 1902; *1st* and *2nd Trials* – evidence of Mrs Crisp; *2nd Trial* – evidence of W.H. Brown and Superintendent Andrews; visit to Providence House, the authors and Stewart Evans, 3 May 1989.

Mrs Dickinson's evidence: *1st* and *2nd Trials*.

Movements of William Harsent: *EADT* 3, 4, 20 June 1902; *Illustrated Police News*, 14 June 1902; *1st* and *2nd Trials* – evidence of William Harsent. At the 2nd trial, Harsent said that James Crisp came to Providence House unsummoned, but his memory was obviously hazy, as he seemed to think he had come with other unidentified interested villagers. At the magistrates' hearing on 19 June he was precise about having fetched James Crisp, and then himself staying with the body.

State of the body and the kitchen, Nunn's and Lay's movements, and medical evidence: *EADT* 3, 4 17, 20 June, 1, 4 July, *1st* and *2nd Trials*: evidence of Drs Lay and Richardson and PC Nunn. Rose's chemise is mentioned in Superintendent Andrews's *Work Journal* (deposited in Suffolk County Constabulary Museum), which also clarifies Nunn's rapid identification of the death as murder.

Paraffin lamp shade: *EMG* 23 Jan 1903 – evidence of Eli Nunn. The shade is usually described as a 'broken globe'. Nunn is quite specific, however, in saying, 'It got broken. It was whole when I took it.' He calls it a 'globe', but an excellent drawing in *The Star*, 23 Jan 1903, shows Nunn in court holding the chimney in his hand, with the candlestick, well, and quite definite mushroom shade on a shelf in front of him.

The broken bottle, matchstick and piece of cloth: *EADT* 3, 4, 17, 20 June, 4, 17 July 1902, *1st* and *2nd Trials*: evidence of Drs Lay and Stevenson. The bottle was variously described (at different hearings and in Superintendent Andrews's *Work Journal*) as 6 oz and 10 oz. Since Dr Lay said it would hold 48 teaspoonfuls, and Mr Wild said it contained half a pint of paraffin (*1st Trial*) we think it was more probably 10 oz.

TWO: THE VILLAGE

The county and country of Suffolk: Ronald Blythe, *Akenfield*, Allen Lane, 1969; Allan Jobson, *Something of Old Suffolk*, Robert Hale, 1978; 'Sudbourne: Portrait of a Village', *Sunday Times Weekly Review*, 29 Jan 1978.

Peasenhall village: *Kelly's Post Office Directory: Suffolk*, 1903; Nikolaus Pevsner, *The Buildings of England: Suffolk*, Penguin, 1964; 'Yeoman' (Allan Jobson), 'Pocket Histories of Suffolk Parishes No. 180 – Peasenhall,' *Suffolk Chronicle and Mercury*, 13 June 1930; E.J.M. Kirby, 'Salute to the Blythburgh Sower', *The Countryman*, Spring 1989, Dr C.E. Lay, MS letter on The Ancient House, Suffolk County Record Office, Ipswich. Ordnance Survey maps: 1″ to the mile, 1860, Sheet 50, Eye; 2″ to the mile, 1903, sheets 38, 39, 49, East Suffolk. Informant: Mr Billy Rowe, conversation with the authors, 5 May 1989.

Congregationalism in Peasenhall: *R. Freeman Buller, Catalogue of Beneficed Suffolk Clergy with Notes* (MS), deposited Suffolk County Archives, Ipswich; *Dictionary of National Biography* (henceforth *DNB*). Informant: Miss Gertie Rose, conversation with the authors and Stewart Evans, 5 May 1989.

Methodism in Peasenhall: Primitive Methodist Circuit Reports, Wangford Circuit, Suffolk Record Office, Lowestoft, FK1/11 6333/29. Wangford Circuit Preaching Plans 1900–3. Informant: Mr Hubert Aldridge, conversations with Keith Skinner and John Gleeson, 24 Aug 1985; with the authors and Stewart Evans, 3 May 1989.

Church and Chapel tensions: *Peasenhall Church Monthly*, September 1899; Peasenhall Charity List, Suffolk Record Office, Ipswich, FC67/L1/8: 1610/55. Informants: Mr Hubert Aldridge, conversation with the authors and Stewart Evans, 3 May 1989; Mr Herbert Denny, conversation with the authors and Stewart Evans, 3 May 1989; Mrs Sue Trovell, conversation with the authors and Stewart Evans, 3 May 1989.

THREE: WILLIAM GARDINER AND ROSE HARSENT

Gardiner, Harsent and Cady family backgrounds and residences: Birth, Marriage and Death Registers, St Catherine's House; Census returns, 1841–81; collected by Keith Skinner, Stewart Evans and Wilfrid Goodman.

Bulcamp Workhouse at Blythburgh: 'A Nice Little Blaze', *The View in Winter*, ed. Ronald Blythe, Penguin, 1981.

Caroline Gardiner Coleman's appearance: information from the Gardiner family.

Suffolk craftsmen: *Akenfield Revisited*, BBC Radio 4, 14 May 1989.

George Cady: Allan Jobson, *An Hourglass on the Run*, Michael Joseph, 1959; Wangford Circuit Primitive Methodist Quarterly Meeting Minutes, Suffolk County Archives, Lowestoft, FK1/11 6333/7 (henceforth QM) 6 Mar 1893; Saxmundham Magistrates' Charge Book, 8 Sep, 10 Dec 1888.

The name **Georgianna [Cady Gardiner]** is spelled as she signed herself in her letter to the *Sun*, 31 Jan 1903. Various certificates spell it in a variety of ways. It was a popular name in various forms (Georgeanne,

Georgeanna, Georgina, etc.) at the time: Mrs Crisp paid to have the spelling of her name on her marriage certificate altered to her own preferred form, 'Georgiana'. Gardiner addresses his wife as 'Georgie' in his letter from prison, and we are told that he and he alone used this diminutive (though friends as well as Georgie were permitted to call him Willie). She herself pronounced her name Georgina, and the five or more children named for her all spelled their name Georgina. (Information from Gardiner family.)

Georgianna's habit of reducing Ettie May's age: noted by John Gleeson, Keith Skinner and Wilfrid Goodman in her evidence at *2nd Trial*.

Gardiner at Newberry's; his character and reputation in the village; and Bob Kerridge: Information from many sources in Peasenhall and district, especially Mr H. Aldridge, Mr H. Denny and Mr W. Rowe, given to the authors, Stewart Evans and Wilfrid Goodman. On Gardiner's respectability and Ernest's resentment; information from the Gardiner family.

Methodist activities: QM.

Sibton Chapel and Wangford Circuit offices held by Gardiner, Rouse, Burgess and others: Suffolk County Archives, Lowestoft, FK1/11 6333/32, Primitive Methodist Connexion, Schedule of Sunday Schools in the Wangford Station; QM, 12 June 1894; *1st* and *2nd Trials*, evidence of John Guy.

We use the form **Rose Anne [Harsent]** as aesthetically pleasing. The forms Roseanne, Rosanna and Rose Annie are also found in various certificates and reports.

Harsent children's school absences: Sibton School Log Book 1874–1904, 2001/1, Suffolk County Record Office, Ipswich.

Billy Rowe on Rose's generosity with her favours: 'An Infamous Address', BBC Radio 4, 8 Mar 1987; Mr Rowe, conversation with the authors, 5 May 1989.

Frederick Davis: Evidence, *1st* and *2nd Trials*.
His quotation from book of Proverbs: R.J. White in *Women of Peasenhall*, Macmillan, 1969, p. 84, suggests the quotation was chapter 5, verse 19.

FOUR: THE SCANDAL

Events at the Doctor's Chapel, Gardiner's subseqent actions and Sibton Chapel Inquiry: *1st* and *2nd Trials* collated with *EADT*, 20 June, 1, 4 July; *EMG* 7 Nov 1902.

Annie Cady in Peasenhall: Register of Marriages. On 4 May 1901, Annie Sarah Cady married James Beckett Culham at Peasenhall Wesleyan Methodist Chapel. William Gardiner was one of the witnesses, and presumably gave her away since her father had died and he was the successful husband of her eldest sibling.

Darkness and poor visibility at the chapel: If the time of nightfall seems unusually early (like the estimated 2.30 a.m. daylight after the thunderstorm the following year) it should be borne in mind that Peasenhall is almost as far east as one can go in England, and the sun's movements are observed much earlier than is the case in the west. Furthermore there was no Daylight Saving: all these summer hours are Greenwich Mean Time.

Daisy May Gardiner: Register of Births and Deaths; Register of Burials, Peasenhall Cemetery, vol. 1. See also ch. 9 and notes for interesting Gardiner family traditions on her death.

Gardiner's Letters to Rose: the text we quote will seem slightly unfamiliar to readers of *NBT*. It is taken from Stewart Evans's collation of *NBT* with more accurate contemporary newspaper reports.

Methodist affairs and Mr Guy: *1st* and *2nd Trials*; QM; Norwich District Committee Minute Books, 1881–1905, Methodist Archives, John Ryland University Library, Manchester (henceforth DC).

Fires at Smyths' Works attributed to Gardiner: Informant, Mr Herbert Denny, conversation with the authors and Stewart Evans, 2 May 1989; *Halesworth Times*, 24 Dec 1901; *EADT* 19 Dec 1901.

Mr Denny on Gardiner family: Conversation with the authors and Stewart Evans, 2 May 1989.

Bob Kerridge's broken engagement: Informant, Mr Herbert Denny, conversation with the authors and Stewart Evans, 2 May 1989; *Illustrated Police News*, 14 June 1902.

Herbert Rouse: *1st* and *2nd Trials*; his anonymous letter wording, collated with *EMG* 22 Jan 1903.

Authors' varying opinions on the scandal: John Rowland, *The Peasen-hall Mystery*, John Long, 1962, says a conclusion must be reached if the case is to be understood (but he signally fails to reach one). Jack Smith-Hughes, *Eight Studies in Justice*, Cassell, 1953, finds Rose and Gardiner guilty, essentially for no other reason than that he thinks all evangelicals are humbugs. Edwin Packer, *The Peasenhall Murder*, Yoxford Publications, 1981, for no apparent reason thinks they were innocent, and Wright and Skinner made the whole thing up for fun.

Village background and scandals, and Skinner's reported words: Mr F. Rowe, conversation with the authors and Stewart Evans, 23 Nov 1989.

Subsequent events: *1st* and *2nd Trials*.

FIVE: THE INVESTIGATION

Superintendent Andrews: *Work Journal*, MS, hand-titled in Gothic lettering *Geo Andrews/Supt of Police/Halesworth*, Police Museum, Suffolk County Constabulary HQ, courtesy the Chief Constable and Inspector Leslie Jacobs; *EADT* 4 Apr 1931; *Halesworth Times* 8 Apr 1931, *The Police Review*, 22 Apr 1904.

Photographing exteriors only: Edwin Packer, *The Peasenhall Murder*, Yoxford Publications, 1981, claims plausibly that the kitchen interior was photographed for the police by F. Jenkins of Southwold. (See also *Police Review* above wherein Jenkins photographed Andrews.)

Rix case: *The Times*, 4 June 1902.

Superintendent Staunton: Staunton family papers; conversation Mr J. Staunton with the authors, 29 June 1989.

His courageous persistence in prosecuting E.R. Hollond JP for man-slaughter: *EADT* 22 Nov 1929.

Chief Constable Jasper Mayne: Weekly Orders to the Suffolk County Constabulary, Constabulary Museum, Martlesham Heath.

Scots Guards' Band at Sports: *EADT* 29 July 1908.

Scarfe and Berry: newspapers variously describe either as Sergeant or Inspector. We have taken their ranks and stations from their Service Records in East Suffolk Police Records, A1465/ 1–3 County Record Office, Ipswich, checked against *Kelly's Directory* entries.

Mrs Culham: Newspapers variously report 'Callum' or 'Cullam'. In fact this is Georgianna's sister Annie Sarah from Leiston, who married James Culham from the Gardiner house in Peasenhall the previous year. See ch. 4 and Sources.

First Inquest Hearing (Swan Inn): *EADT* 4 June 1902.

Second Inquest Hearing (Swan Inn): *EADT* 17 June 1902.

Final Inquest Hearing (Assembly Hall): *EADT* 1 July 1902.

Formal and remanding magistrates' hearings: *EADT* 5, 6, 13 June 1902.

Saxmundham Bench first hearing of case: *EADT* 20 June 1902.

Second hearing: *EADT* 4 July 1902.

Police movements the first week of June, 1902: Testimony of Staunton and Nunn before inquest and magistrates, and *1st* and *2nd Trials*. Testimony of Staunton, Nunn and Mrs Gardiner *2nd Trial*.

Destruction of Gardiner's wages sheets: Mr Fred Rowe, conversation with the authors and Stewart Evans, 23 Nov 1989.

Gardiner in the gantry: Mr Herbert Denny, conversation with the authors and Stewart Evans, 22 Nov 89.

Gardiner's arrest: Mr Billy Rowe, conversation with the authors, 5 May 1989; *1st* and *2nd Trials*, Nunn's evidence; Roger Wilkes, *An Infamous Address*, Grafton, 1989, p. 177.

Rose's funeral: *EADT* 6 June 1902.

James Morris: the name is spelled 'Morriss' in *NBT* and many subsequent authors. We have seen Morris's personal copy of *Carter's Practical Gardener* (pub. 1868), now in the possession of Mr Herbert Denny. Morris has written his name in it, spelled as above.

Mr A.S. Leighton: *EADT* 16 Jan 39; Mr M.D. Hocking, Messrs Gotelee & Goldsmith, letter to Martin Fido, 15 Nov 1989.

Mrs Crisp: Conversations, Mr Billy Rowe with the authors, 5 May 1989; Mr Fred Rowe with the authors and Stewart Evans 23 Nov 1989, Peasenhall School, Minutes of the Board of Managers, 2001/1 Suffolk County Record Office, Ipswich.

Twenty letters in Rose's drawer: At Gardiner's trials the documents were labelled Exhibits A–Z. A was the assignation note and B its envelope. C and D were Gardiner's letters to Rose concerning the scandal. H and I were Gardiner's letters from Paris to Messrs Smyth. E, F and G were probably also Gardiner documents. U–Z were Davis's compositions. These were the only documents discussed until the jury at the end of the first trial asked to see Gardiner's letter from prison to Georgianna, and the prosecution introduced another prison note from Gardiner to Leighton at the end of their case in the second. The rest of the alphabet was apparently taken up with Rose's family letters and the innocuous letter or letters from another man or other men.

SIX: THE FIRST TRIAL

Throughout: *1st Trial*.

Wild and Dickens: *NBT*; R.J. Blackham, *Sir Ernest Wild*, with Introduction by Lady Wild, Rich & Cowan, 1935; Sir Henry Dickens, *Reminiscences*, Heinemann, 1934.

Sir William Grantham: *DNB*; C. Kingston, *Famous Judges and Famous Trials*, Stanley Paul, 1923.

Village belief that Leighton's acoustical test was invalidated by noise from the drill works: Mr Herbert Denny, conversation with the authors and Stewart Evans, 2 May 1989.

Redgrift: Newspapers, *NBT* and succeeding authors repeatedly spell Redgrave. This error presumably rests on misheard dialect pronunciation. True spelling and relationship established from *Kelly's Directory*, Electoral Registers and Census Returns.

Fire in the washhouse for breakfast kettle: Colin Wilson intimates surprise at the Gardiners' lighting a fire on a warm June morning. (*Mammoth Book of True Crime*, Robinson, 1988, p. 3.) It seems the sage of Gorran Haven has never wanted a cup of tea in a village without gas or electricity! The Gardiners boiled their kettle in the washhouse and ate their breakfast in the kitchen.

Evan Edwards: Letter and enclosures from the late Mr Dennis Jaques to Wilfrid Goodman, 16 May 1984. His denial of being influenced by views on capital punishment: *EADT* 27 Jan 1903.

SEVEN: THE SECOND TRIAL

Throughout: *2nd Trial*, further collated with *EMG* 22, 23, 24, 26 Jan 1903, *The Sun* 22, 23, 24, 26 Jan 1903, *The Star*, 22, 23, 24, 26 Jan 1903, *Daily Graphic*, 22 Jan 1903, *Daily Chronicle*, 23, Jan 1903 *Illustrated Mail* 24, Jan 1903, *The People*, 25 Jan 1903, *News of the World*, 25 Jan 1903, *Bury Free Press*, 31, Jan 1903.

Crowd in Ipswich afer first trial: *EADT* 11 Nov 1902.

Editorial opinion: *EMG* 11 Nov 1902.

Gardiner Family Appeal Fund: *EADT* 13, 14 Nov 1902, 31 Jan 1903.

Georgianna's letter: *The Times*, 15 Nov 1902.

Evan Edwards: information Mr Wilfrid Goodman, as notes to ch. 6.

Methodist divisions, positions and disciplinary practices: Wangford Primitive Methodist Circuit Reports 1900–8, Suffolk County Record Office, Lowestoft, FK1/11 6333/29; Wangford Circuit Preachers' Plans 1898–1903, FK1/11 6333/34; QM; DC. DC shows that it was normal for members to be disciplined for misconduct, and 'dismembered' for flagrant misconduct.

Turrell: the name is spelled Burrell in *NBT* and some newspapers. We have preferred the newspaper variant Turrell as slightly commoner in the region.

Edna Carter: *Bury Free Press*, 15 Nov 1884.

Mr Hunt: Superintendent Andrews's *Work Journal*; Mr Hubert Aldridge conversation with the authors and Stewart Evans, 23 Nov 1989; QM.

Mr Sims: *EADT* 23 Jan 1903.

Harry Harsent: Various authors, possibly following *NBT* which sets his age as fourteen, suggest that Harry's confused testimony was a consequence of his extreme youth. In fact he was seventeen and in poor health. He died in 1906. (Register of Births and Deaths; Register of Burials, Peasenhall Cemetery, vol. 1.)

Suffolk migrant labour to Bass's Brewery: George Ewart Evans, *Where Beards Wag All*, Faber, 1970; information, Dr Colin Owen; Mr Wilfrid Goodman.

Burton letter exonerating Gardiner: Mr Wilfrid Goodman notes that a slip of the tongue on Wild's part might have led him to say 'Gardiner' in mistake for 'Goodchild', in which case the argument would be logical.

Sexual intercourse before the murder: Mr Wilfrid Goodman drew our attention to the unique report of Mr Justice Lawrance's examination of Richardson in *News of the World*, 25 Jan 1903. Alderman Jenkins's information: Edwin Packer, *The Peasenhall Murder*, Yoxford Publications, 1980. Mrs Erskine Muir's copy of *NBT*, described by Packer as containing the marginal note on this conversation, was sold by Mrs Packer to Wilfrid Goodman but lost in the post; information Mrs Packer and Wilfrid Goodman.

Hon. John de Grey, Mr Dickens's junior, as chairman of Saxmundham Petty Sessions: Supt Andrews's *Work Journal*, 14 Aug 1902.

Mr Justice Lawrance: *The Times*, 6 Dec 1912.

EIGHT: THE AFTERMATH

Events after the trial, Gardiners' interviews, local and national feeling: *EADT* 27, 28, 30, 31 Jan 1903; *EMG* 27, 30, 31 Jan 1903; *The Sun* 27, 28, 30, 31 Jan 1903; *The Star* 26, 28, 29, 30, 31 Jan 1903; *Daily News* 30 Jan 1903; *Daily Express* 31 Jan 1903; *Bury Free Press* 31 Jan 1903, *Illustrated Mail* 31 Jan 1903.

Execution of Montgomery: *The Star* 26 Jan 1903.

Burgess's daughter, Newberry's daughters: Mr Fred Rowe, conversation with the authors and Stewart Evans, 23 Nov 1989.

Mrs Dickinson supplying oil: Peasenhall Parish Vestry Accounts, Suffolk County Record Office, Ipswich.

Methodist deliberations: QM; DC.

Christianna Hurren: *EADT* 13 Feb, 6 June 1903; *Halesworth Times* 17 Feb 1903; *The Bury Free Press* 13 June 1903, Mr Herbert Denny, conversation with Stewart Evans and Keith Skinner, 10 Aug 1988.

Gardiner Fund final accounts: *Halesworth Times* 24 Mar 1903. Alfonso Skinner's alleged undisclosed evidence: Mrs Dora Pepper, conversation with Keith Skinner and John Gleeson, 24 Nov 1985.

The village band, Mrs Driver's story and Mr Fidler's conversion: Mr Herbert Denny, conversation with Keith Skinner and Stewart Evans, 10 Aug 1988; the authors and Stewart Evans, 2 May 1989.

Hostility to Gardiner in Peasenhall was such that much of his furniture was vandalized by villagers before being sent on to Southall, and had to be buried in the garden at Hartington Rd. Information, Gardiner family.

Mr Harold Mills on Pepper family opinions: conversation with the authors, 3 May 1989.

Taylor's false confession: *The Star* 13, 16 Aug 1904; *Daily Chronicle* 15 Aug 1904.

Deaths of various protagonists: Central Registry of Births, Marriages and Deaths, St Catherine's House, Kingsway and Aldwych; information Mr Billy Rowe, conversation with the authors, 3 May 1989; information Gardiner family.

Alfonso Skinner: known to Keith Skinner and Elizabeth Skinner.

The claim in *East Anglian Magazine*, vol. 26, May 1977, that **Gardiner** returned to local preaching confuses him with a William John Gardiner.

Fred Davis: *Kent and Sussex Courier* 29 May, 1 June 1964; information supplied by Miss Mary E. Davis to Stewart Evans, 13 Apr 1989; Miss Gertie Rose, conversation with the authors 24 Nov 1989.

Wild and Dickens: R.J. Blackham, *Sir Ernest Wild*, Rich and Cowan, 1935; Sir H.F. Dickens, *Reminiscences*, Heinemann, 1934.

Mr Guy's obituary: *Methodist Times*, 13 Mar 1924.

Supt Andrews: *The Police Review* 22 Apr 1904; *EADT* 4 Apr 1931; *Halesworth Times* 8 Apr 1931.

Supt Staunton: Mr John Staunton, written information supplied to the authors, family papers, and conversation with the authors, 29 June 1989.

Brewer: Application for Superannuation No. 53644/24 (110), Post Office Archives; *The London Gazette*, 13 June 1924; *EADT* 14 June 1924 (kindly furnished by Mr Wilfrid Goodman).

Gardiner family at Southall: *Kelly's Directory*; Central Registry of Births, Marriages and Deaths; information, Gardiner family.

Mrs Gardiner taking tea with Mrs Newberry: Mr Herbert Denny, conversations with Stewart Evans, Ray and Joan Cole, 25 Jan 1989; with

Keith Skinner and Stewart Evans, 10 Aug 1988; Mr Fred Rowe, conversation with the authors and Stewart Evans, 23 Nov 1989.

Mrs Gardiner counselling young women: information, Mrs Joan Moore (whose mother worked with one of Gardiner's daughters), conversation with Keith Skinner and John Gleeson, 20 April 1985; information Gardiner family. Observation by John Gleeson.

Gardiner's deathbed: Mrs Joan Moore, conversation with John Gleeson and Keith Skinner, 20 Apr 1985; corrected by Gardiner family. Mrs Moore's story was that Gardiner sang 'Abide With Me', and then swore on the Bible that he had not killed Rose. The family confirmed the astonishing deathbed hymn, but noted that it was 'Jesu, lover of my soul'; gave us the correct last words; and remarked that Ernest (the family member present) would have been deeply offended by any oath of innocence, since he and his siblings had never for one moment doubted it.

NINE: GARDINER: THE CONCLUSIONS

***East Anglian Daily Times* copy as tinder**: we doubt this speculative interpretation of the newspaper under Rose's head. Whoever the murderer was, we don't think he would have believed one newspaper would suffice to start a pyre. He might have been carrying a paper when he visited Rose for any one of a number of reasons – for example, because he wanted to show her some item of mutual interest.

Cecil Lay on Gardiner's shirts: *East Anglian Magazine*, vol. 14, July 1955. See also Mr T.E. Cooke's objection in Sep 1955 that by Mr Lay's dating, Mrs Gardiner should have had no dirty shirt to hand over. We have met this with the suggestion that 'dirty' means 'clean but worn once'.

Stevenson's evidence on the broken bottle: *1st* and *2nd Trials*. Our quotation is from the *1st Trial*.

Methodist awe at thunder: *The Referee*, 1 Feb 1903.

'Graphological analysis' of Gardiner's personality from his handwriting: Patricia Marne, *Crime and Sex in Handwriting*, Constable, 1981.

Thomas Gurrin: *The Police Review*, 19 Aug 1910 (including citation of *The Spectator* of the previous week).

His son: *Kelly's Directories*; *The Times*, 12 Mar 1974.

East Suffolk handwriting of the period: among the sources we have examined are Anglican and Congregationalist archives in the Suffolk Record Offices at Ipswich; records from Smyths' Drill Works and firms of solicitors, with other documents including letters from Dr Lay describing The Ancient House held in the above; Methodist archives held in the Suffolk Record Office at Lowestoft and the John Rylands Library, Manchester; police records at the Suffolk County Constabulary Museum; and various inscribed books, photograph albums and other memorabilia, kindly shown us by old people in and around Peasenhall.

The most unusual feature of the assignation note when compared with contemporary local hands is the deeply notched figure 2 with a serif making the top hook into a V. We eventually found another example of this in Dr Lay's hand – the rest of which was quite different from that of the note.

TEN: THE MURDERER

Accidental death theory: *The Great Stories of Real Life*, ed. Max Pemberton, Newnes, 1924, followed, embroidered and garbled by many subsequent writers.

Speculations about Lay, Crisp and Morris: Edwin Packer, *The Peasenhall Murder*, Yoxford Publications, 1980.

Novel around Evan Edwards: Brian Cooper, *Genesis 38*, Heinemann, 1964.

Wives' conspiracy: R.J. White, *The Women of Peasenhall*, Macmillan, 1969. Although this novel puts forward the ridiculous suggestion that Mrs Crisp and Georgianna engineered the murder, Gardiner family sources argue that Dorothy Erskine Muir, the dedicatee, gave White a certain amount of genuine background information about the family and the village, and that some quite surprising suggestions unconnected with the murder are validated by conversations between William and Georgianna. Perhaps we should stress that the validated suggestions do not include witchcraft and lesbianism as aspects of Peasenhall life.

Bob Kerridge: Registry of Births, Marriages and Deaths; Wangford Primitive Methodist Circuit Archives, Suffolk County Record Office, Lowestoft; information Mrs Ruby Davis, Mr Herbert Denny, Mr Billy

Rowe, Mr Hubert Aldridge.

Fred Davis: Blything Petty Sessions Registers, Suffolk Record Office, Ipswich, Court Registers 1893–1903, BB2/1/1/1; *Halesworth Times*, 11 Feb 1902; Registry of Births, Marriages and Deaths.

Goodchild and Harsent: Information, Mr Wilfrid Goodman. Blything Petty Sessions Registers, BB2/1/1/2 record a court hearing following a fight between Albert Goodchild and William Harsent, but we are reasonably certain that this was another William Harsent, an older bricklayer who shows up on census returns of the period.

Fred Grice: conversations, the authors and Stewart Evans with Mr Herbert Denny, 22 Nov 1989; Miss Gertie Rose, Mr Fred Rowe, 23 Nov 1989; Registry of Births, Marriages and Deaths; D.A. Escott, letter to Keith Skinner, 19 Feb 1990; E. Warren, letter to Keith Skinner 3 Mar 1990; information Mr Herbert Denny 17 Mar 1990.

The runaway farmer's boy: Information Mr Wilfrid Goodman, with notes from the late Dennis Jaques; information Mr Eric Godward, 15 Mar 1990; Mrs Joan Stockeld, 15 Mar 1990; Mr Herbert Denny, 17 Mar, 30 Apr 1990; Mr Fred Rowe, 20 Apr 1990; Mr Billy Rowe and Mr Hubert Aldridge, 1 May 1990. Mr Aldridge was able to identify for us a living son of the young lady, born after her subsequent marriage to another party.

Harry Smith and Mayhew: Information, Mr Fred Rowe, 20 Apr 1990; conversations, the authors with Mr H. Denny and Mr Billy Rowe, 30 Apr 1990; Mr H. Aldridge, 1 May 1990; Registry of Births, Marriages and Deaths.

Bibliography

Aldred, David L., 'Rose of Peasenhall', *East Anglian Magazine*,
  Vol. 40, 1981.
Blackham, R.J., *Sir Ernest Wild, K.C.*, Rich & Cowan, 1935.
Blythe, Ronald, *Akenfield*, Penguin, 1972.
—— *Review in the Winter*, Penguin, 1981.
Bresler, Fenton, 'The Choirmaster's Ordeal', *Sunday Express*,
  26 May 1968.
Church, Robert, *Murder in East Anglia*, Hale, 1987.
Cooper, Brian, *Genesis 38*, Heinemann, 1964.
Dickens, Sir H.F., *Reminiscences*, Heinemann, 1934.
Dictionary of National Biography, OUP, 1930.
East Anglian Magazine, 'Letters to the Editor', Vols. 14, 17, 18, 24,
  27, 36; 1955, 1958, 1959, 1965, 1967, 1977.
Evans, George Ewart, *The Horse in the Furrow*, Faber, 1960.
—— *Where Beards Wag All*, Faber, 1970.
Franklin, Charles, *A Mirror of Murder*, Corgi, 1964.
Freeman, R. Austin (ed.), *Great Unsolved Crimes*, Hutchinson, 1935.
Futter, R.H., 'The Peasenhall Murder', *East Anglian Magazine*,
  Vol. 14, 1955.
Gladstone, Rev. H.H., 'The Unsolved Mystery of Peasenhall', *East
  Anglian Magazine*, Vol. 24, 1964.
Goodman, Jonathan (ed.), *The Country House Murders*, W.H. Allen, 1987.
Henderson, William, *The Trial of William Gardiner* (*Notable British
  Trials*), Hodge, 1934.
Jobson, Allan, *An Hour-Glass on the Run*, Michael Joseph, 1959.
—— 'The Peasenhall Murder', *Suffolk Fair Magazine*, Vol. 2, 1972.
—— *Something of Old Suffolk*, Hale, 1978.
Kelly's Post Office Directories (Suffolk), 1900, 1937.
Kingston, Charles, *Famous Judges and Famous Trials*, Stanley Paul,
  1923.
Lambton, Arthur, *Echoes of Causes Celebres*, Hurst & Blackett,
  1931.

Logan, Guy B.H., *Guilty or Not Guilty?* Stanley Paul, 1928.
Marne, Patricia, *Crime and Sex in Handwriting*, Constable, 1981.
Morland, Nigel, *That Nice Miss Smith*, Muller, 1957.
Owen, Colin, *The Development of Industry in Burton upon Trent*, Phillimore, 1978.
Packer, Edwin, *The Peasenhall Murder*, Yoxford Publications, 1981.
Parrish, J.M. and Crossland, J.R., *The Fifty Most Amazing Crimes*, Odhams, 1936.
Pemberton, Max (ed.), *The Great Stories of Real Life*, Newnes, 1924.
Pevsner, Nikolaus, *The Buildings of England: Suffolk*, Penguin, 1964.
Reeves, Marshall, 'Suffolk Village Mystery', *Master Detective*, June 1987.
Rowland, John, *The Peasenhall Mystery*, John Long, 1962.
Shew, Edmund Spencer, *A Second Companion to Murder*, Cassell, 1960.
Smith-Hughes, Jack, *Eight Studies in Justice*, Cassell, 1953.
Villiers, Elizabeth, *Riddles of Crime*, Werner Laurie, 1928.
White's Suffolk Directories, 1848, 1858.
White, R.J., *The Women of Peasenhall*, Macmillan, 1969.
Wilkes, Roger, *An Infamous Address*, Grafton, 1989.
Wilson, Colin, *The Mammoth Book of True Crime* , Robinson, 1988.

Illustration Credits

Sources for illustrations are as follows:

PLATES 2 & 3   2: photograph by Stewart Evans; 3: diagram by Paul Evans; 4: courtesy of Mrs Kitty Gardiner; 5: photograph by Stewart Evans; 6: courtesy of Mrs Kitty Gardiner

PLATE 4   4: courtesy of Mrs Gladys Wilton; 5: photograph by Martin Fido; 6: courtesy of David Banthorpe

PLATE 5   1: courtesy of Richard Whittington-Egan; 3: courtesy of Mrs Ruby Davis; 4: courtesy of Fred Nunn

PLATES 6 & 7   3: photograph by Stewart Evans; 4: photograph by Stewart Evans; 6: photograph by Keith Skinner

PLATE 9   2: photograph by Stewart Evans; 3 & 4: by kind permission of the Chief Constable of Suffolk

PLATES 10 & 11   1: acc. K421/1 courtesy of Suffolk Record Office; 2: courtesy of Mrs Botwright; 4 & 5: by kind permission of the Chief Constable of Suffolk; 6: courtesy of Dr J. Ryder Richardson

PLATE 12   2: courtesy of Suffolk Record Office

PLATE 13   1: courtesy of Mrs Gladys Wilton

PLATES 14 & 15   8: courtesy of Miss Mary E. Davis; 9: courtesy of Mrs Violet Graves

PLATE 16   2: acc. AD672/1/55 Wilton Collection, courtesy of Suffolk Record Office; 4: courtesy of London Borough of Ealing Local History Collection

Index

30, 31, 36, 40, 90, 157, 170
Kerridge, Mrs Frances 157

Lambert, Arthur, yob 158
Larkin, Charles, accountant and handwriting expert 85–6, 93, 94, 98–9
Last families of Yoxford 18
Lawrance, Sir John Compton (Mr Justice) 104, 105, 107–8, 109, 121, 122, 123, 125–30, 153, 162
Lay, Cecil, shirt explicator 152
Lay, Dr C.E. 5, 6, 7, 16, 41, 42, 43, 48, 51–2, 59, 61, 67, 79–80, 114, 153, 156, 161, 169
Leighton and Aldous, Messrs 51, 62, 63, 74, 119–20, 139
Leighton, Arthur Sadler, solicitor 51, 52, 53, 55, 56–7, 58, 59, 61, 62, 64, 78, 92, 103, 107, 113, 132, 134, 135, 138
Leiston 9, 45, 50, 140
Levett-Scrivener, Capt. Egerton Bagot Byrd, JP 49, 50, 51, 57, 58, 73, 166
London 42, 44, 80, 81, 108, 109, 131, 134, 142
Lowestoft 44, 133
Ludbrook, Henry James, Methodist philanderer 39, 136
Luton 141

maltster's shoes 110, 112, 124
Mann, Frederick, GPO detective 138 139
Manning, Revd John, early Congregationalist 13
Marshall Hall, (Sir) Edward, KC 62, 142
Mayhew, —, wheelwrights' overseer 105, 108, 171
Mayhew, —, gamekeeper of Bruisyard 171
Mayne, Jasper, Chief Constable of Suffolk 44–5, 84, 142, 143

Meads, Mr and Mrs R.J. 156
medicine bottle 4, 42, 48, 51–2, 53, 87, 88, 95–6, 110, 118, 146, 148, 149, 150, 152–3
Methodism 2, 13–15, 20, 69, 126, 138, 143, 153, 157, 170 (*see* also under Norwich; Primitive Methodists; Sibton; Wangford)
Methodist offices 22, 23, 33, 69, 85, 91, 138, 157
migratory workers 110, 112, 162–4
Mill Lane (part of Heveningham Long Lane) 29, 30
Mills, Mr Harold 140
Montgomery, —, Ulster murderer 132
Morris, James, gamekeeper 50, 54, 56, 69, 73–6, 86, 94, 97, 108, 118, 119, 124, 147, 151, 156, 160
Muir, Dorothy Erskine, crime historian 114
Mullens, Harold, solicitor 33, 34, 40, 158

Nash, —, farmer 107
New Road 36
Newberry, Mr, carpenter 20
Newberry, Mrs, her 'naughty' daughters 136
News of the World 114
Norwich Primitive Methodist District Committee 21, 103, 138
Norwood 143
Nunn, PC Eli 6, 45, 46, 48, 49, 50, 54, 59, 60, 61, 63, 64, 67, 72, 77–8, 81, 108–9, 118, 121, 142, 149, 153, 158, 159, 161
– his immediate suspicion of WGLG 41, 42, 43, 52
– his disputed notebook entry 47, 78, 88–9

Old Bailey 44, 131
Onan 29, 39
Osborne Royal Naval Academy 154
Owen, Dr Colin 163